Right to Information
and
Good Governance

About the Author

Rajvir S. Dhaka is currently a Member of Academic Faculty at the Haryana Institute of Public Administration, Gurgaon. He has been keenly interested in the fundamental problems that the discipline of Public Administration offers. With Master's degree in Public Administration and Ph.D. in Political Science from Maharshi Dayanand University, Rohtak, and MBA in HRD from IGNOU, New Delhi, Dr. Dhaka has contributed several articles and research papers and authored books on the latest issues of Public Administration and Good Governance. Dr. Dhaka is the Master Trainer on RTI Act and also, State Nodal Officer, for Department of Personnel and Training (DOPT), Government of India and United Nations Development Programme (UNDP) Sponsored Project on "Capacity-Building for Access to Information". Currently he is also In-charge Examination for the Haryana Subordinate Accounts Service Examination.

Dr. Dhaka's publications include, Participatory Development and Capacity-Building (2000); Humanizing Development Trends in Public Administration (2001); Grassroots Democracy in Action (2004) and Beyond the Veil: Dalit Women in Panchayati Raj (2005).

Right to Information and Good Governance

Rajvir S. Dhaka

CONCEPT PUBLISHING COMPANY Pvt. Ltd.
NEW DELHI-110059

ISBN-13:978-81-8069-659-6 ISBN-10:81-8069-659-6

First Published 2010

Published and Printed by

Concept Since 1974

Concept Publishing Company Pvt. Ltd.
Regd. Office:
A/15-16, Commercial Block, Mohan Garden
New Delhi-110059 (India)
Phones : 25351460, 25351794, *Fax* : 091-11-25357109
Email : publishing@conceptpub.com,
Website: www.conceptpub.com

Editorial Office:
H-13, Bali Nagar, New Delhi-110 015, India.

Cataloging in Publication Data--*Courtesy:* D.K. Agencies (P) Ltd. <docinfo@dkagencies.com>

Dhaka, Rajvir S., 1970-
Right to information and good governance / Rajvir S. Dhaka.
p. cm.
In Indian context.
Includes bibliographical references.
Includes index.
ISBN 13: 9788180696596 ISBN 10: 8180696596

1. Freedom of information--India. 2. Transparency in government--India. I. Title.

DDC 342.540853 22

वजाहत हबीबुल्लाह
मुख्य सूचना आयुक्त
Wajahat Habibullah
Chief Information Commissioner

केन्दीय सूचना आयोग
रूम नं. 306, द्वितीय तल, अगस्त क्रान्ति भवन,
भीकाजी कामा प्लेस, नई दिल्ली-110066
CENTRAL INFORMATION COMMISSION
ROOM NO. 306, 2ND FLOOR,
AUGUST KRANTI BHAWAN,
BHIKAJI CAMA PLACE, NEW DELHI-110066

Foreword

India's Right to Information RTI Act 2005 has been described as a revolution and acclaimed as even the most radical legislation since the introduction of the Constitution of India. The right to information has been a fundamental right of every Indian citizen, being part of the Freedom of Speech and Expression enshrined in Article 19 (1) (a) of the Constitution of India. However, for an Indian citizen there was hardly a speedy and an effective means of actually enforcing this right except to take recourse unwieldy channels of the civil law. Now the RTI Act has changed all that and brought the means of exercising this Right within everyone's easy reach.

This Act has another overriding effect; it is an equalizer making sure that all those who seek to benefit from the public trust by virtue of the position that they may hold, are also rendered fully accountable for that trust. Such public accountability, it goes without saying, is the essence of good governance. What remains now is that more and more Indians become aware of this right and are able to make use of it to benefit themselves, their communities and above all the nation of which we are all so proud.

The publication of "Right to Information and Good Governance" has, therefore, made a timely contribution to the growth of awareness of this vital element of our democratic polity. The former Secretary General of the United Nations Mr. Kofi Annan characterized the strength of democracy in the following words:

> "The great democratizing power of information has given us all the chance to effect change and alleviate poverty in ways we cannot even imagine today. Our task, your task ... is to make that change real for those in need, whatever they may be. With information on our side, with knowledge of a potential for all, the path to poverty can be reversed".

In other words, democracy is the best instrument for good governance provided that democracy is real, which means that there is public participation in governance. The exercise of the right to information is also the means to make that democracy real. The author of the book, Dr. Rajvir Dhaka deserves our congratulations for this excellent work. It is recommended reading not only for those in Government but all those who wish to be active citizens of India's civil society in all its vibrancy.

New Delhi
20th March 2009

(Wajahat Habibullah)

Preface

The enactment of the Right to Information (RTI) Act, 2005 is a laudable step. The Act covers not only the public sector but also the NGOs and the private sector to some extent. In addition to this, it has various other positive features like provision of First and Second Appellate Authorities. It is also one of the toughest legislations in the world, as it is the only RTI Act imposing penalty for any contravention of the provisions of the Act. After completion of three years of its implementation, the response of this Act has been very positive and it has received very wide and warm welcome from the people. People are learning the importance of the power of information in their hands. That is why the people of every section have been seeking information from the different authorities. As a result, Public Authorities and Public Information Officers are becoming increasingly aware of their full responsibilities. It has been a learning experience for each entity involved in the working of the law.

The fact is that Public Authorities are yet to give shape to any time-bound action plan for the implementation of the RTI Act especially *suo moto* disclosure. The reason for this is that, incomplete/insufficient disclosures have no penal consequences for Public Authorities.

Besides experience regarding seeking information is also not very encouraging. Fees charged and the manner of payment is not uniform. Some States like Haryana, charge very high fees which runs counter to the spirit of the Act. There is confusion about the head of accounts to which the amount received as application fees and other fee are to be credited. Most of the PIOs at state and district levels are not truly cooperative and they sometimes force the applicants to withdraw applications.

The Governments, with a view to overcome the problems in its effective use, need to take steps to propagate this Act among the illiterate population living in the villages. The states should increasingly adopt and popularize the use of IT/e-governance. Records in the Government offices need to be digitized and indexed for easy retrieval and access. Video Conferencing should be used extensively for hearing the appeals. Proactive disclosure of public authorities should be audited by a team of Government officials and NGOs.

Further, effective operationalisation of the RTI requires capacity-building of the information providers and seekers both. Capacity-building of the cutting edge level functionaries forms the key element as it facilitates the first interface with the citizens. To ensure that the RTI regime is in tune with the spirit and philosophy of the Act would require institutional mechanism for improved government citizen interface, capacity-building of officials to meet citizen's information requirements and awareness and empowerment of citizens to enable them to exercise RTI in the right earnest.

Keeping in view the importance of the RTI and its increasing use to redress the grievances of the people, more and effective steps at the hands of government are required.

I am confident that this book will prove useful for the government servants, social activists and of course for the students having a keen interest in the latest issues in administration.

This book would not have been possible in the present form without the support and encouragement from various well wishers and friends. First of all, I would like to place on record my deep sense of gratitude to Sh. Wajahat Habibullah, Chief Information Commissioner, Central Information Commission, New Delhi for writing the foreword of this book.

Then I would like to express my sincere thanks to Sh. Pankaj Sehrasehkar, Joint Registrar and Deputy Secretary,

Central Information Commission for his valuable help and advice in shaping this book at the different stages. I would also like to thank various other experts on the subject by interacting with whom I have been benefited immensely at the time of writing this book. I am also indebted to those thousands of trainees from various states in general and Haryana in particular for posing many tricky questions which helped me a lot in enriching my knowledge on the subject. I am indebted to Prof. S.N.Misra, Editor, *Indian Journal of Public Administration* IIPA, New Delhi; Lala Lajpat Rai Chair Professor Madan G. Gandhi, Punjab. University. Chandigarh; Prof. Ranvir Singh, HIRD, Nilokheri; and Prof. D. Banerjea, HIPA for blessing me with their persipicacious comments and suggestions. I am also grateful to Prof. Sushma Yadav, Indian Institute of Public Administration for going through the draft of the book. From the core of my heart I would also like to thank my friends Mr. R.S. Kharb, IAS, Additional Deputy Commissioner, Rewari and Prof. S.B. Bhardwaj , Delhi University and Mr. Sanjiv Batra, Regional Officer, AICTE, New Delhi for inspiring me to write this book.

From the core of my heart, I express my gratitude to Prof. Suresh Misra, HIPA whose work on Right to Information Act proved as *Path Pardarshak* for me. I am especially indebted to the various other sources from which I have taken a lot of help, most importantly, YASHADA (Pune), CGG (Hyderabad), The HCM Rajasthan (Jaipur) and PRIA (New Delhi) material on RTI, Act. The support rendered by my colleague Mr. Devender Singh has been of immense help. I am also thankful to Mr. Puneet Chopra, Mr. Munish Khichi, Mrs. Kamlesh Sharma, Mrs. Amita Gupta and Mrs. Neelam, Mr. Deepak Bajaj for assistance rendered by them. Last but not the least, I am grateful to my family members particularly my elder brother Sh. Attar Singh Dhaka for encouragement and inspiration during the period of writing the book.

Rajvir S. Dhaka

Contents

Contents

1 Right to Information : Genesis and Evolution

Introduction

In recent years, there has been an almost unstoppable global trend towards the recognition and enactment of Right to Information (RTI) by various countries. The inter governmental organisations, civil society and many sections of the people have invariably been behind this trend. It has been widely recognised as a fundamental Human Right, which upholds the inherent dignity of all human beings. The RTI, is now accepted, as a crucial underpinning of participatory democracy. It has now been widely acknowledged as a prerequisite for ensuring accountability and good governance.

It goes without saying, the greater the access of the citizen to information, the greater the responsiveness of the government to community needs. Alternatively, the greater the restrictions that are placed on access to information, the greater the feelings of 'powerlessness' and 'alienation'. Without information, as a matter of fact, people cannot adequately exercise their rights as citizens or make informed choices.

Over the past few years, the 'RTI' has gained increasing prominence both in the Human Rights and the democratic discourse. Since a democratic government must be sensitive to the public opinion, it is necessary that information must be made available by it to the people.

Actually, meaningful substantive democracy ought to be founded on the notion of an informed public that is able to participate thoughtfully in its own governance. Information and knowledge are the instruments of human transformation.

Therefore, without sufficient information, representative democracy is undermined.

Apart from the elections, access to information is vital to enable public to engage their representatives and the bureaucracy on an ongoing basis and to participate effectively in the formulation and implementation of policies and activities purportedly for their benefit. It has the potential to empower the citizen in relation to the state by making administration more accountable and participatory. Besides, it not only ensures greater transparency but also acts as a deterrent against the arbitrary exercise of official powers.

Admittedly effective accountability rests on the peoples' acquaintance with the information. A Government which operates in secrecy tends to lose the faith of the people as much as its own legitimacy and credibility. Openness and full access to information are the two pillars of the democratic state. These equip the citizens to participate meaningfully in the development process.

The governance is undoubtedly strengthened by the RTI. Not only the government but also the corporate houses and industries which operate for profit must also be made to disclose facts of public interest. That is why the RTI has now been recognized as an essential requirements of the good governance. This is evident in the prescriptions provided by the international organizations such as World Bank, International Monitory Fund (IMB) United Nations Development Programme (UNDP) and Asian Development Bank. (ADB).

Despite all this, there had been no specific law for Access to Information in India. The transition from an opaque system of governance, legitimised by the colonial Official Secrets Act, to the RTI took 82 years. Prior to it, free flow of information to the citizens was blocked by an attitude of secrecy due to the old framework of rules. It was further compounded by low levels of literacy and unawareness.

Transparency seems to be the only means for sustaining democratic governance. That is why the RTI has been legislated in about 70 countries of the world and another 30 countries are in the process of doing so. It was in this backdrop that the RTI was enacted in India in 2005. It marks a paradigm shift in Indian democracy. The experience of four years shows that, the response to this Act has been very positive. It has been widely welcomed by the people. They have been seeking various types of information from different authorities. Therefore, an attempt has been made to discuss the various dimensions of its evolution in India along with its salient features and grey areas. Besides the discussion would focus on the major impediments in its implementation and also various suggestions needed for removing them.

Need for Right to Information

The RTI had already received judicial recognition as a part of the Fundamental Right to Freedom of Speech and Expression. The right to information is important for many reasons. Soli Sorabjee had aptly stressed its need for bringing in transparency in administration and public life. According to him, "Lack of transparency was one of the main causes for all pervading corruption and Right to Information would lead to openness, accountability and integrity."

P. B. Sawant has expressed similar views. He holds that, "the barrier to information is the single most cause responsible for corruption in society. It facilitates clandestine deals, arbitrary decisions, manipulations and embezzlements. Transparency in dealings, with their every detail exposed to the public view, should go a long way in curtailing corruption in public life."

The genesis and evolution of the Right to Information Act, 2005

The evolution of the Act may be traced to the following developments and factors:

1. Good Governance

The access to information is cardinal to good governance and the whole mechanism of governance in the country has been vitiated owing to lack of it. According to a paper prepared by the Human Rights Initiative, good governance has eight major facets. It is participatory, consensus oriented, accountable, transparent, responsive, effective and efficient, equitable and inclusive and follows the rule of law. It is an ideal which is difficult to be achieved in its totality. However, to ensure sustainable human development, action must be taken to work towards this ideal. Access to information is a vital factor for achieving the goals of good governance. It promotes transparency and public accountability in the working of government functionaries. The end objective of the RTI is also to achieve good governance.

Actually, the basic premise behind it is that the government should be open and accountable. It should conceal nothing from the people whom it represents. The citizens feel wary when secrecy is claimed even for routine business of administration. Importance of the RTI has therefore, now been recognized as an essential requirement for good governance. This is evident from the prescriptions provided by the international organizations such as World Bank, IMF, UNDP and ADB.

2. The Global Trend

Since the 1980s, the emergence of new democracies after the collapse of authoritarian regimes has given rise to new constitutions that include specific guarantees of the Right to Information. At the same time, older democracies such as the United Kingdom too are seeing the wisdom of enacting such legislation. International bodies like United Nations Organisation, the Commonwealth, Council of Europe and the Organisation of American States have drafted guidelines or model legislation to promote freedom of information. The World Bank, the International Monetary Fund and other donors are also pressing the recipient countries to enact laws for access to information increasing transparency and reducing corruption. As a result, such provisions have been made in about 70 countries of the world.

3. *Democratisation of Governance*

Access to information is the basic requirement in democratization of governance. Despite the LPG regime's stress on curtailing the role of the state, the functions and powers of the government have grown many-fold. These are not always for public good and public interest. There are instances of its use for private gains. In such a scenario, there is always a conflict between power and justice. Therefore, some control mechanism needs to be evolved to discipline the arbitrariness of power to promote justice, equity and fairplay. That is why, L.D. White has observed, "Power in a democracy requires control, greater the power greater should be the control."

RTI is one such device for disciplining the power and ensuring better accountability.

4. *People's Participation*

Governance in a democracy implies that people should participate in the process of governance. For this, they must have the necessary information to make informed choices between available options. The RTI is also expected to improve the quality of decision-making by removing unnecessary secrecy in the decision-making process. The citizens would be enabled to participate in the processes of decision-making and policy formulation on issue of their concern and to know the criteria applied by government agencies for making these decisions.

Transparency is the essence of democracy as it ensures accountability of institutions of governance. Thus the state is not only under obligation to respect the right of the people to information, but should also ensure supply of the same for their meaningful participation.

5. *Public Accountability*

The RTI is necessary to promote a culture of accountability. Accessibility of information pertaining to finances, proceedings and decisions of all the social actors whose activities have an impact on the public, is the guarantee that such actors shall make them accountable. It shall check mismanagement, abuse of discretion, bribery, other forms of corruption and malpractices. Sometimes media reveals a fraud and describes it as a tip of the iceberg which means that more facts are necessary to discover the whole picture of the fraud, and it is only when all the information is revealed that the extent of loss of public money can be evaluated and the persons be made accountable. The RTI Act, therefore, empowers the citizens to make the State and the public sector more accountable to them.

6. *Rule of Law and Right to Information*

Right to information has a rights perspective as well since correct information at the right time reduces the chance of misuse of resources and lessens corruption. It also helps governance function better, makes service providers accountable for their actions, creates participatory and transparent environment for people to contribute in policy formulation and establishing rule of law. It also gives people a legal right to demand entitlements and monitor the use or misuse of funds meant for them. Right to Information regime is also a means for government to empower the poor and inform them about pro-poor policies and safety-net programmes.

7. Combating Corruption

The most effective systemic check on corruption is to enable the citizens to take the initiative to seek information from the state, and thereby to enforce transparency and accountability.

The RTI is, therefore, likely to reduce corruption and increase administrative efficiency. This is because it provides every citizen the enforceable right to question, examine, audit, review and assess government acts and decisions, to ensure that these are consistent with the principles of public interest, probity and justice. The RTI Act would certainly enable the public to obtain access to documents that may otherwise be available only at the discretion of government. The cumulative impact of the availability of such information to the citizen for cheking on corruption and the arbitrary exercise of power, would certainly be momentous.

8. Checking the Misuse of Discretionary Powers

Officers are given discretionary powers for carrying out their duties effectively, and they don't have to depend on seniors for approval. Officials can abuse their discretion to suit various political or vested interests or to misappropriate funds. In absence of legislation on Right to information they tend to be hidden from disclosure. Although it is possible to seek courts intervention to compel disclosure of the information in practice it is not possible for the poor, villagers, due to cost, distance and delays involved. Another problem is the lack of transparency in appointment selection for public posts. The right to information is therefore important to check misuse of administrative discretion and to ensure fairness.

9. Administrative Efficiency

As far as administrative efficiency in government is

concerned, it comprises of conducting the administration without unnecessary delays. It should not have ulterior or corrupt motives while passing orders. Where required or implied, principles of natural justice have to be observed by it. The citizens must be informed by the Government about its functioning. But contrary to this, grievances of citizens in the form of representations or statutory applications or appeals, are kept pending for long periods, sometimes months or years, without disposal in several cases. In some other cases, applications are simply disposed of by saying that the Government or the concerned authority "finds no reason" to accede to the request etc.

Now that the RTI Act requires information about the pendency of the applications, reasons as to why these have not been disposed of or the reasons behind their rejection needs to be given. This is likely to improve the efficiency of various departments.

10. *Creating a more Democratic and Open Society*

There can be no democratic participation in decision-making without transparency and sharing of information. Secretive government is nearly always inefficient. The free flow of information is essential if problems are to be identified and resolved. Furthermore, a secretive governing culture fosters suspicion and encourages rumors and conspiracy theories. In such a culture, the public is likely to treat all government information with skepticism including public education campaigns for example, those dealing with important health issues like HIV/AIDS or those, which may be particularly sensitive. People are more likely to be politically malleable, skeptical of government and its intentions, and resistant to change unless legitimised by informal opinion leaders.

11. *Protection of Civil Liberties*

The Right to information is also essential for protecting

liberties of citizens by making it easier for civil society groups to monitor wrong doings like custodial deaths and abuse of preventive detention legislation. Custodial institutions are some of the most non-transparent in the country. Violations in custody range from deaths in custody, illegal detention and sexual abuse. Effective community monitoring of these institutions is dependent on access to information. Some governments are considering providing the right to information explicitly for prisons.

12. *Reducing Poverty and achieving the Millennium Development Goals (MDGs)*

Legislation on right to information is fundamental to furthering the effective development of society and eradicating poverty. Effective anti-poverty programmes require accurate information on problems hindering development to be in the public domain. Meaningful debates also need to take place around the policies designed to tackle the problems of poverty. Information can empower poor communities to battle the circumstances in which they find themselves and help balance the unequal power dynamic that exists between people marginalised through poverty and their governments. This transparent approach to working also helps poor communities to be visible on the political map so that their interests can be advanced. The right to information is therefore central to the achievement of the MDGs.

13. *Effective Implementation of Government Schemes*

In rural areas, numerous schemes for providing food, housing, employment and education are run by the Central and State Government. These schemes meant for the poorest of the poor in the rural areas are routed through the network of government agencies. There is widespread criticism of these funds being routinely misappropriated or misused on a large scale. In most cases, people do not know about the existence of these schemes. Even if they know, they fail to derive the benefits of these schemes. Furthermore, records are often tampered because no one outside the administration has access to them. By providing entire information on these schemes to the public would make the administration more accountable.

14. *Reforming Administration*

Uncaring, callous, slow, unaccountable and corrupt are among the perceptions by the common people of government servant. Is it true? If yes, to what extent? It is obviously not true of all government servants. A lot of good work is done by the officials but that is often considered as part of his duty the public perception is not too far from the reality. Over the years, he starts regarding every file as another job to be done at his convenience, forgetting that behind every file there is a decision to be taken which would vitally affect some body.

In Government it is known that saying no is the easier alternative and has little consequences for the official almost any body at any level can block a decision. Consequently, corruption today is much more widely prevalent, and spreading. Even with all kinds of Investigative agencies, anti-corruption departments, audits and what not, the mechanism for fixing the responsibility on the government servant is so protracted and gives him so many loopholes that rarely does he end up being convicted. And even when proved, he escapes with a caution or one or two increments being stopped, surviving in the government service to carry on with his game and perhaps with renewed vigor. If they are to be eliminated, many administrative reforms are needed quickly. It is not easy to push reforms in the monolith, called the Government. But the Right to Information opens a new vista altogether. This one single step can help to improve governance in most of its parameters.

15. *Right to Information as a Fundamental Right*

That the RTI is a Fundamental Right flowing from Art. 19(1) (a) of the Constitution is now well-settled. Over the years, the Supreme Court has consistently ruled in favour of the citizen's Right to Know in a number of cases like : Bennett Coleman vis-à-vis Union of India, 1973; Raj Narain *vis-à-vis* Government. of Uttar Pradesh, 1975; S.P. Gupta *vis-a vis* Union of India 1982 and People's Union for Civil Liberties (PUCL) *vis-a vis* Union of India, 2004.

In all these cases, Supreme Court pronounced that the citizens of this country have the Right to Freedom and Speech under Article 19(1) (a) of the Constitution and this Right is not complete unless and until the citizens have the Right to Know. The Right to Information was further elevated to the status of a Human Right by the Schedule Caste in 2004 case of 'People's Union for Civil Liberties vis-à-vis Union of India' judgment.

16. *Media's Effectiveness*

The citizens resort to the media like newspaper, radio, television etc. for day to day information about government activities. The media serves as a link between the citizens and government. So, it is essential that media have access to information. The media's right to information is not a special privilege, ut rather an extension of the public's right to know. The lack of a right to access official information causes many problems for the media. Balanced reporting becomes difficult when denied the primary sources of information. In absence of exact information they provide biased news, suppress or distort information. By providing right to information, media and citizens would together make the government more accountable.

17. *Movement for Transparency*

The Right to information has not come on a platter and there have been many activists and citizens' groups whose continuous struggle and efforts and movements have brought about this change. A mass based organization, called the Mazdoor Kissan Shakti Sangthan (MKSS), movement led by Aruna Roy, in May 1990 took an initiative to organize people, in a very backward region of Rajasthan : Bhim Tehsil, to assert their Right to Information by asking for copies of bills and vouchers and names of persons who have been paid wages mentioned in muster-rolls on the construction of school, dispensaries, small dams and community centers. It spread quickly to other areas of Rajasthan and to other States. The attempts of Harsh Mandar the then Divisional Commissioner of Bilaspur, Madhya Pradesh in 1996 to throw open the registers of Employment Exchanges and the records of Public Distribution System to the citizens or the agitation led by Anna Hazare in Maharashtra in 2001 are some the examples.

Consequently the National Campaign for People's Right to Information (NCPRI) which became a broad-based platform for action was formed in the late-1990s. As the campaign gathered momentum, it became clear that the Right to Information has to be made legally enforceable.

Right to Information : The International Perspective

At present, the RTI exists in about 70 countries either in the Constitution or through specific laws. Another 30 countries are in process of enacting such legislation. However, there are still many states, including democracies, where people are still denied access to information. UNDP's conditional laws have compelled many countries to enact the relevant legislations. It has been of the view that people's awareness on RTI directly impacts the life of the people.

United Nations

Freedom of information was recognised as a Fundamental Human Right by the UN at the first session of the UN General Assembly in 1946. It adopted Resolution 59(1) which states: "Freedom of information is a fundamental human right and ... the touchstone of all the freedoms to which the UN is consecrated."

In ensuing international instruments on Human Rights, freedom of information was made a part of the Fundamental Right of Freedom of Expression, which included the right to seek, receive and impart information. In 1948, the UN General Assembly adopted the Universal Declaration of Human Rights (UDHR) which guarantees Freedom of Opinion and Expression: "Everyone has the right to freedom of opinion and expression; this right includes freedom to hold opinions without interference and to seek, receive and impart information and ideas through any media and regardless of frontiers." This declaration recognizes freedom of expression including Freedom of Information and free press as Fundamental Human Right.

Article 19(2) of the International Covenant on Civil and Political Rights adopted by General Assembly in 1966 states: "Everyone shall have the right to freedom of expression; this right shall include freedom to seek, receive and impart information and ideas of all kinds, regardless of frontiers, either orally, in writing or in print, in the form of art, or through any other media of his choice".

Article I of the UNESCO Declaration of 1978 on 'Fundamental Principles Concerning the Contribution of Mass Media to Strengthening Peace and International Understanding, to the promotion of Human Rights and to Countering Racialism, Apartheid and Incitement of War' states:

"The strengthening of peace and international understanding, the promotion of human rights and the countering of racialism, apartheid and incitement to war demand a free flow and a wider and better balanced dissemination of information".

Article II of the Declaration states:

> "...the exercise of freedom of opinion, expression and information, recognized as an integral part of human rights and fundamental freedoms, is a vital factor in the strengthening of peace and international understanding..."

Article 10 of the Convention states: "... to combat corruption, each (member state) shall, in accordance with fundamental principles of its domestic law, take such measures as may be necessary to enhance transparency in its public administration, including with regard to its organization, functioning and decision-making processes and take measures for:

(a) Adopting procedures or regulations allowing members of the general public to obtain, where appropriate, information on the organization, functioning and decision-making processes of its public administration and, with due regard for the protection of privacy and personal data, on decisions and legal acts that concern members of the public;
(b) Simplifying administrative procedures, where appropriate, in order to facilitate public access to the competent decision-making authorities; and
(c) Publishing information, (including) periodic reports on the risks of corruption in its public administration."

Article 13 of 'UN Convention against Corruption' identifies '(i) effective access to information for public;

(ii) undertaking public information activities contributing to non-tolerance of corruption (including conducting public education programmes) and (iii) respecting, promoting and protecting the freedom to seek, receive, publish and disseminate information concerning corruption...' as important measures to be taken by Governments for ensuring the participation of society in governance.

In 1993, the UN Commission on Human Rights established the office of the UN Special Rapporteur on Freedom of Opinion and Expression. Part of the Special Rapporteur's mandate is to clarify the precise content of the right to freedom of opinion and expression.

Besides these international instruments the Regional Human Right treaties like the European Convention of Human Rights, 1950; the African Charter on Human and Peoples, Rights 1981; the Inter-American Declaration of Principles of Freedom of Expression 2000 and Declaration of the Principle of Freedom of Expression in Africa, 2002, have reiterated Article 19 of the Universal Declaration of Human Rights, 1948 by adopting Freedom of Expression and Information as a fundamental human right.

The Commonwealth

In 1980, the Commonwealth Law Ministers meeting in Barbados stated that "public participation in the democratic and governmental process was at its most meaningful when citizens had adequate access to official information". More recently, the Commonwealth has taken a number of significant steps to elaborate the content of that right. In March 1999, the Commonwealth Expert Group Meeting in London adopted a document setting out a number of guidelines on the Right to Know and Freedom of Information as a Human Right, including the following: Freedom of information should be guaranteed as a legal and enforceable right permitting every individual to obtain records and information held by the executive, the legislative and the judicial arms of the State, as well as any government-owned corporation and any other body carrying out public functions. These principles and guidelines were endorsed at the Commonwealth Heads of Government Meeting in November 1999.

1992 Rio Declaration on Environment and Development: Principle 10 of the 1992. Rio Declaration on Environment and Development recognised the fact that access to information on the environment, including information held by public authorities, is the key to sustainable development and effective public participation in environmental-governance. Agenda 21, the 'Blueprint for Sustainable Development', the companion implementation document to the Rio Declaration, states: "Individuals, groups and organisations should have access to information relevant to environment and development held by national authorities, including information on products and activities that have or are likely to have a significant impact on the environment, and information protection measures."

At the national level, several countries have laws which codify, at least in part, Article 10 of the Rio Declaration. In Colombia, for example, Law 99 of 1993, on public participation in environmental matters, includes provisions on the right to request information. Likewise, in the Czech Republic, there is a constitutional right to obtain information about the state of the environment, which has been implemented through a number of environmental protection laws.

In 1998, as a follow-up to the Rio Declaration and Agenda 21, Member States of the United Nations Economic Commission for Europe (UNECE) and the European Union signed the legally binding Convention on Access to Information, Public Participation in Decision-Making and Access to Justice in Environmental Matters (the Aarhus Convention). It recognises access to information as part of the right to live in a healthy environment, rather than as a free-standing right. However, it does impose a number of obligations on States which are consistent with international standards — for example, it requires States to adopt broad definitions of 'environmental information' and 'public authority', exceptions must be subject to a public interest test, and an independent body with the power to review refusals of request for information must be established.

Right to Information in Different Countries

Although freedom of information laws have been existing since 1766, when Sweden passed its Freedom of the Press Act, the last 10 years have seen an unprecedented number of states striving to become more transparent and more prompt in legislating on the access to information. In Western Europe, only Germany and Switzerland lack legislation. Nearly all the Central and Eastern European countries have adopted laws as part of their democratic transitions. Almost a dozen Asian countries have either enacted laws or are in the process of doing so. Similarly, in South and Central America, several countries are considering such laws. Many countries in Southern and Central Africa are following South Africa's lead, for formulating freedom of information laws.

Sweden's Freedom of the Press Act required the disclosure of official documents upon request. The Freedom of the Press Act, now a part of the Swedish Constitution, provides among other things that "every Swedish subject shall have free access to official documents". While Chapter 2 sets out the exceptions to free access, it also, in most cases, provides for a right to appeal against refusals to grant access to the courts. Another country with a long history of freedom of information legislation is Colombia, whose 1888 Code of Political and Municipal Organisation allowed individuals to request documents held by government agencies or in government archives.

Finland also has a law on the Right to Information since 1951 on publicity of documents. France too has accepted the principle of citizen's access to information. The accountability of public servant is a constitutional right in it. The implementing legislation of 1978 provides for an independent administrative authority, the Commission on Access to Administrative Documents. Norway and Denmark have also statutorised public access to official information. Norway has the Freedom of Information Act of 1970 besides the constitutional right to access the public documents. Denmark has the Access to Public Administration Files Act, 1985.

In USA the foundation of openness and right to information lay in the Constitutional Fundamental Right of Free Speech. The statutory framework for it is provided in the Freedom of Information Act, in 1966 and its statutory cousins, the Privacy Act, 1974 and the Sunshine Act, 1976. Freedom of Information Act makes disclosure a rule and non-disclosure an exception. Individuals have been given the right to access information and in case the information is withheld, the government has to justify the reason for the same. In case of denial of access to documents, the individuals have a right to seek injunctive relief. However, all the states as well as the District of Colombia and some territories have enacted similar legislations requiring disclosure of information by the agencies of the state and local governments.

In U. K., the Freedom of Information Act (FoIA) was passed on November 30, 2000. It gives a general right to public of access to all types of 'recorded' information held by public authorities, sets out exemptions from that general right, and places a number of obligations on public authorities. The Act applies only to 'public authorities' and not to private entities. Public authorities are, however, broadly defined in the Act, and they include not only Government Departments, local authorities and many other public bodies, (such as the Post Office, National Gallery and the Parole Board), but also schools, colleges and universities. Private entities such as spin-off companies, those are wholly or largely owned by a 'public authority' are also subject to the Act. The Act is enforced by the Information Commissioner who oversees both Freedom of Information and Data Protection legislation. The Act applies only to England, Wales and Northern Ireland. There is a separate Freedom of Information Act, 2002 for Scotland.

The concept of secrecy has almost lost its relevance in the Commonwealth countries like Canada, Australia and New Zealand. Canada has the Access to Information Act, 1985 and complementary Privacy Act, 1983. The Access to Information Act provides complete procedure of disclosure of information to person applying and requires the government departments to maintain a register, providing the kind of information, which is available to the public and have the register available for the public consultation. The Act gives every person who is a Canadian citizen, or a permanent resident a right to request for any record under the control of a government institution. A request for access to a record under this Act shall be made in writing and in sufficient detail to the government institution that has control of the record. Australia and New Zealand are having law on Freedom of Information since 1982.

In Asia, the Philippines recognised the right to access information held by the State relatively early, passing a Code of Conduct and Ethical Standards for Public Officials and Employees in 1987. A Code on Access to Information was adopted in Hong Kong in March 1995. In Thailand, the Official Information Act came into effect in December 1997. The Act on Disclosure of Information by Public Agencies came into effect in 1998 in South Korea. The Law Concerning Access to Information Held by Administrative Organs was enacted in April 2001 in Japan. Pakistan promulgated the Freedom of Information Ordinance in 2002. Instead of Information Commission there is Ombudsman in Pakistan. There are many exemptions, like file notings, intermediary opinion and private-personnel information. Rules not yet notified and information request procedure is very difficult and moreover, this ordinance does not cover Punjab and NWFP, therefore, is not an effective instrument of accessing the information. Nepal was the second country in the region after India, to introduce the full-fledged right to information in the form of Right to Information Act in July, 2007, though the Act not effectively implemented. Bangladesh recently (6th April, 2009) notified RTI Act in the Gazette. This ordinance is heavily borrowed from the Indian RTI Act, 2005. There is no Right to Information Law in Sri Lanka. However, Article 10 of the Constitution of Sri Lanka gives its citizen freedom of thought, conscience and religion while, Article 14, entitles Sri Lankan citizens to the freedom of speeches and expression. However, unlike Article 10, Article 14 is subjected to restiction.

South Africa remains the only African country to have actually passed freedom of information legislation. The 1996 Constitution of the Republic of South Africa is perhaps unique, not only in the breadth of its guarantee of freedom of information, but also in that it requires the adoption of national legislation to give effect to this right, within three years of its coming into force. The enabling legislation, the Promotion of Access to Information Act, came into effect in March 2001.

An insight into the international scenario reveals that there has been a trend from administrative practice of secrecy to freedom of information all over. As already underlined a number of counties all over the world have enacted legislations for access to information and many are in the process of doing so. The objectives behind these enactments are to ensure transparency, openness and fairness in the functioning of government. Most of the legislations are based on the premise that except for exceptional matters like security, defence of the nation etc., there is no room for secrecy in affairs of the Government.

Access to Information in India : The Legal Provisions

Various Indian laws provide for the right to access

information in specific contexts. Section 76 of the Indian Evidence Act, 1872, contains what has been termed a 'Freedom of Information Act in embryonic form'. This provision requires public officials to provide copies of public documents to anyone who has a right to inspect them.

The Factories Act, 1948, provides for compulsory disclosure of information to factory workers "regarding dangers including health hazards and the measures to overcome such hazards", arising from their exposure to dangerous materials. While this is an excellent provision, in practice it is violated with impunity. The Environment (Protection) Act 1986 and the Environmental Impact Assessment Regulations provide for public consultation and disclosure in various circumstances. Although this provision is meant to facilitate citizen input, in fact it is too limited and the environmental groups had to go to the courts to get more complete disclosure.

Regardless of these provisions, the system of Governance in India has traditionally been opaque, with the State retaining the colonial Official Secrets Act (OSA) and continuing to operate in secrecy at the administrative level. The OSA enacted in 1923 still retains its original form, apart from some minor amendments in 1967. Two important aspects have been dealt in the Act-Espionage and disclosure of secret official information. Section 5, is also called as the catchall provision of the Act, preventing disclosure of all official information. Under this Section, any official document can be marked as 'confidential' to prevent its disclosure to the public. The disclosure per se has been made punishable irrespective of the purpose of disclosure or the prejudicial effect it is going to have on the national interest. Both, the person who is communicating and the person, who is receiving the official information, are guilty under the Act. Person guilty under the Act is punishable with imprisonment, which may extend to three years or fine or both.

The point to decide whether the information is secret or

not lies solely with the government. Government by classifying any document as secret can prohibit public access to it. The Central Civil Service Conduct Rules, 1964 bolster the provisions of the OSA by prohibiting government servants from communicating any official document to anyone without authorisation. Section 123 of the Indian Evidence Act, 1872 also prohibits the giving of evidence from unpublished official records without the permission of the head of the relevant department, who is free to grant or to withhold such permission as he or she sees fit.

It is, therefore, essential to introduce consequential changes in the provisions of the different laws having negative implications on the free flow of information.

The Constitutional Development of RTI in India

At the outset, it may be said that, there was no specific right to information in the Constitution of India. The Right to Information has been read with the Fundamental Rights the Right to Freedom of Speech and Expression (Article 19(1)(a)) and the Right to Life and Personal Liberty (Article 21) contained in Chapter Three of the Constitution. In case of infringement of these rights one can approach the Supreme Court under Article 32 of the Constitution and High Court under Article 226 of the Constitution. These rights have received dynamic interpretation by the Supreme Court over the years and can truly said to be the basis for the development of the Rule of Law in India.

That the right to information is a fundamental right flowing from Art. 19(1) (a) of the Constitution is now well-settled. The legal position with regard to the right to information has developed through several Supreme Court decisions given in the context of the Right to Freedom of Speech and Expression, which has been said to be the obverse side of the Right to Know, and one cannot be exercised without the other. Over the years, the Supreme Court has consistently ruled in favour of the citizen's right to know. The nature of this right and the relevant restrictions thereto, has been discussed by the Supreme Court in a number of cases.

Further, Article 21 of the Constitution guarantees to every citizen the Right to Life and Personal Liberty. The citizens cannot exercise this right to protect their lives unless they are informed about threats to their lives, the measures being taken by the concerned authorities and the measures available to them. Without this information, the right becomes totally meaningless. Bhopal gas tragedy is a living example wherein many lives could have been saved if the people living near the plant site had been provided complete information about the hazards of the plant and how they can protect themselves from the MIC gas.

Article 51A (g) imposes a duty on every citizen to protect and improve environment.

> "It shall be the duty of every citizen of India to protect and improve the natural environment including forests, lakes, rivers and wildlife and to have compassion for living creatures"

Again this duty becomes meaningless if the citizens are denied information on important aspects of natural environment, various projects being taken up by the government which are going to effect the environment and the policies of the government on environmental issues. The right to know has also been reaffirmed in the context of environmental issues that have an impact upon people's very survival. Several High Court decisions have upheld the right of citizens' groups to access information where an environmental issue was concerned.

The fact that the Right to Information is included in the Constitutional guarantees of freedom of speech and expression has been recognised by Supreme Court decisions and its need for performance of Fundamental Duties has further deepened the roots of Right to Information as a Constitutional Right. The development of the Right to Information as a part of the Constitutional Law of the country started with petitions of the press to the Supreme Court for the enforcement of certain logical implications of the right to freedom of speech and expression such as challenging governmental orders for control of newsprint, bans on distribution of papers, etc.

The above referred landmark case was Bennett Coleman & Co. *vs.* Union of India, 1973, in which the petitioners, a publishing house bringing out one of the leading dailies challenged the government's newsprint policy which put restrictions on acquisition, sale and consumption of newsprint. This was challenged as restricting the Petitioner's rights to freedom of speech and expression. The court struck down the newsprint control order saying that it directly affected the Petitioner's right to freely publish and circulate their paper. In that, it violated their right to freedom of speech and expression. The judges also remarked, "It is indisputable that by freedom of the press meant the right of all citizens to speak, publish and express their views" and "Freedom to Speak and Expression" includes within its compass the right of all citizens to read and be informed."

The dissenting judgment of Justice K.K.Mathew also noted, "The freedom of speech protects two kinds of interests. There is an individual interest, the need of men to express their opinion on matters vital to them and a social interest in the attainment of truth so that the country may not only accept the wisest course but carry it out in the wisest way. Now in the method of political government the point of ultimate interest is not in the words of the speakers but in the hearts of the hearers".

In State of U.P *vs.* Raj Narain, 1975 the Supreme Court said, " While there are overwhelming arguments for giving to the executive the power to determine what matters may prejudice public security, those arguments give no sanction to giving the executive exclusive power to determine what matters may prejudice the public interest. Once considerations of national security are left out there are few matters of public interest which cannot be safely discussed in public". Justice K.K.Mathew went further to say, "In a government of responsibility like ours, where all the agents of the public must be responsible for their conduct, there can be but few secrets. The people of this country have a right to know every public act, everything that is done in a public way, by their public functionaries. They are entitled to know the particulars of every public transaction in all its bearing. The right to know which is derived from the concept of freedom of speech, though not absolute, is a factor which should make one wary, when secrecy is claimed for transactions which can, at any rate, have no repercussion on public security. To cover with veil of secrecy, the common routine business is not in the interest of the public. Such secrecy can seldom be legitimately desired. It is generally desired for the purpose of parties and politics or personal self-interest or bureaucratic routine. The responsibility of officials to explain or to justify their acts is the chief safeguard against oppression and corruption".

The Supreme Court in S.P. Gupta *vs*. Union of India, 1982 decided by seven-judge bench, added a fresh, liberal dimension to the need for disclosure in matters relating to public affairs. In the instant case it was held that in regard to the functioning of Government, disclosure of information must be the ordinary rule while secrecy must be an exception, justifiable only when it is demanded by the requirement of public interest. It was further held that the disclosure of documents relating to the affairs of the State involves two competing dimensions of public interest, namely, the right of the citizen to obtain disclosure of information, which competes with the right of the state of protecting the information relating to its crucial affairs. In addition it was also held that in deciding whether or not to disclose the contents of a particular document, a Judge must balance the competing interests and make his final decision depending upon the particular facts involved in each individual case. It is important to note that it was conceded that there are certain classes of documents which are necessarily required to be protected such as Cabinet Minutes, documents concerning the national safety, documents which affect diplomatic relations or relate to state secrets of the highest importance and the like in respect of which court would ordinarily uphold government's claim of privilege. However, even these documents have to be tested against the basic guiding principle, which is that wherever it is clearly contrary to the public interest for a document to be disclosed, then alone it is in law immune from disclosure.

In Dinesh Trivedi *vs.* Union of India, 1997 the Supreme Court while making a reference to the State of U.P. *vs.* Raj Narain and S.P. Gupta *vs.* Union of India held that in modern Constitutional democracies, it is axiomatic that citizens have a right to know about the affairs of the Government which, having been elected by them, seeks to formulate sound policies of governance aimed at their welfare. However, like all other rights, even this right has recognized limitations; it is by no means, absolute. Transactions, which have serious repercussions on public security, secrecy can legitimately, be claimed because it would then be in public interest that such matters are not publicly disclosed or disseminated.

In Secretary, Ministry of I&B, Government. of India *vs.* Cricket Association of Bengal, 1995 case the right to impart and receive information from electronic media was included in the freedom of speech by Supreme Court. The airwaves were held to be public property and hence distribution of these waves between government and private channels was to be done on an equitable basis.

In People's Union for Civil Liberties *vs.* Union of India, 2004 case, the Right to Information was further elevated by the Supreme Court to the status of a human right, necessary for making governance transparent and accountable. It held that people have every right to know the background of the contesting candidates for assembly and parliament. It also emphasized that governance must be participatory.

In the area of civil liberties, the courts have built up the right to have a transparent criminal justice system free from arbitrariness. In Prabha Dutt *vs.* Union of India, the Supreme Court held that excepting clear evidence that the prisoners had refused to be interviewed, there could be no reason for refusing permission to the media to interview prisoners in death row.

Repeated violations of civil rights by the police and other law enforcement agencies have compelled the courts to give, time and again, directions to the concerned agencies for ensuring transparency in their functioning in order to avoid violations like illegal arrests and detention, torture in custody and the like.

The Supreme Court has also given details of the procedural safeguards for arrest and custody. Most of these directions translate into the right of the accused or his kin to have access to information regarding his arrest and detention such as preparation of a memo of arrest to be counter-signed by the arrestee and a relative or neighbour, preparation of a report of the physical condition of the arrestee, recording of the place of detention in appropriate registers at the police station, display of details of detained persons at a prominent place at the police station and at the district headquarters, etc. Developments in administrative law further strengthened the right.

Thus, the above judgments cut across freedom of the individual, privacy, freedom of the press, duties of governments, duties of public authorities, right to seek disclosure of information about candidates contesting in elections and so on and so forth and also to the exceptions contained in Art. 19(2) of the Constitution. The overall impact of these decisions has been to establish clearly that the people's right to know is embedded in the provisions guaranteeing fundamental rights in the Constitution.

Legislating the Right to Information

Objections to the Official Secrets Act have been raised ever since 1948, when the Press Laws Enquiry Committee recommended certain amendments. In fact, the Act has been used time and again to suit the purposes of the government.

In 1977, a Working Group was formed by the Janata Party government to look into the possibilities of amending the Official Secrets Act. Unfortunately, the Working Group did not recommend changes, as it felt the that Act related to the protection of national safety and did not prevent the release of information in the public interest; despite overwhelming evidence to the contrary, Official Secret act remained unaltered.

In early 1989, V. P. Singh's National Front Government came to power and declared its decision to make Right to Information a fundamental right. He expressed his intention in April 1991 at the 20th Conference of Ministers of Information and Cinematography, when he said, "An open system of governance is an essential prerequisite for the fullest flowering of democracy. Free flow of information from the Government to the people will not only create an enlightened and informed public opinion but also render those in authority accountable. In the recent past, we have witnessed many distortions in our information system. The veil of secrecy was lowered many a time not in the interest of national security, but to shield the guilty, vested interests or gross errors of judgments. Therefore, the National Front Government has decided to make the Right to Information a Fundamental Right."

A Committee set up in 1989 by the National Front Government recommended limiting the areas where government information could be hidden and opening up of all other spheres of information. As most of the members of the Committee were bureaucrats, something different was not expected, so no legislation followed from these recommendations.

Finally, the focus of citizens' groups shifted from demanding merely an amendment to the Official Secrets Act, to its replacement by a comprehensive legislation towards the Right to Information. The initiative for the Right to Information was taken by a mass based organization, the Mazdoor Kisan Shakti Sangathan (MKSS) in early nineties in a very back ward region of Rajasthan—Bhim Tehsil. This agitation for transparency was started by asking for copies of bills and vouchers and names of persons who have been paid wages mentioned in the muster rolls for the construction of school, dispensaries, small dams and community centers in the Block Development & Panchayat Officer office. After years of knocking at officials' doors and despite the usual apathy of the State Government, MKSS succeeded in getting photocopies of certain relevant documents. Misappropriation of funds was clearly obvious. MKSS organized several *Jan Sunwai* (People's hearing), between December 1994 and April 1995, in Rajasthan. This grassroot movement spread very fast to other areas of Rajasthan and to other States establishing firmly that information is power and people should have the right to official information.

Subsequently, the National Campaign for People's Right to Information (NCPRI) formed in the late-1990s became a broad-based platform for action. As the campaign gathered momentum, it became clear that the right to information had to be legally enforceable. It was demanded that information that cannot be denied to Parliament or state legislatures cannot be denied to a citizen either.

In 1996, Justice P. B. Sawant, the Chairman of the Press Council of India, drafted the bill keeping in view the dire need of the day and the observations made by eminent persons that in a democracy, it is the people who are the masters and those utilizing public resources and exercising public power are their agents. Interestingly, this in turn derived significantly from a draft prepared earlier by a meeting of social activists, civil servants and lawyers at the Lal Bahadur Shastri National Academy of Administration, Mussoorie in October, 1995. One important feature of the Press Council draft legislation was that it affirmed in its preamble the constitutional position that the Right to Information already exists under the Constitution, as the natural corollary to the Fundamental Right to Free Speech and expression under Article 19(1) of the Constitution. It stated that the legislation merely seeks to make explicit provisions for securing to the citizen this right to information.

The Drafts Bill was submitted to the Government of India on 1996. The core of the Bill is Clause 3 which says:

(i) Every citizen shall have the Right to Information from public body;
(ii) It shall be the duty of the public body to maintain all records duly catalogued and indexed;
(iii) The public body shall be under a duty to make available to the person requesting information, as it is under an obligation to obtain and furnish and not withhold any information or limit its availability to the public except the information specified in Clause 4; and
(iv) All individuals whether citizens or not, shall have the right to such information that affects their life and liberty.

Information was defined as any fact relating to the affairs of the public body and included any of the records relating to its affairs. The right to information included inspection, taking notes and extracts and receiving certified copies of the documents. Significantly, the term 'public body' included not only the state as defined in Article 12 of the Constitution of India for the purposes of enforcing Fundamental Rights. It also incorporated all undertakings and non-statutory authorities, and most significantly a company, corporation, society, trust, firm or a co-operative society, owned or controlled by private individuals and institutions whose activities affect the public interest. In effect, both the corporate sector and the NGOs were sought to be brought under the purview of this proposed legislation.

Like the restriction on fundamental rights, under the Art. 19 (2) of the Constitution, the bill says that Right to Information is subject to restrictions on grounds of the security of the State, friendly relations with foreign States; public order; investigation of an offence or which leads to incitement to an offence', personal or medical information of a private nature and trade and commercial secrets protected by the law. The Bill also enumerates the procedure for the enforcement of this right. The officer in charge will be held responsible in the event of refusal of information, and information must be furnished within 30 days of application. The officer must provide solid reason for any refusal and appeal against refusal should be made to the principal civil judge of the region.

However, the most significant provision was that information which cannot be denied to the Parliament or the State Legislature shall not be denied to a citizen. The draft legislation laid down penalties for default in providing information, in the form of fines as personal liability on the person responsible for supplying the information. It also provided for appeals to the local civil judiciary against failure or refusal to supply the desired information.

Next came the Consumer Education Research Council (CERC) draft, by far the most detailed proposed freedom of information legislation in India. In line with international standards, it gave the right to information to anyone, except "alien enemies", whether or not they were citizens. It required public agencies at the federal and state levels to maintain their records in good order, to provide a directory of all records under their control, to promote the computerisation of records in interconnected networks, and to publish all laws, regulations, guidelines, circulars related to or issued by government departments and any information concerning welfare schemes. The draft provided for the outright repeal of the Official Secret Act. This draft didn't make it through Parliament either.

Finally in 1997, a Conference of Chief Ministers resolved that the central and state governments would work together on transparency and the right to information. Following this, the Centre agreed to take immediate steps, in consultation with the states, to introduce freedom of information legislation, along with amendments to the Official Secrets Act and the Indian Evidence Act, before the end of 1997. The Central and State governments also agreed to a number of other measures to promote openness. These included establishing accessible computerised information centres to provide information to the public on essential services, and speeding up ongoing efforts to computerise government operations. such as land records, passports, investigation of offences, administration of justice, tax collection, and the issue of permits and licences.

In 1997, two states passed right to information legislation (Tamil Nadu and Goa). Keeping in view the burning problem, the Department of Personnel Government of India, constituted a Working Group on January 2, 1997 under the chairmanship bureaucrat and consumer activist H.D. Shourie to draft a legislation for consideration of government. The working group on the 'Right to Information and promotion of open and Transparent Government' submitted its comprehensive and detailed report and the draft Bill on Freedom of Information on 24 May 1997.

The salient features of the 1997 Bill :

(i) When enacted, it will also apply to State governments

over riding State legislations to the extent they clash with the Central legislation;

(ii) A fee would be paid by the citizen while seeking information from Government, and the officer or the department concerned can be held responsible and taken to a Consumer Court for not providing the information within the prescribed time limit of 30 days;

(iii) Every Government department should appoint a Public Information Officer for this purpose;

(iv) Section 5 of the Official Secrets Act should be suitably amended to make it easier for a citizen to obtain official information, and information can be withheld only in respect of especially 'exempted' items;

(v) Clauses 123 and 124 of the Indian Evidence Act which inhibit public officials from submitting information to Courts, should be suitably amended; and

(vi) The basis and the procedure for classification of official documents (as 'top secret', Secret' and 'confidential' should be suitably amended so that availability of information to the public becomes the rule rather than the exception.

Not only the Central and the State Ministries, but also public sector undertakings, municipal bodies and panchayats and other bodies substantially funded by Government, would come within the purview of the Act.

The Working Group Report, was advanced on the Press Council draft in one respect. It explicitly brought the judiciary and legislatures under the purview of the proposed legislation. Many of the positive aspects of the Press Council legislation were excluded or diluted in the Shourie's draft. Most importantly, it widened the scope of exclusions to enable public authorities to withhold 'information, the disclosure of which would not sub serve any public interest'. This single clause broke the back of the entire legislation, because in effect public authorities would then be empowered to withhold disclosure of incriminating information in the name of public interest. This simulation could have been avoided if the powerful clause of Press Council Legislation, which provided that only such information that can be denied to Parliament or the legislature can be withheld from the citizen, was not included.

The Shourie's draft also made no provisions for penalties in the event of default, rendering the Right to Information toothless. Appeals were allowed to consumer courts. The Act defined public authorities more narrowly to exclude the private sector and all NGOs which are not 'substantially funded or controlled' by government.

The Press Council of India, the Press Institute of India, the National Campaign for People's Right to Information and the Forum for Right to Information unanimously submitted the Resolution on February 20, 1998 to Government of India for amending the proposed bill.

Main Points of the 1998 Resolution

(i) The Right to Information should also be extended in respect of companies, NGOs and international agencies whose activities are of a public nature and have a direct bearing on public interest;

(ii) The law must contain strong, penal provisions against willful and wanton withholding or delay in supplying information or deliberately supplying misleading or inaccurate information;

(iii) The law must contain an appeal mechanism of an independent nature to provide reliable redress to any citizen dissatisfied with any decision of a public authority under this law;

(iv) The categories of information, which can be restricted or withheld by the Government, are too wide in the draft Bill. In particular, the restriction on disclosing internal nothings and official correspondence between public officials and offices has no justification whatsoever;

(v) Similarly the restriction on confidential communications between the State and Centre and their agencies have no justification, unless they harm public interest; and

(vi) The restriction on disclosure of the record of discussions of Secretaries and other public servants also needs to be removed. However, this draft also went into cold storage due to the fall of two United Front Governments;

Freedom of Information Bill 2000

The BJP led National Democratic Alliance reworked on the Shourie's draft to finalise the Freedom of Information Bill, 2000. It was introduced in the Lok Sabha on July 25, 2000. However, after the president's signature this Act could not be notified in the Government Gazette.

This Freedom of Information Bill included some provisions that were not in the Shourie draft, such as the requirement that urgent requests in cases involving life and liberty should get a response within 48 hours. Various provisions of the Act were similar to that of the RTI Act except on the points on which it has been criticized.

The Act has been criticised on the followings main points: It reinforces the controlling role of the government official, who retains wide discretionary powers to withhold information. For example, requests for information involving "disproportionate diversion of the resources of a public authority" can be shot down by the public information officer. This leaves open the danger that government officials might be transformed from gatekeepers of the Official Secrets Act to gatekeepers of the Freedom of Information Act.

The most scathing indictment of the Act has come from

the critics who focus on the sweeping exemptions it permits viz. restrictions on information relating to security, foreign policy, defence, law enforcement and public safety. The Act also excludes Cabinet papers, including records of the Council of Ministers, secretaries and other officials. Information shared between the Centre and States were not subject to disclosure. These exemptions effectively shielded the whole process of decision-making from mandatory disclosure.

There was neither penalty provision nor provision for Information Commission. So there is no compelling reason for the official concerned to provide answers. Instead, the law provides for two internal appeals within the government machinery and, in addition, blocks access to civil courts. Private bodies were kept out of the purview of this Act.

Legislation in States Prior to the RTI Act

Inspired and encouraged by the exercises taken up by the Press Council of India, Working Group and the Central Government and under popular pressure, the State Governments also started preparing draft legislation on Right to Information. Before the Freedom of Information Bill, 2000 introduced in the Lok Sabha on 25 July, 2000, a number of States had already introduced the Bill on Right to Information, .

Clause (18) of the Bill empowered the State Government to make rules to implement the provisions of the Act. On the matters relating to the fee payable to obtain information from any organization, the authority to be prescribed before which appeal may be referred against the decision of the Public Information Officer and any other matter which is required to be prescribed.

Tamil Nadu was the first to introduce the RTI Act on 17 April 1996. Modeled on a draft legislation recommended by the Press Council of India, it stipulated that the authorities should part with information within 30 days of its being sought. All Public Distribution System shops in the State were asked to display details of available stocks. The government departments brought out citizens' charters listing information on what the public was entitled to know and get. The statute was, however, not clear about application on Panchayat Unions, Municipalities and Panchayat. It was full of exemptions and inadequacies and failed to evoke much response from the public, NGOs and other concerned activists.

Goa was the second State to enact the RTI legislation in 1997. It was a progressive legislation with the few categories of exceptions. It also provided for urgent processing of requests pertaining to life and liberty and a penalty clause. Besides, private bodies executing government works were also brought in its purview. However, one notable weakness is that it has no provision for pro-active disclosure by government.

In Karnataka, access to information already existed through the Karnataka Freedom of Press Bill 1988. Its essential features were: (i) immunity to a journalist from disclosure of the source of information (ii) right to access to public documents and (iii) penalty for causing hurt to a journalist on duty. But the Bill did not see the light of the day. Karnataka took some more steps to provide access to information to the public way back in 1997 and for this purpose government departments issued executive orders. These were replaced by the Karnataka RTI Act, 2002 and Rules were notified in July 2002 to operationalise it. This apart from containing standard exception clauses covering 12 categories of information, and limited provisions for pro-active disclosure, contains a penalty clause and provides for an appeal to an independent tribunal.

Maharashtra also enacted the Right to Information Act, 2000 due to sustained pressure from social activist and anticorruption crusader Anna Hazare in Maharastra. It had nine sections and 22 categories of exemptions but no provisions for appellate authority or penalties for withholding or destroying information. It empowered the citizens with the RTI about various government schemes, their stages of implementation and other details. It has been recognized as the most progressive piece of legislation. The Act not only brings government and semi-government bodies but also state public sector units, co-operatives, registered societies (including educational institutions) and public trusts within its purview. It provides for a fine also for not furnishing information on Public Information Officer. For wilful incorrect, misleading and incomplete information, the PIO may also be subject to disciplinary action. A council comprising of senior members of government, members of the press and representatives of NGOs was to be set up to monitor the workings of the Act and to review its functioning at least once every six months.

Delhi passed Delhi Right to Information Act in 2001 modeled on the Goa Act. Competent authority in the Public Authority are provide information within 30 days of receiving the application. It contained the standard exceptions and provided for an appeal to an independent body, i.e. Public Grievances Commission and the State Council for Right to Information. It is also prescribed for a penalty for false or deliberately tampered information. This Act is still in operation in Delhi but used mainly for grievances redressal.

Rajasthan passed the Right to Information Act in 2000. It had 13 sections and provided for 10 categories of exemptions, and in total had 13 sections of which 10 established categories of exemptions. Besides having weak penalty provisions, it gave too much discretionary power to bureaucrats. Despite this, the right to information movement thrives at the grassroots level in Rajasthan, due to systematic campaigns waged by concerned groups and people's growing awareness of their own role in participatory governance.

Assam also passed the Assam Right to Information Act in 2001, following a number of executive orders dealing with access to information regarding public distribution system, development programmes, and pollution awareness. In Madhya Pradesh the RTI Bill, 1998 was passed in 2002. It aimed at providing transparency in the administration. But even before its enactment, the local authorities acquired the access to information in certain places like Bilaspur and Korba. The Divisional Commissioner, Bilaspur allowed the citizen the access to the details of Public Distribution System. Meanwhile the other states like, Kerala and Gujarat had also decided to introduce the RTI Bills in their respective assemblies.

The *Jammu & Kashmir Right to Information Act, 2004*, was enacted on 7 January, 2004. The *Rules to the Act* were issued on June 30, 2005. In September 2007, the Jammu & Kashmir Assembly passed the *Jammu & Kashmir Right to Information (Amendment) Act*, which was duly notified in the Jammu & Kashmir Gazette in January 2008. The Amendment Act, 2008 includes for several amendments to the original 2004 Act to bring it closer in-line with the (Central) RTI Act, 2005, though it has been criticized by citizen's groups for "watering down" its key provisions.

The Amendment Act, 2008 is technically "in force" but several provisions have not been implemented as the accompanying Amendment Act Rules have not yet been issued. Most importantly, the prescribed Jammu & Kashmir State Information Commission has not yet been constituted and appointed. Until that time, the RTI Act, 2004 is the effective governing legislation for the Right to Information with the Government of Jammu & Kashmir, with appeals directed to the General Administration Department as prescribed under the J&K RTI Act, 2004. Though the state subjects and residents of Jammu & Kashmir may still seek information within Jammu & Kashmir from the Union

Government and its offices in the state under the (Central) RTI Act, 2005, as they are governed by the Central Act and not by state-level legislation.

Again the Jammu of Kashmir government tabled the J&K RTI Bill, 2009 in the Jammu & Kashmir Legislative Assembly on 7th March, 2009. The Bill if passed will replace the current J&K RTI Act, 2004 as amended by the J&K RTI (Amendment) in Act 2008. The Bill contains provisions that are similar to the RTI Act, 2005 enacted by the Parliament and would bring J&K Act at par with the Central RTI Act.

Note : As such, the (Central) RTI Act, 2005 applies to the whole country except to the State of Jammu & Kashmir as Jammu & Kashmir is accorded special provisions under Article of the Constitution, which exempts most legislation passed in the Parliament from automatically applying to the Jammu & Kashmir. Instead, under the Constitution of Jammu & Kashmir, the State's own Legislative Assembly has the option of (a) voting to "extend" a Union Act to its own state using a special legislative procedure, (b) voting to enact a state-specific law of its own using the traditional state-level drafting process, or (c) simply ignoring the Union Act altogether.

Objections to the Official Secrets Act have been raised since Independence. Serious efforts in the direction of amending OSA began in 1977. Before the Freedom of Information Bill, 2000 introduced in the Lok Sabha, a number of States had already introduced the Bill on Right to Information. It was in this backdrop that the RTI was enacted in India in 2005. It marks a paradigm shift in Indian democracy.

RTI Act, 2005

Ultimately, the Parliament of India passed legislation on Right to Information in 2005. It is a landmark legislation in

Indian context. It is in consonance with provisions of International Covenants on the issue and has brought India in line with other development democracies of the world. Right to Information Act, 2005 was passed by both the Houses in the Summer Session of the Parliament and received assent of President on June 15, 2005. Around 150 amendments were introduced in the original draft. The Act replaces relatively weak and ineffective legislation, the Freedom of Information Act, 2002.

Summing Up

There is a visible global trend towards the recognition of the Right to Information (RTI) by various countries, inter-governmental organisations, civil society and many sections of the people. Over the past few years, the 'RTI' has gained increasing prominence in the Human Rights discourse as well as the larger democratic discourse. Since a democratic government must be sensitive to the public opinion, for which information must be made available by it to the people. It goes without saying, the greater the access of the citizen to information, the greater the responsiveness of government to community needs. Actually, meaningful substantive democracy ought to be founded on the notion of an informed public that is able to participate thoughtfully in its own governance. Information and knowledge are the instruments of transformation. Therefore, without sufficient information, representative democracy is undermined. RTI has also been widely acknowledged as a requisite for ensuring accountability and good governance.

Effective accountability rests on the peoples' acquaintance with the information. A system that operates in secrecy tends to lose the faith of the people as much as its own legitimacy and credibility. Openness and full access to information are the two pillars of the democratic state. These equip the citizens to participate meaningfully in the development process.

Governance is undoubtedly strengthened by the RTI. That is why the RTI has now been recognized as an essential requirement of the good governance.

RTI has been granted in about 70 countries of the world and another 30 countries are in the process of doing so. Sweden was the first country to enact a law on freedom of information since 1766. In Western Europe, only Germany and Switzerland lack legislation. Nearly all Central and Eastern European countries have adopted laws as part of their democratic transitions. Almost a dozen Asian countries have either enacted laws or are in the process of doing so. Similarly, in South and Central America, several countries are considering such laws. Many countries in Southern and Central Africa are following South Africa's lead, for formulating freedom of information laws.

That the RTI is a Fundamental Right flowing from Article 19(1) (a) of the Constitution is now well-settled in our country. Over the years, the Supreme Court has consistently ruled in favour of the citizen's Right to Know in a number of cases. Various Indian laws provide for the right to access information in specific contexts.

Regardless of these provisions, the system of governance in India has traditionally been opaque, with the State retaining the colonial Official Secrets Act (OSA) and continuing to operate in secrecy at the administrative level. It is, therefore, essential to introduce consequential changes in the provisions of the different laws having negative implications on the free flow of information. At the outset, it may be said that, there was no specific right to information in the Constitution of India. The transition from an opaque system of governance, legitimised by the colonial Official Secrets Act, to the RTI took 82 years.

REFERENCES

Practical Guidance: Note on Right to Information, UNDP, October 2003.
Practical Guidance: Note on Right to Information, UNDP, October 2004.

United Nations and General Assembly Resolution 217 (III) A of 1948.
United Nations and General Assembly Resolution 2200 A (XXI) of 1966.
Bennett Coleman *v.* Union of India , AIR 1973 SC 60.
State of UP *v.* Raj Narain, (1975) 4 SCC 428.
S.P. Gupta *v.* UOI, AIR 1982 SC 149.
Secy., Ministry of I&B, Government of India *v.* Cricket Assn. of Bengal , (1995) 2 SCC 161.
Handbook on Right to Information Act, 2005, Right to Information Cell, Yashwantrao Chavan Academy of Development Administration, Raj Bhavan Complex, Baner Road, Pune
People's Union for Civil Liberties *v.* UOI, 2004 (2) SCC 476.
Governance and Accountability in the Public Sector, speech by Hon'ble Lianne Dalziel, 2003 (www.scoop.co.nz).
See Importance of Human Right to Information – A Key to Good Governance by Ms. Prabha, S.D. College , Muzaffarnagar, UP, contained in chapter 27 of the book, Good Governance in India , edited by C.P. Barthwal.
Anu Kumar — RTI: Background and Perspective, Info Change News and Features, June 2003.
P. Slogh & C. Rodrigues – Indias RTI movement makes a breakthrough, *Open Government: A Journal on Freedom of Information*, vol. 1, 21 March 2005.
G. Prasanna Kumar & Suresh Misra – Democratizing Governance: Right to Informationa Opportunities and Challenges.
Sapna Chadah – Right to Information Regime in India: A Critical Appraisal, *IJPA*, vol. LII, No. 1, Delhi, January to March 2006.
"What is Good Governance" (July 2001).
Harsh Mander and Abha Singhal Joshi, The Movement for Right to Information in India: People's Power for the Control of Corruption.
Y.K. Sabharwal, Right to Information, Issues of Administrative Efficiency, Public Accountability and Constitutional Governance.
Jaytilak Guha Roy, Right to Information Initiatives and Impact, Occational paper, IIPA, New Delhi, March, 2006.
Suchi Pande and Shekhar Singh, Right to Information Act, 2005: A Primer, National Book Trust, India, New Delhi, 2008.
R.S. Tolia, Towards a Transparent and Accountable Uttarakhand (Handbook), Uttarakhand Information Commission, Dehradun, Uttarakhand, 2007.
B.P.Maithani, Some Grey Areas of the RTI Act, Uttarakhand Information Commission, State Coordinator, RTI Cell, Dehradun, Uttarakhand, 2007.
PRIA, Analysis of judgements of the Central Information Commission on the Right to Information Act, 2005, New Delhi, October 2007.
Report of National Sub Committee of CIC on Implementation of RTI Act, 2005, New Delhi, July, 2008.

http:// *www.cic.gov.in/Conference/Program.htm* (Recommendations of the Three National Conventions i.e. 2006, 2007 and 2008.).

A Guide to Right to Information, IC Centre for Governance.

The Right to Information Act, 2005.

"J&K RTI Act 2004 (Official Copy)" (PDF). Government of Jammu & Kashmir, GA. http://jkgad.nic.in/roi/JK-RTI-Act-2004.PDF. Retrieved on 2007-09-14.

"SRO 181, Right to Information Rules (Official Copy)" (PDF). Government of Jammu & Kashmir. http://www.jkgad.nic.in/roi/JK-RTI-Rules-2005.PDF. Retrieved on 2008-10-29.

"State Level RTI: Jammu and Kashmir". Commonwealth Human Rights Initiative (Delhi Office). http://www.humanrightsinitiative.org/programs/ai/rti/india/states/jammu_kashmir.htm. Retrieved on 2008-10-29.

Bukhari, Shujaat. "J&K RTI Act amended, State to have Information Commission soon". *The Hindu (newspaper)*. http://www.hindu.com/2007/09/02/stories/2007090256000900.htm. Retrieved on 2008-10-29.

Nayak, Venkatesh. "Jammu and Kashmir Right to Information (Amendment) Bill, 2007: An Analysis with Recommendations for Improvement" (PDF). Commonwealth Human Rights Initiative (Delhi Office). http://www.humanrightsinitiative.org/programs/ai/rti/india/states/jk/jk_rti_bill_2007_chri_submission2.pdf. Retrieved on 2008-10-29.

JK_rti_bill_2009_chri_analysis.pdf

2 Salient Features and Deficiencies

The RTI Act confers on all citizens the right to seek information and makes it the duty of the public authorities to disseminate the same for better governance and accountability. It covers the Central and State Governments, Panchayati Raj Institutions, local bodies and recipients of government grants but does not apply to the intelligence and security organizations except if the information relates to the allegations of corruption. The Prime Minister said that it would usher in a new era of performance and transparency to benefit the common man in the complex modern world and empower the people to judge if the government was functioning in public interest. It gives public-spirited people an instrument to prevent misuse of public power and funds. He said that the intention was to enlarge the interface between people and government and not to paralyse the administration.

Preamble to the Act

The Preamble to the Act says that it has been enacted for establishing "the practical regime of Right to Information for citizens to secure access to information under the control of public authorities, in order to promote transparency and accountability in the working of every public authority, the constitution of a Central Information Commission and State Information Commissions and for matters connected therewith or incidental thereto".

It further points out that democracy requires an informed citizenry and transparency in information to contain corruption and to hold governments and their instrumentalities accountable to the governed. The Preamble also says that, in some cases, revelation of information in actual practice is likely to conflict with other public interests including efficient operations of the Governments, optimum use of limited physical resources and the preservation of confidentiality of sensitive information. The Act proposes to harmonise these conflicting interests while preserving the paramountcy of the democratic idea by providing the needed exemptions.

Salient Features of the Right to Information Act, 2005

- The Act provides all citizens the right to information, subject to the provisions of the Act.
- It covers all *the three tiers i.e. central, state and local government and also the three branches i.e. legislative, executive and judiciary of the government.*
- It applies to *"Public Authorities"* established or constituted by or under the Constitution; by any law made by the appropriate Government or, any other body owned, controlled or substantially financed directly or indirectly by' the appropriate Government, and includes non-government organizations, substantially financed by the government.
- The ambit, covers even the private bodies and their information can be accessed through the controlling public authority.
- The Act provides that information of the third party can be accessed after giving ten days notice to the third party.
- It casts an obligation on Public Authorities to grant access to information and to publish certain categories of information. Public Authorities are also supposed to maintain their record in the indexed and cataloged manner. The responsibilities about suo-moto disclosure/publication 'by public authorities have been considerably enlarged .

- The Act lays down the machinery for the grant of access to information. The Public Authorities are required to designate Public Information Officers and Assistant: Public Information Officers for dealing with requests for information and··· also to assist persons' seeking: information .
- Provision has been made for transfer of a request by a public, authority to another public authority, wherein the subject' matter/information is held by the latter.
- A time limit has been prescribed for compliance with requests for information under the Act, viz. 30 days for normal information; 40 days for third party information; life and liberty information in 48th hours and information relating to human rights violation in 45 days.
- The Act provides that in case PIO rejects the application, he/she is bound to give reasons of such rejection; the period within which can appeal against such rejection may be referred as well as the particulars of the appellate authority.
- The Act excludes the time taken for calculation and intimation of fees from the time frame.
- The Act prescribes for reasonable fee for providing information. Also, no fee to be charged from persons who are below poverty line. Further, information to be provided free of charge where the response time limit is not adhered to.
- Certain categories of information have been exempted from disclosure. The categories, by way of illustration, include, information likely to affect security of the State, strategic, scientific or economic interests of the State, detection and investigation of offences, public order, conduct of international relations and Cabinet papers. Trade or commercial secrets, information the disclosure of which would

cause breach of privilege of Parliament of State Legislature and personnel information which has no relationship with public activity and could cause unwarranted invasion of the privacy of any person are also exempted from disclosure. However, exemptions provided are not absolute and withholding of information must be balanced against disclosure in the public interest. Information is to be released even if harm is shown to the public authority if the public benefit in knowing the information outweighs the harm that may be caused by disclosure.

- The Act contains a provision for reveal of certain information, which is otherwise, exempted from disclosure on completion of 20 Years after the incident.
- The Act also incorporates the principle of severability.
- Envisages creation of an independent non-judicial machinery, viz., Central Information Commission and State Information Commissions comprising a Chief Information Commissioner and Information Commissioners to decide 2nd stage appeals. At the same time, there is no hierarchy of Commissions.
- Legal framework for exercise of powers by the Commission defined in the Act.
- The Commission while inquiring into any matter has the same powers as are vested in a civil court while trying a suit under the Code of Civil Procedure.
- The Act provides a two-tier Appellate Forum. First appeal to departmental officer senior to the Public Information Officer. The second appeal to be made to the Commission .
- On a request for information being refused, the applicant can prefer an appeal to the prescribed authority within 30 days of the decision; the time limit for disposal of appeal being also 30 days extendable

RTI Act : Main Sections at a Glance

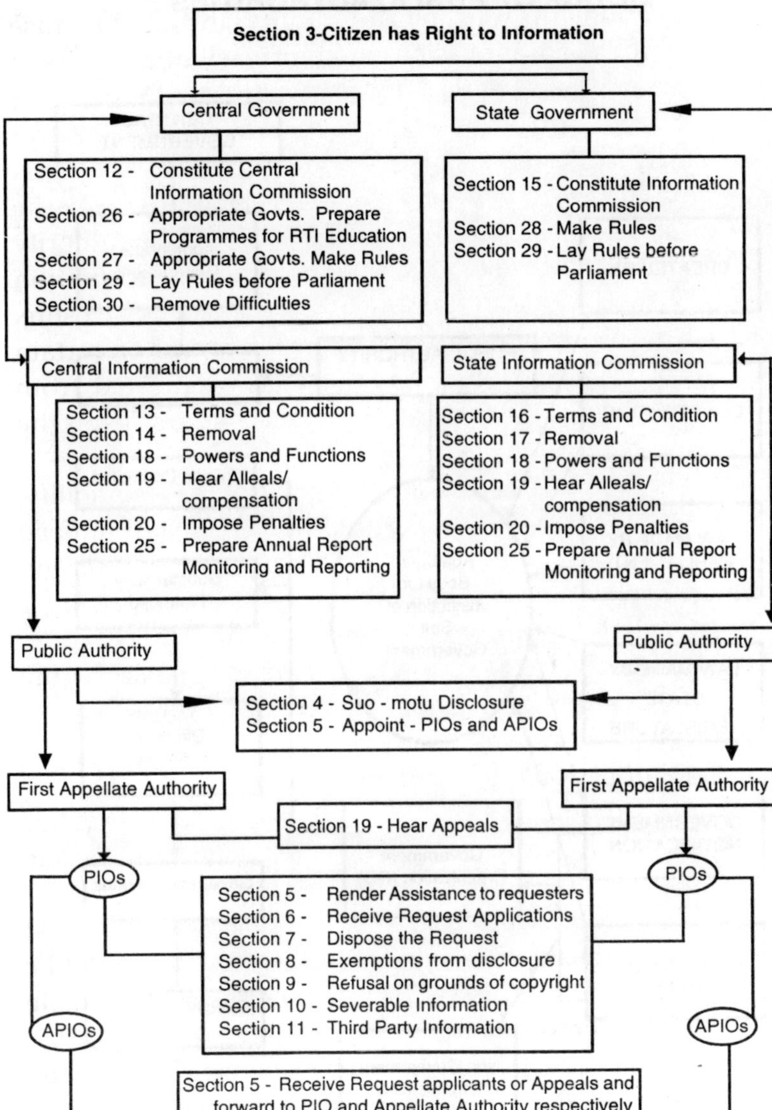

* Some other sections

Extent and commencement of the Act-1

Definitions : Appropriate Government - 2a; Competent Authority - 2e; Information - 2f; Public Authority - 2h; Records - 2i; Right to information - 2j; Third Party - 2n;

Protection of action taken and good faith for PIO-21; Act has overriding effect - 22; Bar on Jurisdiction of court - 23; and doesn't apply to listed agencies - 24.

Source : Handbook on Right to Information Act, 2005, Yashada, Pune

SET UP OF PUBLIC AUTHORITIES

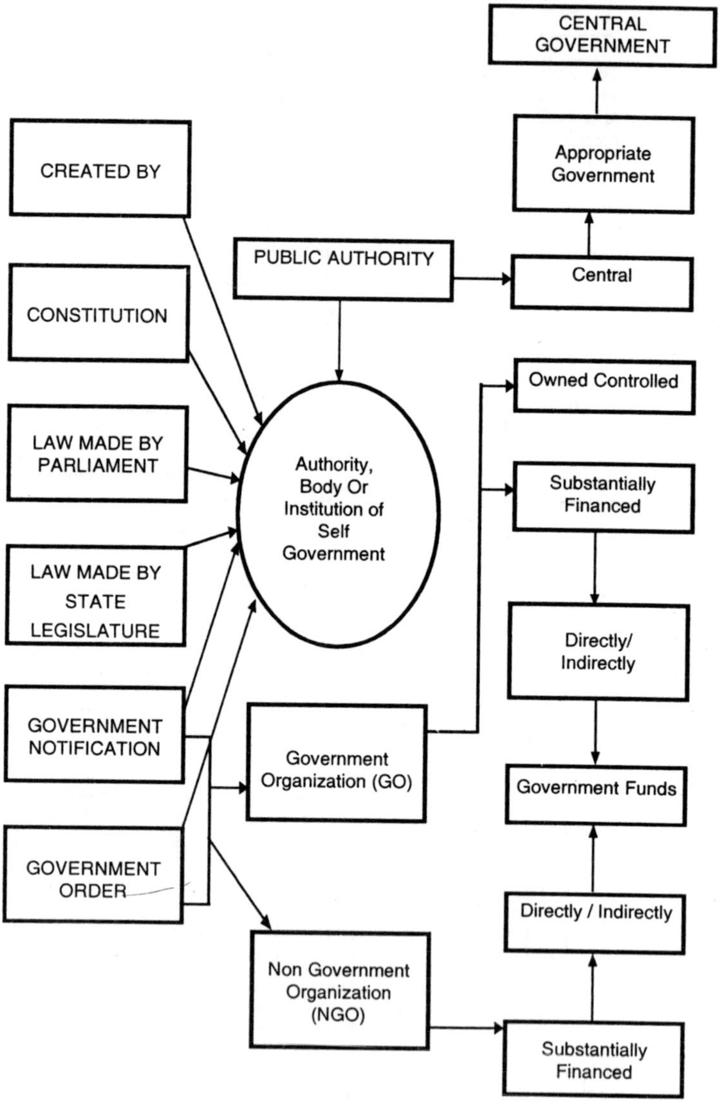

Source : Handbook on Right to Information Act, 2005 Yashada, Pune.

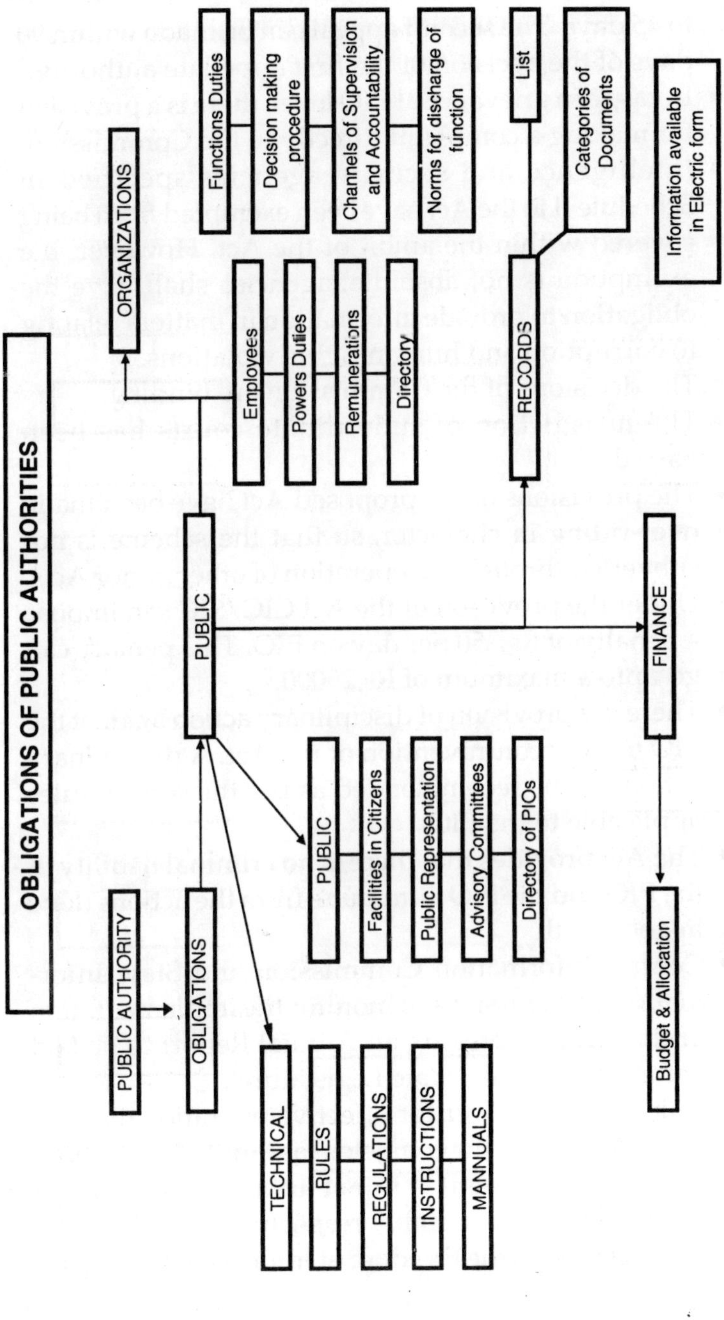

Source : Handbook on Right to Information Act, 2005, Yashada, Pune.

to 45 days. The second appeal can be made within 90 days of the decision of the first appellate authority.

- In case of a grievance at PIO level, there is a provision for making a complaint directly to the Commission
- Intelligence and security agencies specified in Schedule II to the Act have been exempted from being covered within the ambit of the Act. However, the exemption is not absolute; agencies shall have the obligation to provide information in matters relating to corruption and human rights violations.
- The decisions of the Commission are binding.
- The jurisdiction of subordinate courts has been barred.
- The provisions of the proposed Act have been made over-riding in character, so that the scheme is not subverted through the operation of other minor Acts.
- Under the provision of the Act CIC/SIC can impose a penalty of Rs.250 per day on PIO. This penalty can go upto a maximum of Rs,25000.
- There is a provision of disciplinary action against the PIO for any contravention of the Act. A disciplinary action can be recommended as per the service rules applicable to the PIO.
- The Act provides that there is no criminal liability of the PIO and the PIO is immune from the actions done in good faith.
- Central Information Commission and State Information Commissions to monitor the implementation of the Act and prepare an Annual Report to be laid before Parliament/State Legislature .
- Rule making power for effective operationalisation of the Act is with the competent authority i.e. Central/ State Government subject to the approval of Parliament and Assembly respectively.
- The Act repeals the Freedom of Information Act, 2002.

Some Deficiencies in the RTI Act

Inspite of being very exhaustive and with all its positive features, the RTI Act suffers from some weaknesses which has impeded its uniform and effective implementation during the last three years. These deficiencies are discussed below:

I. Missing Definitions

Substantial Financing

The Act does not define the word "substantially financed". Though some Information Commissioners both at the Centre and the State level are of the view that since the word control is there in the definition of public authority so why the need of the definition of substantial financing has not aroused as one can have the information of public authority even if it has not been financed because it is controlled by some agency or department under certain existing Act. However, the substantial financing has created a lot of confusion for the user and providers of information under the Act. Therefore, it should have been amplified by way of an explanation. This omission will result in different interpretations of the term by different states and public authorities.

There is another dimension to this issue. The expression Non-Governmental Organisations as used in the Act is ambiguous. The NGOs, are a class and category apart from the other private sector organisations. The use of the phrase 'Non-Governmental Organisations' creates an illusion that the Act is applicable only to NGOs because they receive funds under various projects and schemes of the Government as partners in implementation. There are many other private institutions specially the Government aided private schools and colleges who believe that they should not be designated as public authority on the spurious argument that they belong to the private sector.

Similarly, there is problem with identification and interpretation of the organisations which are indirectly financed by the appropriate Government. The Act does not provide any guidance on the criteria for identifying these. Tax concessions, various subsidies, infrastructure facilities, acquisition and allotment of land on concessional cost etc. are various ways by which indirect benefits are extended to private sector. There is therefore, need to further substantiate the conditions implying 'substantially financed' directly or indirectly by the Governmental. Instead of using the phrase 'Non-Governmental Organisations substantially financed', the Act should have laid down not only public bodies but also private companies, corporations, societies and trusts owned or controlled by private individuals whose activities affect the public interest. It could have been more explicit than the phase Substantially Financed Non-Governmental Organisations.

No provision for ensuring the fulfilment of obligations on public authorities

The Act also imposes certain obligations on public authorities in Section 4. Primarily, these relate to (a) proper maintenance and upkeep of records, and (b) suo motu dissemination of information through publication of information directories about the functions and functioning of each public authority. But, the public authorities, have generally been treating this provision as optional rather than compulsory. The dictionary meaning of obligation is binding power, written bond, duty, some thing that obligates one to a course of action, etc. But it appears that in the absence of any penalty clause, the task is not viewed as an obligation. This gives rise to the question: What option the Information Commission has if the Public Authority does not comply with this provision? Unless enforced, these obligations will remain only on paper.

Life and Liberty

The Act does not define the information falling under life and liberty. Sikkim has defined life and liberty in its RTI rule as if the information requested relates to a person's confinement, internment, arbitrary detention, imminent death at the hands of the State or another individual, torture or violation of due process rights. Moreover, there is no provision for relatively speedier disposal of appeals/ complaints regarding information pertaining to 'Life and Liberty' unlike 48 hours time stipulated for providing such information. The Act should be amended to include such provisions.

II. Confusion about First Appellate Authority

The Section 19(1) provides for the designation of an appellate authority at the Public Authority level who is an officer senior in rank to the Public Information Officer (PIO). However, the Act is silent about the powers and functions of the first appellate authority. As a result, there is confusion about the role and responsibility of the first appellate authorities.

Moreover, the Act does not in a way, make the first appeal mandatory when it says that any person aggrieved by the decision of the PIO may prefer an appeal to such officer who is senior in rank to her/him. In general perception, an applicant is supposed to appeal with the Information Commission only after she/he has exhausted all options. The Act does not support this perception. It is not clear whether the information commission can entertain an appeal when the first appeal has not been preferred by the appellant.

Another paradox that arises from this confusion is about the status of the First Appellate authority *vis-a-vis* the information commissioner. Since both are appellate authorities under the Act, the Information Commission can not summon and force the attendance of the first Appellate

Authority and compel him to give evidence and produce the documents. This lack of clarity needs to be corrected for efficient and effective implementation of the Act.

III. Appeal Procedure

Section 19(9) of the Act states that the information commission shall give notice of its decision, including right to appeal to the complainant and the public authority. It does not make clear whether the right to appeal can be exercised at the commission level itself. It will be better if the cases and situations in which review petitions may be filed for reconsideration of the decision of a single commissioner bench or by two or more commissioners bench or by a full commission are specified.

IV. Overlapping of the Grounds of Appeal and Complaints

The grounds of a complaint under Section (u/s) 18 and for an appeal u/s 19 are over lapping. Separate grounds should be there for appeals and complaints. Three clauses of Section 18 (1) i.e. Clause (b) relating to refusal of access to information; (c) relating to no response to the request for information within the stipulated time; and (e) relating to giving incomplete, misleading or false information may be deleted as these grounds are basically for exercising appellate powers u/s 19.

V. Contempt Provisions

Section 19(7) of the Act states that the decision of the Information Commission shall be binding. But it is not supported by 'Contempt of Court' provision to enforce compliance of its decision by the public authority. Due to the absence of such a provision there are instances of non-compliance of orders passed by the Commission. Power of contempt should be given to the Information Commissions so as to implement their orders. Specific provisions may be included in the RTI Act itself for dealing with contempt proceedings. In the absence of any contempt provision under the RTI Act, it is suggested that the compensation clause under Section 19(8) (b) of the Act can be invoked against the public authorities for non-compliance of the Commission's decisions. The amount of penalty imposed or compensation awarded by the Commission should be made recoverable. For this purpose, head of the erring public authority/ Appellate authorities can be treated as deemed CPIO/SPIO and thereby invoking penalty provisions under Section 20(1) of the RTI Act.

VI. Information Commissions and Powers of Civil Courts

Information Commissions have been conferred powers of a civil court u/s 18(3) under the Civil Procedure Code, 1908. The powers of civil court u/s 18(3) have been given only for limited purposes. These do not cover powers concerning execution of decrees and recovery of fine etc. The ICs powers of civil courts may be incorporated into a separate section within the same Chapter V so that it becomes applicable to all proceedings (including enquiry , appeal and penalty proceedings). Similarly, the provisions under Section 19 (7) and 19(8) may be incorporated in separate sections in Chapter V so that these powers can be applied in case of all proceedings before the Commission. Similarly, there is no uniformity of procedure of enquiry, the procedure for hearing under Section 19 and for conducting enquiry u/s 18 which points should be clearly outlined.

VII. No Time Limit for IC to Decide the Appeals

Unlike the time limit for the First Appellate Authority for giving decisions on appeals, the Act does not provide for any time limit to decide the appeal. Due to the absence of this provision, ICs are very often not giving the decisions on appeals on time and not only this the disposal rate is also not very good. To avoid any delay in disposal of appeals, there should be a provision regarding the time limit in the Act.

VIII. Public Interest

While interpreting the provisions of this Act, it is necessary to understand the meaning of the phrase 'public interest' which has been used liberally but not defined anywhere in the Act. It is clear from Section 8 that most or all exemption provisions should pass through a public interest balancing test which require disclosure if the public interest considerations favouring disclosure out weigh those favouring non-disclosure.

This calls not only for defining public interest but also devising methods and techniques of measuring the importance of the public interest objectively. Unless it is done, the PIOs may use public interest rider arbitrarily to disclose or withhold information selectively. Given an all pervading spectrum of the concept of public interest, it would be useful if the phrase is contextually defined in the Act with an explanatory note.

Concluding Remarks

The enactment of the RTI Act, 2005 is a bold step. The Act covers not only the public sector but also the NGOs and the private sector to some extent. In addition to this, it has various other positive features like provision of First and Second Appellate Authorities. It is also one of the toughest legislations in the world, as it is the only RTI Act imposing penalty for any contravention of the provisions of the Act.

However, mere conferment of the right is not enough. Its successful implementation in the true spirit is needed. The revision and review of legislations contrary to this right is required. Suitable amendments in the conduct rules for public servants, attitudinal change in the behaviour of the bureaucracy, creation of efficient information management system, more frequent use of this right by press and will of the citizens are also required.

Many loopholes need to be plucked. However, despite the weaknesses, it is a Magna Carta for introducing reforms in the governance in the country and will go a long way in strengthening the roots of democracy by introducing transparency and accountability in governance.

REFERENCES

RTI Act. 2005

B.P. Mailhani, some Grey Areas of the RTI Act, (Monographs) Uttarakhand Information Commission, State Coordination RTI Cell, Dehradun, Uttarakhand.

Suchi Pande & Shekhar Singh, Right to Information Act, 2005 : A Primer, National Book Trust, India, New Delhi, 2008.

Report of National Sub. Committee of CIC on Implementation of RTI Act, 2005, New Delhi, July, 2008.

Sapna Chadha, Right to Information Regime in India : A Critical Appraisal IJPA, Vol. LII, No. I, Delhi, January-March, 2006.

3 Administrative Authorities Created Under the Act : Their Role and Responsibilities

Section 5 (1) of the Act requires a Public Authority to designate "as many" officers as Central Public Information Officer or the State Public Information Officer, as the case may be, in all administrative units and offices under it as may be necessary to provide information to persons requesting for the same. They were to be designated within 100 days of the enactment of the Act.

Similarly, Central or State Assistant Public Information Officers are to be designated at "each sub-divisional level or other sub-district level" to receive applications or appeals and forward them on to the concerned Public Information Officers, Designated Appellate Officers and the Information Commission [Section 5(2)]. This is to ensure that the public can apply for information in their own local areas without the need for traveling long distances to the offices of the Public Information Officers.

Duties and Responsibilities

The Act prescribes the obligations of a Public Information Officer (PIO), Assistant Public Information Officer (APIO) and other officers as follows:

Public Information Officer

- To deal with requests from persons seeking information and render reasonable assistance to the persons seeking such information, taking the assis-

Flow chart of APIO's duties and responsibilities

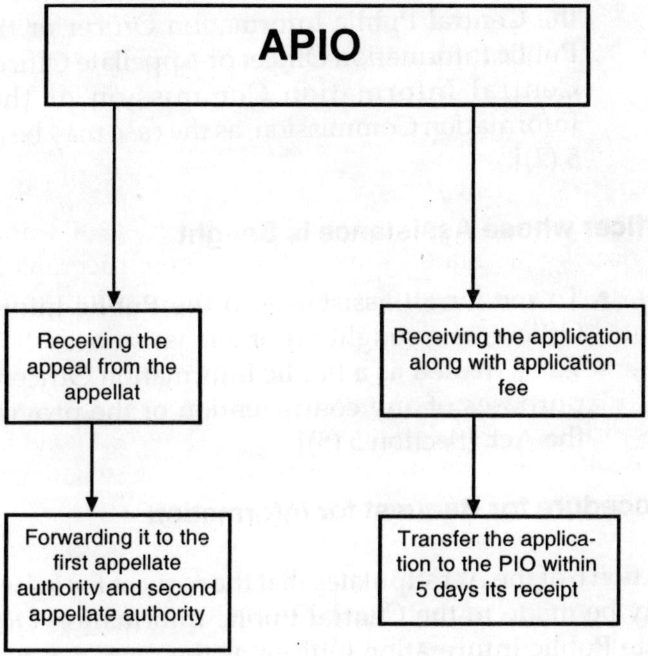

tance of any other officer, if considered necessary by him or her for the proper discharge of duties [Section 5(3) & 5(4)];

- To render 'all reasonable assistance', where request for information cannot be made in writing, to the person making the request orally to reduce the same into writing [Section 6(1)];
- To dispose request for information under the Act, either providing the information requested on payment of prescribed fee or rejecting the request for reasons to be specified within the time period stipulated under the Act [Section 7(1)].

Assistant Public Information Officer

- To receive applications for information or appeals under the Act for forwarding the same forthwith to the Central Public Information Officer or the State Public Information Officer or Appellate Officer or the Central Information Commission or the State Information Commission, as the case may be [Section 5 (2)].

Officer whose Assistance is Sought

- To render all assistance to the Public Information Officer who sought his or her assistance;
- To be treated as a Public Information Officer for the purposes of any contravention of the provisions of the Act. [Section 5 (5)]

Procedure for Request for Information

Section 6 of the Act stipulates that the request for information may be made to the Central Public Information Officer or State Public Information Officer, as the case may be, of the concerned public authority or given to the Central Assistant Public Information Officer or State Assistant Public Information Officer, as the case may be.

The request for information can be made as follows:

- In writing or through electronic means in English or Hindi or in the official language of the area in which the application is being made;
- Oral request to be reduced to writing with assistance sought from Public Information Officer, where such request cannot be made in writing;
- To specify the particulars of the information being sought by the applicant;

- To be accompanied by fee as prescribed under the rules made under the Act;
- Applicant not to be required to give reason for requesting the information or any other personal details except those that may be necessary for the purpose of contacting.

- RTI application format for 'application' (Form A) is given in the Haryana Right to Information Rules, 2005 in the Annexure-IV at page no. 323-24.

Deposit of Further Fee

- On receipt of an application the PIO/APIO shall give a receipt in token thereof to the applicant.
- On receipt of the application the PIO/APIO shall scrutinize the application and shall assess how much fee is required to be paid by the applicant for obtaining the information.
- The fee assessed shall be informed to the applicant by the PIO/APIO in (Form B -Given in Haryana RTI Rules, 2005 in the Annexure-IV) within a period of seven days from the receipt of the application.
- In case the applicant fails to deposit the requisite fee within a period of fifteen days after the issuance of the intimation given to him it shall be constructed that the applicant is no longer interested in obtaining the information sought for and his application be deemed to have been filed.

- There is no time limit for depositing the additional at the Centre level.

Disposal of Request for Information

Section 7 of the Act makes provisions regarding the disposal of request for information as follows:

- request for information shall be disposed by the Public Information Officer within;
- 30 days of receipt in general cases and 48 hours of receipt in cases where the information sought for concerns the life or liberty of a person [section 7(1)];
- a period of 5 days shall be added in computing the response time where an application for information is given to an Assistant Public Information Officer [Section 5(2)];
- request to be deemed to have been refused by the Public Information Officer, if decision on the request for information is not given within the period specified as above [Section 7(2)];
- where a decision is taken to provide the information on payment of any further fee representing the cost of providing the information, the Public Information Officer shall send an intimation in Form B to the person making the request, giving: (a) the details of further fees representing the cost of providing the information as determined by him or her, together with the calculations made to arrive at the amount in accordance with fee prescribed, requesting him/her to deposit that fees, and the period intervening between the despatch of the said intimation and payment of fees shall be excluded for the purpose of calculating the period of 30 days, and (b) information concerning the right of the person making request with respect to review the decision as to the amount of fees charged or the form of access provided, including the particulars of the appellate authority, time limit, process and any other forms [Section 7(3)];
- where access to the record or a part thereof is required to be provided under the Act and the person to whom access is to be provided is ensorily disabled, the Public Information Officer shall provide assistance to enable access to the information, including providing such

assistance as may be appropriate for the inspection [Section 7(4)];

- where access to information is to be provided in the printed or in any electronic format, the applicant shall pay the fee prescribed [Section 7(5)];
- before taking any decision to provide information, the Public information Officer shall take into consideration the representation made by a third party [Section 11(1)];
- where a request has been rejected, the Public Information Officer shall communicate to the person making the request—

  (i) the reasons for such rejection;
  (ii) the period within which an appeal against such rejection may be preferred; and
  (iii) the particulars of the appellate authority [Section 7(8)].

Fees and Costs to be Charged

The Act prescribes the following fees and costs to be charged from persons making request for information:

(1) Cost: Section 4 (4) – Cost of medium: electronic or print or print cost price.
(2) Fee: Section 6 (1) – Fee accompanying application of request for information.
(3) Fee: Section 7 (1) – Fee as prescribed under rules for furnishing information.
(4) Fee: Section 7(3) – Further fee representing the cost of providing the information requested as determined by PIO.
(5) Fee: Section 7 (5) – Fee prescribed under rules for supply of information in printed or electronic format. [Fees under Section 7 (3) and Section 7 (5) can be combined together.] Other charges and costs, if any,

need to be specified while disposing requests for information.

No fee shall be charged from the persons who are of Below Poverty Line (BPL) as may be determined by the appropriate Government [Section 7(5)]; Further, the person making request for information shall be provided the information free of charge where a public authority fails to comply with the stipulated time limits for disposal of request applications [Section 7(6)].

Scale of Fees

The Administrative Reforms Department, Government of Haryana vide notification No. 5/4/2002— IAR dated 28th October, 2005 has, under the Haryana Right to information Rules, 2005, prescribed an application fee of rupees fifty for a request for obtaining information under Section 6(1). This could be in cash against proper receipt or by treasury challan or by demand draft or by Indian Postal Order payable to the reciept head/account number of the concerned public authority.

The Haryana Right to Information Rules, 2005 provide that the public authority may also charge the following as fees for providing information under Section 7(1):

(a) Rs 10 for each page (in A4 or A3 size paper) created or copied.
(b) actual charges or cost of a copy in larger size paper.

Further, for providing information under Section 7(5), the prescribed fee pattern is:

(a) for information provided in floppy - Rs 50.
(b) for information provided in diskette – Rs 100.
(c) for information provided in printed form at the price

fixed for such publication or Rs. 10. per page for extracts from the publication

(d) for inspection of records, no fees for the first hóur; and a fee of Rs 10 for each fifteen minutes in excess of first hour.

* Fee charged at the Central level as well as in the different states is given in Annexture V.

Form of Access to Information

Section 7 (9) provides that information shall ordinarily be provided in the form in which it is sought unless it would "disproportionately divert the resources of the public authority or would be detrimental to the safety or preservation of the record in question".

The information provided to an applicant, to the extent possible, has to be in the form which is easily understandable to him or her. The information becomes more meaningful if the same is given in the local language.

An aspect to be considered here is: whether any information supplied under this Act could be properly stamped as, for example, 'supplied under RTI Act' for easy identification of such material supplied.

Time Limits for Disposal of Requests

Section 7 (1) requires that the information requested by an applicant to a PIO shall be furnished "as expeditiously as possible". The time limits prescribed under the Act for disposal of requests for information are as follows:

Information up to 20 Years

Section 8(3) of the Act stipulates that subject to exemptions relating to information linked to sovereignty, integrity and security matters, breach of privilege of Parliament or the State Legislature and cabinet papers, any information relating to any occurrence, event or matter which has taken place, occurred or happened 20 years before the date on which any request is made, shall be provided to any person making a request under the Act. However, where any question arises as to the date from which the period of 20 years has to be computed, the decision of the Central Government shall be final, subject to the usual appeals provided for in the Act.

Protection of Copyright

Section 9 of the Act provides that a Public Information Officer may reject a request for information where such a request for providing access would involve an infringement of copyright subsisting in a person other than the State.

Access to Part of Record

Section 10 provides that where a request for access to information is rejected on the ground that it is in relation to information which is exempt from disclosure, access may be provided to that part of the record "which does not contain any information which is exempt from disclosure under the Act" and "which can reasonably be severed from any part that contains exempt information". Where access is granted to a part of the record the Public Information Officer shall give a notice to the applicant under Section 10 (2), informing—

(a) that only part of the record requested, after severance of the record containing information which is exempt from disclosure, is being provided;
(b) the reasons for the decision, including any findings on any material question of fact, referring to the material on which those findings were based;

(c) the name and designation of the person giving the decision;

(d) the details of the fees calculated by him or her and the amount of fee which the applicant is required to deposit; and

(e) his or her rights with respect to review of the decision regarding non-disclosure of part of the information, the amount of fee charged or the form of access provided, including the particulars of the Appellate Officer or the Information Commission, time limit, process and any other form of access.

Third Party Information

"Third Party" is defined under the Act to mean a person other than the citizen making a request for information and the public authority to whom the request is made. It could be a private individual or a public authority [Section 2 (n)]. Section 11 of the Act requires that if the information sought by the citizen pertains to a record or part thereof relates to, or has been supplied by a third party and if it is not treated as confidential by that third party, the PIO is at liberty to provide the same to the applicant.

If, however such above information is treated as 'confidential' by that third party, the following steps will have to be taken:

- The PIO gives a written notice to the third party, within 5 days of receipt of the application, and conveys his intention to disclose the information or record while requiring the third party to make a submission, within 10 days from the date of receipt of such notice, regarding whether the information should be disclosed or not.
- The third party should, within 10 days from the date of receipt of notice from the PIO, make a representa-

tion in writing or orally against the proposed disclosure and give written notice to the third party.
- The PIO can, within 40 days after the receipt of application for information, if the third party has been given an opportunity to make representation, make a decision on disclosure and give a written notice to the third party.
- The third party is entitled to prefer an appeal against the decision of the PIO.

Except in the case of "trade or commercial secrets protected by law", disclosures involving third party information may be allowed, if the public interest in disclosure outweighs the importance of any possible harm or injury to the interests of such third party. If the third party is a private individual, the PIO has to be very cautious and properly weigh the consequences as privacy of an individual is important and protected under Section 8 (1) (j).

Steps for Disposal of Requests

The procedure to be followed by the PIO right from the stage of receipt of application for information till the disposal involves a number of steps as follows:

- receives application along with the application fee.
- scrutinizes the application received and the fees prescribed.
- If required, renders reasonable assistance to the applicant by reducing the oral request in writing.
- Registers the application in the Inward Register.
- Issues acknowledgement/receipt to the applicant.
- Transfers the application/part of it to another public authority, if required.
- Informs the applicant about such transfers.
- Makes necessary entries in the Register being maintained.

- Considers the representations of a 'third party', if any.
- In case of rejection, conveys reason for it, the period within which the appeal may be preferred and the details of the Appellate Authority to whom appeal can be preferred.
- Sends intimation to the applicant, the further fee, representing the cost of providing the information, to be paid along with its calculations.
- Also intimates about the modalities of deposit of fee, the right of the applicant for review of the fees charged and appeal against the calculation or the form of access.
- Wherever required, provides assistance to citizens for inspection of works, documents, records and taking samples of material.
- Waives fees for citizens Below Poverty Line.
- Retains record on each application, disposal etc. so that materials as required may be furnished to appellate authorities in case first/second appeal is preferred.

Inspection of Work/Record/Taking Sample(s)

Right to Information includes, inter alia, inspection of work, documents, records, taking notes, extracts and certified samples of material. In consultation with the concerned sections/divisions/offices in Government Departments, PIOs may fix a day or two of the week for applicants to take samples and for inspection of material. Such an arrangement may not disturb the work in the section/division/office and the citizen would also be aware of the days of visit to the PIO/Public Authority. The General Clauses Act, 1897 defines: 'document': shall include any matter written, expressed or described upon any substance by means of letters figures or marks, or by more than one of those means which is intended to be used or which may be used, for the purpose of recording that matter.

Grounds for Rejection of Requests

(a) Section 8 (1): Exemptions from disclosure of information. There is no obligation on the part of a PIO to give any citizen the following:

(a) Information where disclosure would prejudicially affect the sovereignty and integrity of India, the security, strategic, scientific or economic interests of the State, relation with the foreign State or lead to incitement of an offence;

(b) Information expressly forbidden to be published by any court of law or tribunal or the disclosure of which may constitute contempt of court;

(c) Information, the disclosure of which would cause a breach of privilege of Parliament or State Legislature;

(d) Information including commercial confidence, trade secrets or intellectual property where disclosure would harm the competitive position of a third party, unless larger public interest warrants the disclosure of such information;

(e) Information available to a person in his fiduciary relationship, unless larger public interest warrants the disclosure of such information;

(f) Information received in confidence from a foreign Government;

(g) Information, the disclosure of which would endanger the life or physical safety of any person or identity the source of information or assistance given in confidence for law enforcement or security purposes;

(h) Information which would impede the process of investigation or apprehension or prosecution of offenders;

(i) Cabinet papers including records of deliberations of the Council of Ministers, Secretaries and other officers; and

(j) Personal information, which would cause unwarranted invasion of the privacy of the individual unless larger public interest justifies the disclosure of such information.

(The information which cannot be denied to the Parliament or State Legislature shall not be denied to a person making request for the same). However, a PIO may allow access to information if public interest in disclosure outweighs the harm to the protected interest.

(b) **Section 9:** Infringement of the copyright subsisting in a person other than the State. This is the only absolute exemption. Here, the PIO need not consider the public interest in disclosure.

(c) **Section 11:** Third party information treated as confidential by the concerned and involving the case of trade or commercial secrets protected by law and other third party information where the public interest in disclosure does not outweigh the importance of any possible harm or injury to the interests of such third party.

(d) **Section 24:** Information of exempted intelligence and security organisations except information pertaining to allegations of corruption and human rights violations.

Procedure for Rejection of Requests

A PIO is required under the Act to either provide the information, on payment of the requisite fee or reject the request within the time limit prescribed. The Act stipulates that where a request for information is rejected by the PIO, the PIO will communicate the decision to the person making the request along with:

(i) the reasons for rejection.

(ii) the period within which an appeal against such rejection may be preferred (within 30 days of the date of the rejection)

(iii) the particulars of the Appellate Authority.

Delays and Incomplete Information

In the case of delay in providing the requisite information to the person seeking the same or if the information provided is incomplete, such an eventuality could be a basis for appeal. Therefore, the PIO, in addition to maintaining registers for receipt of requests for information and disposal of such requests, will also have to develop checklists and keep a check on the pendency and/or completeness of the information provided. This is important because the burden of proving that the PIO acted reasonably and diligently would be solely on the PIO himself or herself and that would certainly require production of documentary evidence.

Check Slip for PIOs

To enable the PIOs to discharge their functions effectively, it will be useful for the PIOs to be ready with the following:

- Full details of the administrative unit/office/organisation.
- Full details of the department of which the public authority is a part.
- Information proactively published by the public authority.
- Information made available electronically.
- Annual report and other documents published by the public authority.
- Names, addresses and other details of the Appellate Authorities.
- Designated Appellate Officers and Information Commission.
- The contact details of the other Public Authorities, PIOs and APIOs.
- Proforma for the receipt of application for request of information.

- Forms for receipt of fees and acknowledgement, communication of decision including rejection.
- Proper seating arrangements to facilitate easy accessibility of citizens to information handbooks, portals, websites, etc.
- Register for receipt, acknowledgements — separately for inward and outward and roznama.
- Checklist for monitoring the disposal, pendency and disposal of the applications for information.
- Arrangements for inspection of records/taking samples by persons making requests and fix a particular day or two in the week for the above purposes and be ready with an appropriate contingency plan.

Some Important Tips for PIOs

The PIOs need to constantly keep the following in mind:

- Information which cannot be denied to the Parliament or the State Legislature shall not be denied to any citizen.
- Notwithstanding the exemptions permissible under Section 8 (1) of the Act, access to information is to be allowed, if public interest in disclosure outweighs the harm to the protected interest.
- The Right to Information Act, 2005 overrides the Official Secrets Act, 1923.
- Any material relating to occurrence, event or matter, which has taken place, occurred or happened 20 years before the date of the application has to be given to the applicant.
- Access to information should not involve an infringement of copyright subsisting in a person other than the Sate.
- Information supplied by a third party can be provided by the PIO subject to legal safeguards under Section11.

- The burden is on the PIO to prove before the Information Commission in appeal that he acted reasonably and diligently. He has to support the same with documentary evidence.
- The PIO is personally liable to pay penalty if the same is imposed by the Information Commission while deciding on complaints and appeals.

Dealing with APIOs and Other Departments

The PIO has to keep in constant touch with the APIOs. The appointment of APIOs has been envisaged under the Act to enable citizens to make request for information from sub-district/district levels to the place of location of the PIOs. Where an application or an appeal is received by the APIO, a period of 5 days is to be added in computing the time limit for response.

The APIOs need to inform the PIO from time to time about the status of the applications received along with date of receipt, sent to PIOs, the fees paid, etc. Similarly, the PIO needs to inform the concerned APIOs about the information provided, information denied, the grounds for denial, applications wherein the decision has extended beyond the prescribed time limit, etc.

Public Information Officer (PIO) may transfer the request for information either in totality or partially to another public authority if the subject matter pertains to that other Public Authority. Similarly, a PIO could get a request transferred to him from another Public Authority. In both the cases, a period of 5 days is to be added in computing the time limit for response.

The responsibility of the PIO does not cease when a request is transferred to another public authority. While transferring he/she has to concurrently inform the applicant about the same. He/she is also required to keep a record of transfer in his/her Outward Register for future reference and monitoring. Coordination between the two public authorities in such cases would also enable the PIOs concerned to present the correct picture before the Appellate Officer or Information Commission, as the case may be, if and when the applicant prefers an appeal.

Dealing with Citizens

With the Right to Information Act, 2005 firmly in place, disclosure is the rule and secrecy or exemption is an exception.

The Act confers a right to 'information' and not just 'records' or 'documents'. "Information" is defined by the Act very broadly. Right to Information includes inspection, covering taking of samples by a citizen. Keeping the importance attached to the citizens' Right to Information, the Act bars the courts from entertaining any suit application or other proceeding in respect of any order made under this Act and no such order shall be called in question "otherwise than by way of an appeal under this Act". Seeking information is the citizen's right and an applicant making a request for information cannot be asked to give any reason for requesting the information or any other personal details except those that may be necessary for contacting that applicant. There is provision of compensation to the citizens.

An individual's right to privacy, however, is protected under the Act. The exemption accorded to private information under the Act reflects the underlying public interest to protect personal privacy and prevent "unwarranted invasion" of the same.

The PIOs are required to render reasonable assistance to applicants for information.

The help from the PIO to citizens could be in any form as stated below:

- Where a citizen is unable to make a request in writing,

FLOW CHART OF PIO'S DUTIES AND RESPONSIBILITIES

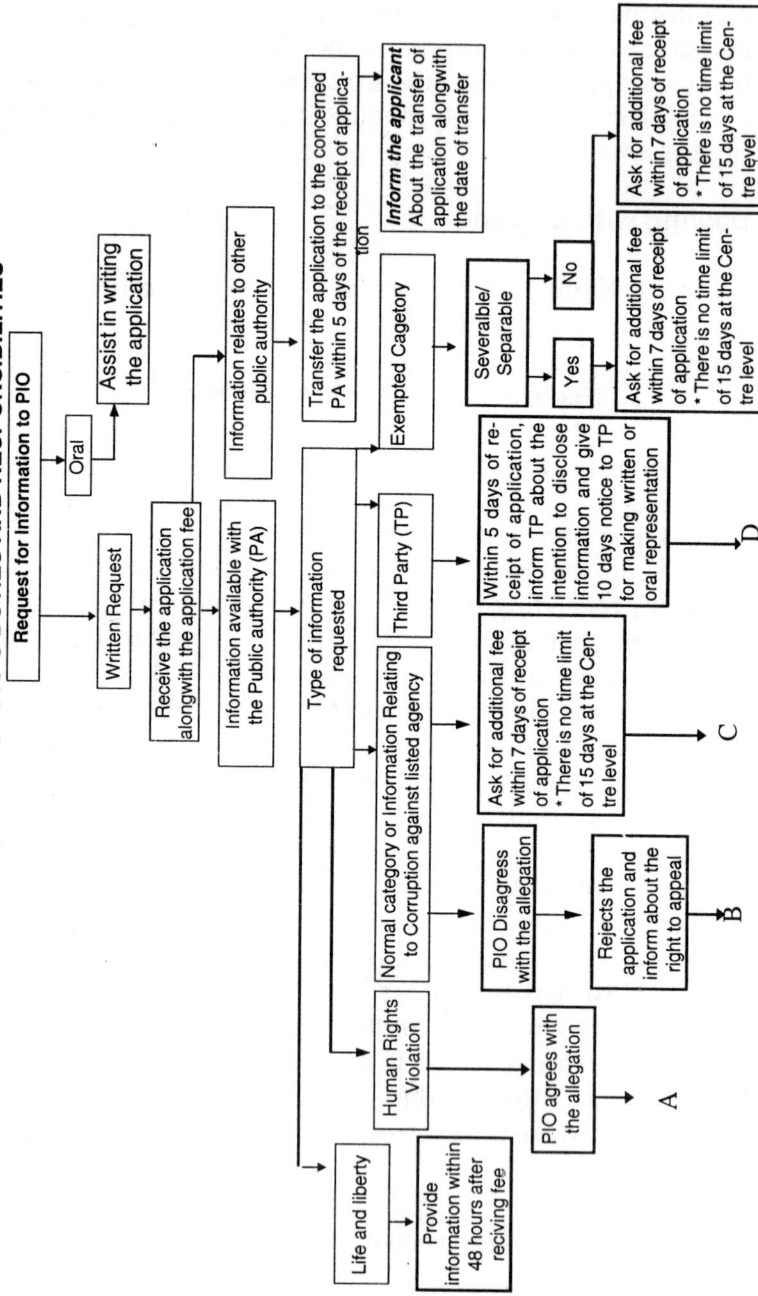

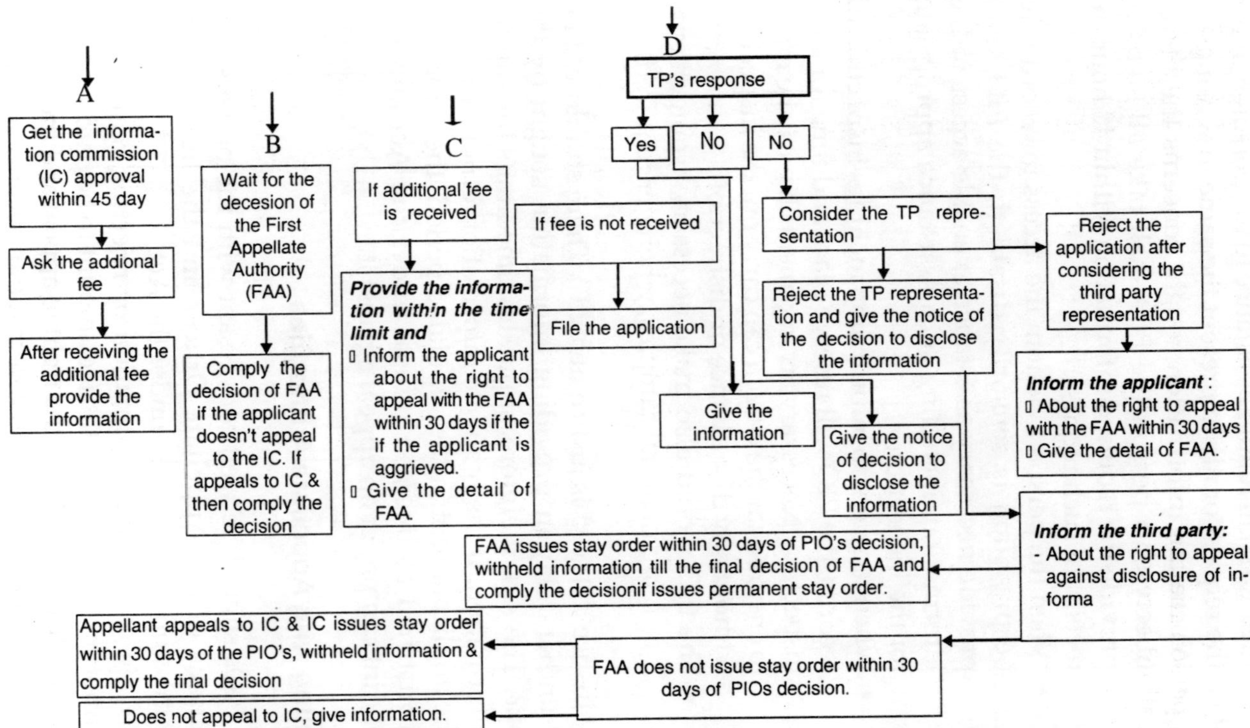

* In Haryana, PIO has to give a notice of 15 days for depositing the additional fee. This provision of 15 days time for additional fees is not there in other state and the centre level.

** Time Limit : Normal category information 30 days.

the PIO shall render assistance to the person making the request orally to present the same in writing.

- Where the information sought concerns the life or liberty of a person the PIO shall take all steps to provide the required information within 48 hours of receipt of such request.
- When the person to whom the access to record is to be provided is sensorily disabled, the PIO shall provide necessary assistance to enable access to the information, including such assistance appropriate for the inspection.
- When the right to information includes inspection of records, the PIO will reserve place and time for such inspection. Necessary arrangements have to be made to ensure that the citizen can carry out the inspection without any disturbance or distraction.
- The PIO would also make necessary arrangements for giving material samples, wherever required.

"Justice delayed is justice denied". There should not be any undue delay in providing information sought by the public. The Act, therefore, stipulates time limits for supply of information. If the requisite information is not provided to the applicant within the stipulated period, the same will be construed as deemed refusal under the Act and the applicant can prefer an appeal against it.

Dealing with Appellate Authorities

The PIOs should be well conversant with the powers and functions of the Appellate Officer and the Information Commission as envisaged under the Act.

While conveying information or rejecting request for information or conveying the fee amount to be paid etc., the PIO is required to indicate the right to appeal and the details of the Appellate Authority to whom the applicant can appeal.

This amounts to paving the way for appeal to be preferred, if considered necessary by the applicant, and getting ready for meeting the requirements of the Appellate Authority.

The State / Central Information Commission (as the case may be) is mandatorily required to impose a penalty on an erring PIO, if in its opinion the PIO has without any reasonable cause:

(i) Refused to receive the application for information.
(ii) Not furnished information within the specified time, or
(iii) Malafidely denied the request for information or
(iv) Destroyed the information which was the subject matter of the request, or
(v) Obstructed in any manner the furnishing of the requested information.

In the event of the above, the Information Commission shall impose a penalty of Rs. 250 per day on the PIO till application is received or information is furnished subject to the total amount of such penalty not exceeding Rs.25000. The Information Commission shall recommend for disciplinary action against the PIO under the service rules applicable to him in certain cases. If he/she persistently violates the provisions of the Act, without any reasonable cause.

The Information Commission is legally bound to give an opportunity to the PIO to be heard before deciding to impose a penalty. The PIO has, therefore, to prepare himself/ herself to justify the action taken by him/her and prove that he/she acted reasonably and diligently. It is needless to say that the PIO keeps public interest paramount all the time. When it comes to making a decision to determine public interest versus private interest, it is important that the PIO makes a decision after considering all possible aspects of the issues at hand – the *pros and cons* and the legal position.

Guidelines for Authorities and Officers

It will be proper for the appropriate Government/public authorities to prepare guides/ manuals for Public Authorities/Public Information Officers and Assistant Public Information Officers/Appellate Officers. A simplified "Dos and Don'ts" list in official language of the area could be prepared by every public authority for use as a check list by the APIOs, PIOs and Appellate Officers.

As time proceeds, more and more information may be made available in the electronic form to citizens by the public authorities. All the APIOs, PIOs, and Appellate Officers may be provided access to computer facility and networks; and adequate training in the use of computers and information systems for retrieval of information may also be provided to them.

Capacity Building Programmes

The Public Information Officer plays a pivotal role in the implementation of the Right to information Act, 2005. The compliance with various provisions of the Act requires a certain level of preparedness on part of the PIO. He/she should have complete knowledge of and experience in office procedures. He/she should have adequate knowledge of record management systems in the public authority, including retrieval of information from the internet. He/she needs to know the structure, functions and delegation of powers within the organization. He/she should be well-versed with the organization chart, the levels of disposal of cases, appeals etc. He/She should be fully conversant with all the provisions of the Act.

The PIO should be good in negotiations with the public, colleagues, third parties and others so that he/she could have smooth interactions with all these stakeholders and effectively attend to his/her duties. The PIO should also have good drafting skills so as to be able to issue well-reasoned orders.

The tasks required to be performed as PIO, for an official, will be in addition to the work he/she performs as an officer of the public authority. The PIO should be able to judiciously apportion time available with him/her to the various activities entrusted to him/her and RTI-related work. Availability of inadequate time cannot be a justification for delay in the disposal of requests for information or for supply of incomplete information.

The PIOs need to be prepared, motivated and trained in right to information, office procedures, information management, good governance, change management etc.from time to time.

Similarly, Appellate Officers and other officers should be trained regularly. Simultaneously, training and awareness programmes need to be launched to address the demand side issues like mobilisation of people, civil society action, legal literacy etc.

Source: A Manual for Public Authorities, Information Officers and Appellate Authorities, CCG, NIA, Capacity Building for Access to Information, June 2006. Modified as per Haryana Government Notifications

4 Judicial Authorities Created Under the Act : Their Powers and Functions

The Act provides two channels of appeals against the decision of a PIO on the request for information by a citizen – an internal or 'first' appeal to a designated "officer senior in rank' to the PIO – the first appellate authority (called "Appellate Officer" in this Hand Book) as notified by the Public Authority and a 'second' appeal to the Information Commission. The Act also provides for preferring complaints to the Information Commission regarding non-implementation of the legal provisions.

If an applicant is aggrieved by the decision of a PIO, he or she can make an appeal to the Appellate Officer who, as required by law, would be an "officer senior in rank" to the PIO. A second appeal, against the decision of the Appellate Officer, lies to the Information Commission.

The prescribed format for appeal as per Haryana Right to Information Rules, 2005 is given at page 325.

First Appellate Authority

The Act does not define the first appellate authority precisely. Under Section 7(b), it refers to "appellate authority" to whom appeal can be made by a person whose request has been rejected. Section 19 (1) refers to first appeal being made to such "officer who is senior in rank to the Central Public Information Officer or State Public Information Officer, as the case may be". The Information Commission is also the second appellate authority. Thus, in this Hand Book we use the term "Appellate Officer" to connote the appellate authority to whom first appeal can be preferred under the

Act. Needless to say that the Appellate Officer must be an officer superior to the PIO such that he is fully conversant with the work of the organization, the subjects dealt with by it and the functions discharged by various PIOs. The number of designated Appellate Officers in a Public Authority could be small as compared to the number of PIOs. One Appellate Officer could easily meet the requirement of appeals arising out of the decisions of a number of PIOs. However, keeping the nature of responsibilities to be discharged under the Act and the structure and functions of the organisation at various levels in view, each Public Authority has to determine the number of senior officers to be designated as appellate authorities, the levels of such officers and the PIOs against whose decisions they would hear appeals. As the Appellate Officers could be transferred, they may be notified as appellate authorities by designation.

A question arises whether the head of a public authority himself or herself can be an appellate authority to hear first appeals. There may be distinct advantages if the head of a public authority is also the Appellate Officer due to the reasons that he or she:

1. Is fully conversant with the functioning of the organisation.
2. Would be the best judge to command various sources of information of the authority and meet the access requirements of the public.
3. Can present to the parent department a complete and correct picture regarding the state of implementation of the Act by the authority.
4. Would usually have first hand knowledge of the operation of the Act within his/her organisation.
5. Would be in a position to explain to the next appellate authority, i.e. the Information Commission regarding the reasons behind the outcomes of first appeals.
6. The fact that he/she is the Appellate Officer may

inculcate a sense of responsibility on the part of PIOs in the authority to be responsive to the requests of citizens for information.

Furthermore as the head of the authority, analysing the type of information sought from the organization, he or she can be in a better position to determine additional areas requiring proactive disclosure/publication.

The advantages listed above may be weighed against factors such as whether the head of the public authority would be in a position to devote time for deciding time-consuming appeals, given the nature and extent of his/her workload. The departments concerned may take appropriate decisions weighing the *pros and cons*. However, it should be kept in mind that appeal lies to the Information Commission against the decisions of the Appellate Officers and therefore, the levels of the latter should be reasonably high.

Disposal of First Appeals

Section 19 (1) and (2) of the Act stipulate that any person who, does not receive a decision on request for information within the stipulated time or is aggrieved by a decision of the Public Information Officer including communication of fees to be paid may within 30 days from the expiry of such period or from the receipt of such a decision prefer an appeal to the designated Appellate Officer, senior in rank to the Public Information Officer. The Appellate Officer may admit the appeal after the expiry of the period of 30 days if he or she is satisfied that the appellant was prevented by sufficient cause from filing the appeal in time. Where an appeal is preferred against an order made by a Public Information Officer to disclose third party information, the appeal by the concerned third party shall be made within 30 days from the date of the order.

The Act prescribes that the appeal shall be disposed of within 30 days of the receipt of the appeal or within such extended period not exceeding a total of 45 days from the date of filing thereof, as the case may be, for reasons to be recorded in writing.

Information Commissions

Section 12 and Section 15 of the Act provide for the Constitution of the Central Information Commission (CIC) and State Information Commission (SIC) respectively to exercise powers conferred on it by the Act (Chapter V, Sections 18-20). The setting up of these Commissions to ensure the effective implementation of right to information regime in the country is one of the most important provisions of the Act. Its importance can be judged from the fact that the long title of the Act itself makes a mention about the Commissions.

The key provisions for the Central and State Information Commissions relate to the following:

- the (Central / State) Information Commission shall consist of: (a) the Chief Information Commissioner / State Chief Information Commissioner, and (b) such number of (Central / State) Information Commissioners, not exceeding 10, as may be deemed necessary [Section 12 (1) and Section 15 (1)];
- the Chief Information Commissioner/State Chief Information Commissioner and (Central/State) Information Commissioners shall be appointed by the President/Governor on the recommendation of a committee consisting of—

  (i) the Prime Minister / Chief Minister, who shall be the Chairperson of the Committee;
  (ii) the Leader of Opposition in the Lok Sabha / State Legislative Assembly; and

(iii) a Union Cabinet Minister/Cabinet Minister in the State to be nominated by the Prime Minister/Chief Minister (Section 12 (3) and Section 15 (3));

- each Commission would function as an autonomous body exercising the powers conferred on, and performing the functions assigned to it under the Act (Section 12 (4) and Section 15 (4));
- the general superintendence, direction and management of the affairs of the Commission shall vest in the Chief Information Commissioner/State Chief Information Commissioner who shall be assisted by the respective Information Commissioners (Section 12 (4) and Section 15 (4));
- the Chief Information Commissioner/State Chief Information Commissioner and every Information Commissioner shall hold office for a term of five years from the date of entering upon office or till attaining the age of 65 years whichever is earlier (Section 13 and Section 16);
- the Chief Information Commissioner/State Chief Information Commissioner or any Information Commissioner shall be removed from office only by order of the President/Governor on the ground of proved misbehaviour or incapacity after the Supreme Court, on a reference made to it by the President / Governor, has, on inquiry, reported that the Chief Information Commissioner/State Chief Information Commissioner or any Information Commissioner, as the case may be, ought on such ground be removed (Section 14 (1) and Section 17 (1));
- the Central/State Government shall provide the Chief Information Commissioner/ State Chief Information Commissioner and the Information Commissioners with such officers and employees as may be necessary for the efficient performance of their functions under

the Act and the salaries and allowances payable to and the terms and conditions of service of the officers and other employees appointed for the purpose of the Act shall be such as prescribed (Section 13 (6) and Section 16 (6)).

The Act empowers the Central Information Commission and State Information Commission, as the case may be, to receive and inquire into complaint from any person relating to access to information under the control of public authorities, including imposing penalties on the erring PIOs and recommending disciplinary action against them. They are the authorities to deal with and dispose of appeals against the decisions of the designated appellate officers, including imposing penalties on and recommending disciplinary action against the erring PIOs. They may also make recommendation to public authorities not conforming with the provisions or the spirit of the Act, specifying the steps to be taken for promoting such conformity.

The Right to Information Act, 2005 envisages that the Information Commissions play the role of "remedy provider", "enforcer" and "educator" as elsewhere in the world.

Inquiry into Complaints

Section 18 (1) of the Act stipulates that the Information Commission shall receive and inquire into a complaint from any person —

(a) who has been unable to submit a request to a Public Information Officer either by reason that no such officer has been appointed under this Act, or because the Assistant Public Information Officer has refused to accept his or her application for information or appeal under the Act for forwarding the same to the Public Information Officer or Appellate Officer or the Information Commission as the case may be;

(b) who has been refused access to any information requested under the Act;
(c) who has not been given a response to a request for information or access to information within the time limit specified under the Act;
(d) who has been required to pay an amount of fee which he or she considers unreasonable;
(e) who believes that he or she has been given incomplete, misleading or false information under the Act; and
(f) in respect of any other matter relating to requesting or obtaining access to records under the Act.

The Commission may initiate an inquiry in respect of complaint, if satisfied that there are reasonable grounds to inquire into the matter. Section 18 further stipulates that while inquiring into a complaint, the Commission shall have the same powers as are vested in a civil court while trying a suit under the Code of Civil Procedure, 1908, in respect of the following matters, namely:—

(a) summoning and enforcing the attendance of persons and compel them to give oral or written evidence on oath and to produce the documents or things;
(b) requiring the discovery and inspection of documents;
(c) receiving evidence on affidavit;
(d) requisitioning any public record or copies thereof from any court or office;
(e) issuing summons for examination of witnesses or documents; and
(f) any other matter which may be prescribed.

Further, the Commission, during the inquiry of any complaint under the Act, may examine any record to which the Act applies which is under the control of the public authority. No such record may be withheld from it on any grounds notwithstanding anything inconsistent contained in any other Act of Parliament or State Legislature, as the case may be.

Disposal of Second Appeals

Section 19 (3) of the Act provides that a second appeal against the decision of the Appellate Officer shall lie within 90 days from the date on which the decision should have been made or was actually received, with the Information Commission. The Information Commission may admit the appeal after the expiry of the period of 90 days if it is satisfied that the appellant was prevented by sufficient cause from filing the appeal in time. If the decision of the Public Information Officer against which an appeal is preferred relates to information of a third party, the Information Commission shall give a reasonable opportunity of being heard to that third party.

Onus of Proof

Section 19 (5) of the Act provides that in any appeal proceedings, the onus to prove that a denial of a request was justified shall be on the Public Information Officer who denied the request.

Decisions in Second Appeals

The Act provides that appeal filed before the Information Commission shall be decided by it in accordance with the prescribed procedure and its decision shall be binding.

The Information Commission has the power to—

(a) require the public authority to take any such steps as may be necessary to secure compliance with the provisions of the Act, including—

(i) by providing access to information, if so requested, in a particular form;

(ii) by appointing a Public Information Officer;

(iii) by publishing certain information or categories of information;

(iv) by making necessary changes to its practices in relation to the maintenance, management and destruction of records;

(v) by enhancing the provision of training on the right to information for its officials; and

(vi) by providing it with an annual report in compliance with clause (b) of subsection (1) of section 4;

(b) require the public authority to compensate the complainant for any loss or other detriment suffered [Section 19 (8) b];

(c) impose any of the penalties provided under the Act; and

(d) reject the application [Section 19 (8)].

The Information Commission is legally bound to give notice of its decision, including any right of appeal, to the complainant and the public authority.

Though it is for the concerned Government to give appropriate operational and budgetary autonomy to the Central and State Information Commission (as the case may be), every pubic authority needs to gear itself to provide all required support to the Information Commission. Among other things, to enable the Commission to arrive at consistent decisions, the public authority's information base has to be comprehensive and available in easily retrievable form and in a format which is also understandable.

The number of second appeals preferred would directly be proportionate to the way public authorities identify appropriate officials as PIOs and Appellate Officers, designate them in adequate numbers, the way they publish information proactively and finally the extent and quality of training imparted to the Public Information Officers and the Appellate Officers. In this regard, the Information

Commissioners may have to be like 'roving' ambassadors and be on the move to see for themselves the manner in which the provisions of the Act are being implemented at various levels: State, District and Local.

Procedure to be followed in Deciding an Appeal

The Haryana Right to Information Rules, 2005 prescribes the procedure for deciding appeal by the Information Commission. Accordingly before deciding an appeal the Commission shall :

(a) serve notice to the concerned persons;
(b) entertain any evidence in support of appeal, which may be oral or in writing form from concerned persons;
(c) examine on oath or by having affidavits from the persons concerned;
(d) persue or inspect the documents or any records or copies;
(e) inquire through the authorized officer the facts of an appeal or may require facts in detail, if it so deems appropriate hear the PIO or any other senior officer who had decided the first appeal as the case may be; and
(f) receive evidence on affidavits from the PIO or any senior officer who had decided the first appeal or from any other person from whom the evidence may be deemed necessary.

Mode of Serving Notice

The Commission may serve notice to the persons concerned in any of the following modes;

(a) by hand delivery through process server.
(b) by registered post with acknowledgement due.
(c) by publication in the newspaper.

Order by the Commission

The Rules require that the Order of the Commission shall be made in writing and pronounced in the presence of the concerned persons. The party concerned may obtain the copy of the order from the commission.

Imposition of Penalty

Section 20 (1) of the Act provides that the Commission, while deciding a complaint or appeal, shall impose penalty on erring PIOs in cases where the PIO has, without any reasonable cause:

- refused to receive an application for information; or
- has not furnished information within the time specified [u/s 7(1)]; or
- malafidely denied the request for information; or
- knowingly given incorrect, incomplete; or misleading information; or
- destroyed information which was the subject of the request; or
- obstructed in any manner in furnishing the information.

The scale of the penalty to be imposed is Rs.250 each day till application is received or information is furnished subject to the total amount of such penalty not exceeding Rs.25,000. The Information Commission is legally bound to give the Public Information Officer a reasonable opportunity of being heard by the Commission before any penalty is imposed on him or her.

The burden of proving that a Public Information Officer acted reasonably and diligently shall be on himself or herself.

Disciplinary Action

Section 20 (2) of the Act provides that the Commission shall, while deciding a complaint or appeal, recommend for disciplinary action against the Public Information Officer under the service rules applicable to him or her in cases where the PIO has, without any reasonable cause and persistently:

- failed to receive an application for information; or
- has not furnished information within the time specified; or
- malafidely denied the request for information; or
- knowingly given incorrect, incomplete; or misleading information; or
- destroyed information which was the subject of the request; or
- obstructed in any manner in furnishing the information.

Monitoring and Reporting

Section 25 (1) of the Act provides that the Central Information Commission or the State Information Commission shall after the end of each year prepare a report on the implementation of the provisions of this Act during that year and forward a copy to the appropriate government.

Importance of Public Interest

The Right to Information Act, 2005 calls for a paradigm shift in the approach to governance. It is an Act which will be implemented by the people and acted upon by the Government. The larger public interest will always be more important than private or protected interest. Only such Information which could lead to unwarranted invasion of the privacy of the individual may be denied by the PIO. Overall, if the public interest in disclosure to the citizen outweighs the harm to the protected interest, then the public authority will have to provide information and not reject the request for the same by the citizens.

FLOW CHART OF APPEAL/COMPLAINT

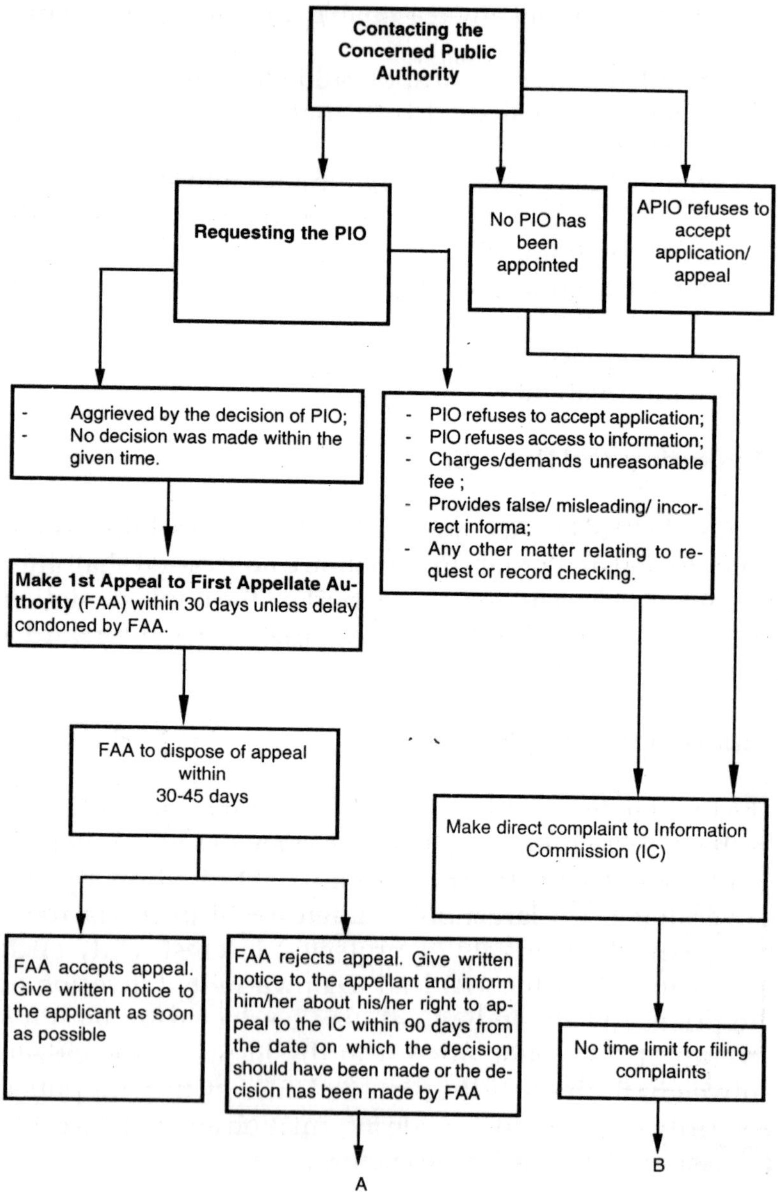

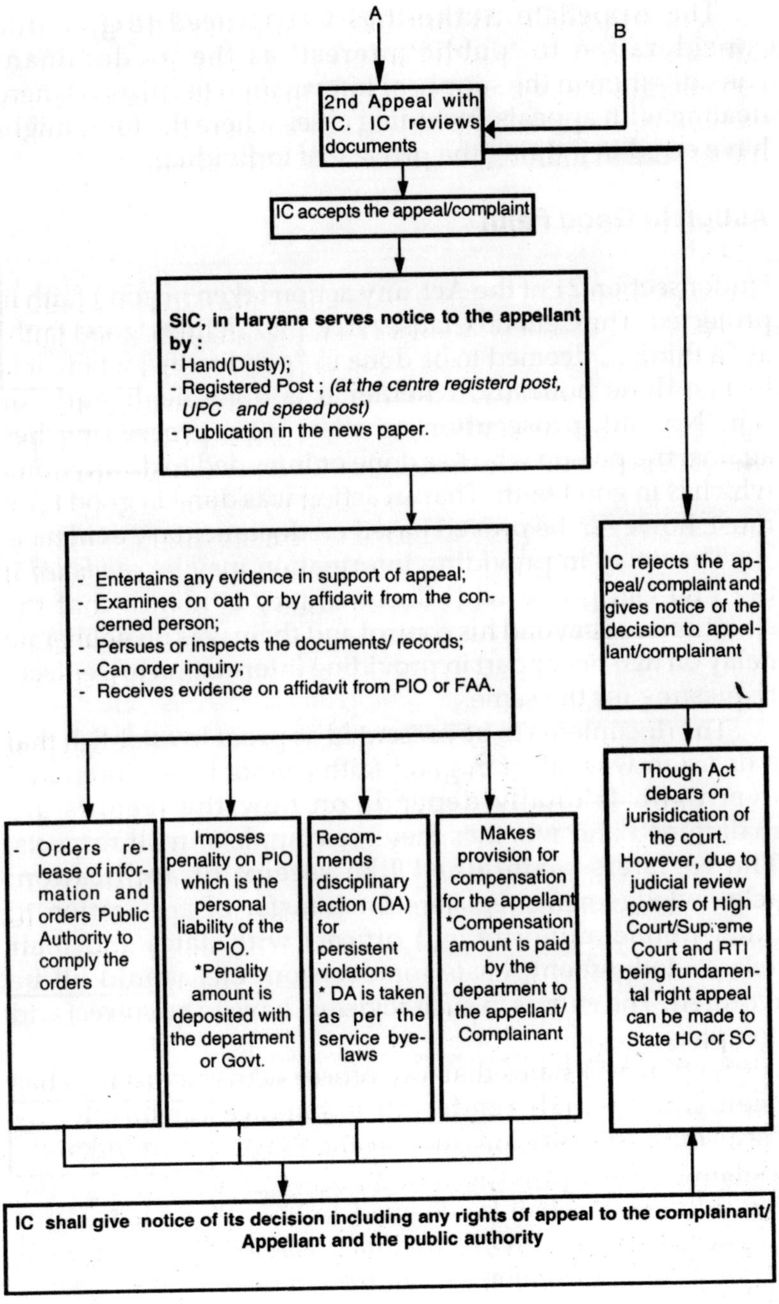
A
B
2nd Appeal with IC. IC reviews documents
IC accepts the appeal/complaint
SIC, in Haryana serves notice to the appellant by :
- Hand(Dusty);
- Registered Post ; (at the centre registerd post, UPC and speed post)
- Publication in the news paper.
- Entertains any evidence in support of appeal;
- Examines on oath or by affidavit from the concerned person;
- Persues or inspects the documents/ records;
- Can order inquiry;
- Receives evidence on affidavit from PIO or FAA.
IC rejects the appeal/ complaint and gives notice of the decision to appellant/complainant
- Orders release of information and orders Public Authority to comply the orders
Imposes penality on PIO which is the personal liability of the PIO. *Penality amount is deposited with the department or Govt.
Recommends disciplinary action (DA) for persistent violations * DA is taken as per the service bye-laws
Makes provision for compensation for the appellant *Compensation amount is paid by the department to the appellant/ Complainant
Though Act debars on jurisidication of the court. However, due to judicial review powers of High Court/Supreme Court and RTI being fundamental right appeal can be made to State HC or SC
IC shall give notice of its decision including any rights of appeal to the complainant/ Appellant and the public authority

The Appellate Authorities would need to give due consideration to 'public interest' as the predominant consideration in the supply of information to citizens where dealing with appeals, including cases where the PIOs might have erred in judging the privacy of individual.

Action in Good Faith

Under section 21 of the Act, any action taken in good faith is protected. The General Clauses Act, 1897 defines 'good faith' as "a thing … deemed to be done in "good faith", where it is in fact done honestly, whether it is done negligently or not."No suit, prosecution or other legal proceeding lies against the person who has done or intended to do anything which is in good faith. That an action was done in good faith must, however, be proved based on documentary evidence.

The delay in providing information may be *condoned* if the PIO can prove with documentary evidence that the situation was beyond his control and there was no deliberate delay on his/her or part in providing information to a citizen, requesting for the same.

The documents to be presented as proof to establish that a decision was taken in good faith cannot be got prepared overnight. It totally depends on how the records are maintained and whether they are complete in all respects. The registers maintained like receipt of application, acknowledgement, registers for transfer of application to other public authority and officers with dates and their acknowledgement, basis for decision, etc. would all be required. The entries in such registers have to be correct and complete.

Section 5(5) states that any officer whose assistance has been sought shall render all assistance to the PIO by furnishing information, and in the event of any default/violation of any provisions of the Act by such other officer, the said officer shall be deemed to be a PIO. Hence, it is important for the PIO to maintain acknowledgements for requests of information sought from other officers.

Since the Information Commission is to hear evidence, peruse and inspect documents and receive evidence for arriving at a decision on an appeal, if a decision is taken in good faith by the PIO, he/she is to be provided ample opportunity to defend him / herself with supporting records.

Well Reasoned Order

Where the Information Commission, at the time of deciding an appeal or complaint, is of the opinion that the PIO has, among others, malafidely denied the request for information it will then impose a penalty. However, before imposing the penalty, the Commission would give reasonable opportunity to the PIO of being heard.

The onus to prove that a denial of request was justified is on the PIO, who denied the request. This burden of proof under Section 19 (5) has to be supported by documentary evidence.As per the provision of Section 7 (8) of the Act, the PIO, when rejecting a request has to communicate (to the person making a request) the following:

1. The reason for such rejection.
2. The period within which an appeal can be preferred, and
3. The particulars of the Appellate authority to whom appear can be preferred.

Similarly, for the requests where information is provided, he/she is equired to intimate the amount of fees to be paid, the details of fees levied and also that the decision of levying a certain amount of fee can be appealed against, details of Appellate Authority and the period within which the appeal could be preferred.

While providing requisite information or rejecting the request, the PIO has to issue well reasoned communications. The reasons are to be given in proper order and the rights of the citizen to appeal are to be explicitly stated.Such communication should clarify the pcsition to the applicants and enable theAppellate Authority to identify the cause for rejection or basis for fee determination etc. It will also help the Commission in issuing its decision(s) wherever appeal(s) have been preferred.

Principles of Natural Justice

The procedure for deciding an appeal by an Appellate Authority or the Information Commission must take into account the application of the principles of natural justice.

No person should be condemned unheard. Both the sides will have to be given opportunity to be heard and also to submit any document etc. for perusal and inspection by the concerned, during appeal. Fair play will thus be an essential ingredient of any decision taken. The procedure for deciding appeal prescribed under the Central Information Commission (Appeal Procedure) Rules, 2005 by the Government of India does not provide any scope for arbitrariness in arriving at a decision or in imposing a penalty. Necessary notices will have to be given by the Information Commission and the stipulated procedure framed under rules will have to be followed in the disposal of appeals. For this purpose, as has been suggested, the Information Commissioners act like 'roving' ambassadors, undertaking tours to observe for themselves how various public functionaries are performing their duties under the Act and whether the citizens are actually able to exercise their right to information. The Commissions should definitely ensure that they uphold the principles of natural justice in disposing appeals.

Source: A Manual for Public Authorities Information Officers andAppellate Authorities, CGG, NIA, Capacity Building for Access to Information, June 2006.. Modified as per *Haryana Government Notifications.*

5 Haryana State Information Commission: Organisational Setup

A key objective of the Right to Information Act, 2005 is to promote transparency and accountability in the working of every public authority in the country. The Act mandates a legal-institutional framework for setting out the practical regime of right to information for every citizen to secure access to information held by or under the control of public authorities. It prescribes mandatory disclosure of certain information to citizens and designation of Public Information Officers in all public authorities to attend to requests from citizens for information within stipulated time limits. It provides for appeal to designated appellate officers against the decisions of Public Information Officers. It also mandates the constitution of a Central Information Commission and State Information Commissions to enquire into complaints hear second appeals and guide the implementation of the Act.

The setting up of Information Commissions at the Central and State levels to ensure the effective implementation of the right to information regime in the country is one of the most important provisions of the Act. The role played by the respective Commissions is likely to have a significant effect on whether or not the Act is implemented in letter and spirit by the public authorities operating at different levels. Apart from exercising the statutory functions entrusted to the h the Information Commissions are expected to act as "friend, philosopher and guide" to citizens in exercise of their right to information, and to public authorities in the discharge of their duties to make information accessible to the people.

In order to ensure the effective implementation of Right

to Information Act, 2005, the State Government on 31st October 2005 by notification in the Official Gazette, constituted a body known as the State Information Commission, Haryana to exercise the powers conferred on, and to perform the functions assigned to, it under this Act and also appointed Shri G.Madhavan, IAS (Retired) as the first Chief Information Commissioner of the State Information Commission, Haryana. He was sworn in on 1st November 2005 and the State Information Commission came into existence from this day and by a coincidence the State of Haryana also came into existence on this very day in the year 1966. Later on vide notification dated 5th May 2006, Ms Meenaxi Anand Chaudhry, IAS (Retired) was appointed as State Information Commissioner in the newly constituted State Information Commission, Haryana. She was sworn in on 9th May 2006. Subsequently, five more state information commissioners namely Mr. Asha Sharma, IAS (Retd.) Lt. Gen. J.B.S. Yadav, Sh. Ashok Mehta, Sh. M.R. Ranga, Sh. Prem Veer Singh were inducted. They were sworn in on 3rd January 2008.

Work Distribution

The allocation of work between the Chief Information Commissioner and the State Information Commissioners under Section 15, sub-section 4 of RTI Act, 2005 is as follows:

(i) *Chief Information Commissioner : Sh. G.Madhavan*

(a) Raj Bhavan, Hospitality, High Court/Subordinate Courts and General Administration (CS Establishment).
(b) Home including CID and Vigilance.
(c) Revenue, Consolidation and Rehabilitation.
(d) Town and Country Planning, Urban Estates and HUDA.

(e) Industries, HSIDC, HFC.
(f) All other departments not mentioned against Sr. No. ii to vii

(ii) *State Information Commissioner(MAC)*

Mrs. Meenxi Anand Chaudhry

(a) Agriculture, Horticulture and Cooperation.
(b) Higher Education/ Universities.
(c) PWD (B&R and Public Health).
(d) Excise and Taxation.
(e) Power.

(iii) *State Information Commissioner(AS)*

Mrs. Asha Sharma

(a) Health, Ayurrveda and Medical Education.
(b) Food & Supplies.
(c) Technical Education.
(d) Industrial Training & Vocational Education.

(iv) *State Information Commissioner(JBSY)*

Lt. Gen. (Retd) J.B.S.Yadav

(a) Haryana Public Service Commission.
(b) Printing and Stationery Department.
(c) Animal Husbandry, Dairy Development and Fisheries.
(d) Transport and Housing.
(e) Irrigation/HSMITC
(f) Department of Secondary Education

(v) *State Information Commissioner(AM)*

Sh. Ashok Mehta

(a) Forest & Wild Life Preservation and Enviornment.
(b) Sports and Youth Affairs.
(c) Urban Development/Municipal Administration.
(d) Architecture, Archaeology & Museums.
(e) Consumer Forums

(vi) *State Information Commissioner(MRR)*

Sh. M.R.Ranga

(a) Women & Child Development.
(b) Development & Panchayats.
(c) Rural Development.
(d) Labour & Employment.
(e) Social Justice & Empowerment/Social Welfare.

(vii) *State Information Commissioner(PS)*

Sh. Premveer Singh

(a) Mines & Geology.
(b) Law, Jails & Judicial.
(c) Staff Selection Commission
(d) Primary Education/Board of School Education
(e) State Finance Commission/State Election Commission/Elections Department
(f) Finance & Planning, Tourism, Culture and Public Relations.

(ii) The powers and duties of its officers and employees

Section 15 (4) provides that the general superintendence, direction and management of the affairs of the State

Information Commission shall vest in the State Chief Information Commissioner who shall be assisted by the State Information Commissioners and may exercise all such powers and do all such acts and things which may be exercised or done by the State Information Commission autonomously without being subjected to directions by any other authority under this Act.

Section 18 of the Act spells out the powers and functions of the State Information Commission.

(1) It shall be the duty of the State Information Commission to receive and inquire into a complaint from any person—

(a) who has been unable to submit a request to a Public Information Officer either by reason that no such officer has been appointed under this Act, or because the Assistant Public Information Officer has refused to accept his or her application for information or appeal under the Act for forwarding the same to the Public Information Officer or appellate officer of the Information Commission as the case may be;
(b) who has been refused access to any information requested under the Act;
(c) who has not been given a response to a request for information or access to information within the time limit specified under the Act;
(d) who has been required to pay an amount of fee which he or she considers unreasonable;
(e) who believes that he or she has been given incomplete misleading or false information under the Act; and
(f) in respect of any other matter relating to

requesting or obtaining access to records under the Act.

(2) Where the State Information Commission is satisfied that there are reasonable grounds to inquire into the matter, may initiate an enquiry in respect thereof.

(3) The State Information Commission shall, while inquiring into a complaint, have the same powers as are vested in a civil court while trying a suit under the Code of Civil Procedure, 1908, in respect of the following matters, namely:— summoning and enforcing the attendance of persons and compel them to give oral or written evidence on oath and to produce the documents of things; requiring the discovery and inspection of documents; receiving evidence on affidavit; requisitioning any public record or copies thereof or any court or office; issuing summons for examination of witnesses or documents; and any other matter which may be prescribed.

(4) Notwithstanding anything inconsistent contained in any other Act of Parliament or State Legislature, as the case may be the State Information Commission may during the inquiry of any complaint under this Act, examine any record to which this Act applies which is under the control of the Public Authority, and no such record may be withheld from it on any grounds

(ii) Section 19 [(7), (8), (9) & (10)] of the Act highlight the powers of the Commission pertaining to the decision in appeals:

- The information Commission to decide appeals in accordance with the prescribed procedure and its decision shall be binding;
- In its decision, the State Information Commission has the power to—

(a) require the public authority to take any such steps as may be necessary to secure compliance with the provisions of the Act, including—

(i) by providing access to information, if so requested, in a particular form;
(ii) by appointing a Public Information Officer;
(iii) by publishing certain information or categories of information;
(iv) by making necessary changes to its practices in relation to the maintenance, management and destruction of records;
(v) by enhancing the provision of training on the right to information for its officials; and
(vi) by providing it with an annual report in compliance with clause (b) of sub-section (1) of section 4.

(b) require the public authority to compensate the complainant for any loss or other detriment suffered;
(c) impose any of the penalties provided under the Act; and
(d) reject the application.

- The information Commission shall give notice of its decision, including any right of appeal, to the complainant and the public authority.
  The Commission may also impose penalty on and/ or recommend for disciplinary action against erring Public Information Officers [Section 20(1), (2)]
- Where the State Information Commission, at the time of deciding any complaint or appeal is of the opinion that the Public Information Officer, has, without, any reasonable cause, refused to receive an application for information or has not furnished information within the time specified under sub-section (1) of

section 7 or malafidely denied the request for information or knowingly given incorrect, incomplete or misleading information or destroyed information which was the subject of the request or obstructed in any manner in furnishing the information, it shall impose a penalty of Rs. 250 each day till application is received or information is furnished, so however, the total amount of such penalty shall not exceed Rs. 25,000.

- the Public Information Officer shall be given a reasonable opportunity of being heard by the Commission before any penalty is imposed on him or her;
- the burden of proving that a Public Information Officer acted reasonably and diligently shall be on himself/herself;
- where the Information Commission, at the time of deciding any complaint or appeal is of the opinion that the Public Information Officer, has, without any reasonable cause and persistently, failed to receive an application for information or has not furnished information within the time specified or malafidely denied the request for information or knowingly given incorrect, incomplete or misleading information which was the subject of the request or obstructed in any manner in furnishing the information, it shall recommend for disciplinary action against the Information Officer under the service rules applicable to him or her.

(iii) *Procedure followed in the decision-making process, including channels of supervision and accountability.*

(iv) *The norms set by it for the discharge of its functions; and*

(v) *The rules, regulations, instructions, manuals and records, held by it or under its control or used by its employees for discharging its functions.*

The State Information Commission, Haryana discharge its function according to norms as under :

(1) Provisions made in the Right to Information Act, 2005 for disposing of various complaints or Appeals received in the Commission.
(2) Any amendment received for the implementation of Right to Information Act, 2005 from the Central or the State Government.
(3) The Haryana Right to Information Rules, 2005.
(4) Punjab Civil Service Rules for disposing of service matters of the employees posted with the Commission.
(5) Punjab Financial Rules for disposing of financial matters.
(6) Policy instructions of the State Government issued from time to time.

There is no time limit fixed in the Act for disposal of second Appeals/Complaints received by the Commission. However, the Commission has been disposing off such matters expeditiously. It shall be the endeavor of the Commission that such matters are finalized with in a maximum period of 3 months of their receipt in the Commission.

(vi) *A statement of the categories of documents that are held by it or under its control :*

(1) The files of complaints received from the complainants under section 18(2) of RTI Act, 2005 for inquiring into the matter and their final disposal.
(2) The files of appeals received from the Appellants under section 19(3) of RTI, Act, 2005 and their final disposal.
(3) Files advising the applicants to take action as provided under the act to get the delivery of information more expeditiously.
(4) Personal files of staff functioning in the State Information more expeditiously.

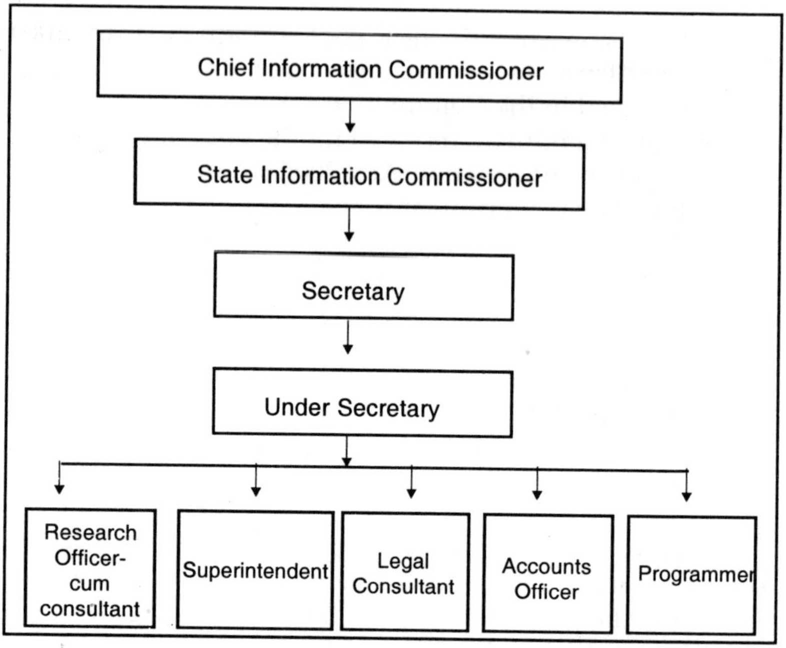

(5) Files of accounts on account of expenditure incurred out of the budget allocated to the State Information Commission, Haryana.

(vii) The particulars of any arrangement that exists for consultation with or representation by the members of the public in relation to the formulation of its policy or administration thereof

The Main function of the State Information Commission is to implement Right to Information Act, 2005 by providing for setting out the practical regime of right to information for citizens to secure access to information under the control of a public authority, in order to promote transparency and accountability in the working of every public authority. There is no arrangement for consultation with or representation by members of the public in relation to the formulation of its policy or administration thereof in the Commission.

(viii) *Statement of the boards, councils committees and other bodies consisting of two or more persons constituted as its part or for the purpose of its advice and as to whether meetings of those boards, councils, committees and other bodies are open to the public, or the minutes of such meetings are accessible for public.*

-Not applicable-

(ix) *A directory of its officers and employees*

(x) *The monthly remuneration received by each of its officers and employees, including the system of compensation as provided in its regulations.*

Sl. No.	*Nomenclature of Post*	*Sanctioned Pay Scale*
1.	Once Chief Information Commissioner	Rs. 90000 minus pension, plus Allowances +18% D.A. + 200 CCA + furnished accommodation i.e. as sanctioned to the Election Commissioner of India
2.	Six State Information Commissioner	Rs. 80000 minus pension, + 16% D.A. + 2000 CCA + HAR 15% of Rs. 80000 i.e. to the Chief Secretary of State
3.	One Secretary	Rs. 15000-400-18300 (Old Pay Scale)
4.	One Sr. Secretary to CIC	Rs. 1000-325-16000-400 Spl. Pay (Old Pay Scale)
5.	One Under Secretary	Rs. 1000-325-13900 +Sp. Pay (Old Pay Scale)
6.	One Research Officer-cum-Consultant	Rs. 7450-225-10500 (Old Pay Scale)
7.	One Superintendent	Rs. 6500-10500 Spl. Pay (Old Pay Scale)
8.	One Account Officer	Rs. 6500-10500 (Old Pay Scale)
9.	Programmer	Rs. 6500-10500 (Old Pay Scale)
10.	One Private Secretary to SIC	Rs. 6500-10500+200 Spl. Pay (Old Pay Scale)

(Contd...)

(Contd...)

11. Three Post of Personal Assistants	Rs. 5400-80000+150 Spl. Pay (Old Pay Scale)
12. Two Post of Assistants	Rs. 5450-8000+60 Spl. Pay (Old Pay Scale)
13. One Post of Accounts Assistant	Rs. 5450-8000+60 Spl. Pay (Old Pay Scale
14. Two Post of Readers	Rs. 5450-8000+60 Spl. Pay (Old Pay Scale)
15. One Jr. Scale Steno	Rs. 4000-6000+40 Spl. Pay (Old Pay Scale)
16. Two Steno Typists	Rs. 3050-4590+100 Spl. Pay (Old Pay Scale)
17. Four Clerks-cum-computer operators	Rs. 3050-4590+40 Spl. Pay (Old Pay Scale)
18. Four Drivers	Rs. 4000-6000+300 Spl. Pay (Old Pay Scale)
19. Eleven Peons	Rs. 2550-3200+30 Spl. Pay (Old Pay Scale)

(xi) *The budget allocated to each of its agencies, indicating the particulars of all plans, proposes expenditures and reports on disbursement made.*

In Haryana, The State Information Commission was set up with effect from 1.11.2005. To run the establishment of the newly constituted Commission, the State Government made the following provisions in the Head of Account 2070-Other Administrative Services—

Non Plan—

(xii) *The manner of execution of subsidy Programmes, including the amounts allocated and the details of Beneficiaries of such programmes;*

Not applicable to the State Information Commission, Haryana.

(xiii) *Particulars of recipients of Concessions, permits or authorization granted by it.*

Not applicable to the State Information Commission, Haryana.

(xiv) *Details in respect of the information, Available to or held by it reduced in an electronic form;*

Nil

(xv) *The particulars of facilities available to the citizens for obtaining information, including the working hours of a library or reading room, if maintained for public use;*

Like any other Public Authority Information concerning the Commission and its working can be obtained under the Right to Information Act, 2005. In view of the paucity of the space it is not possible to provide arrangement for a library or reading room for the public at large at present

(xvi) *The names, designations and other Particulars of the Public Information Officers;*

State Information Commission, Haryana

SCO No. 70-71, Sector 8C, Chandigarh

Telephone No. 0172-2726568, Fax. No. 0172-2783834

Sl. No.	*Name & Designation*	*Address*	*Tel. No.*	
			Office	*Residence*
1.	G. Madhavan, Chief Information Haryana	12, Sector-7 Chandigarh	2726568	2793628
2.	H.C. Bansal, Sr. Secy./CIC	1250, Sector-11 Pkl.	2726568	2579154
3.	Meenaxi Anand Chaudhary, State Information Commissioner	287, Sector-16, Chandigarh	2783621	2543505
4.	Tripta Sharma, PS/SIS	1033, Sector-20B Chandigarh	278621	2716250
5.	Ltd. Gen. (Retd), JBS, Yadav State Information Commissior	–	2720116	96788891127
6.	Om Parkash	749, Sector-7 Chandigarh	2720116	2794051

(Contd...)

(Contd...)

7.	M.R. Ranga, State Information Commissioner	–	2720115	9878891123
8.	M.P. Kamboj,	819, Sector-17, Pkl	2720115	2850339
9.	Premveer Singh, State information Commisioner	–	2720117	9878891126
10.	Usha Saini, PS/SIC	3885, Sector-22, Chandigarh	2720117	2702885
11.	Chander Sekhar, Secretary	720, Sector-7, Chandigarh	2725494	2794554
12.	Yoga Dutt Chugh, Under Secretary	M. Majra	2783670	2735810
13.	K.L. Sharma, R.O.-cum-Consultant	2184, Sector-27, Chandigarh	2540621	2638808
14.	Sh. K.V. Setia, Accounts Officer	1434 Sector-39, Chandigarh	2783670	2696632

(xvii) Such other information as may be prescribed and thereafter update these publications every year.

The Commission will be very soon launching its own web site. Information pertaining to the activities of the Commission including its orders in various public hearings conducted from time to time would be put on the web site for information of all concerned.

Sousce: http://cicharyana.gov.in

6 Accountability : Landmark Decisions of CIC and SIC (Haryana)

Through Right to Information Act, 2005 a legal, workable and practical regime has been set up to help citizens in securing access to information under the control of public authorities with a view to promoting transparency and accountability in the working of every public authority. The citizen requesting for information has two tier appellate remedy for any grievance under the Act, including lack of response and rejection or receipt of incomplete information or even charging of unreasonable fee for providing information.

Central Information Commission (CIC) headed by Central Chief Information Commissioner is Apex statutory body at the centre. In the States there exists State Information Commission, headed by State Chief Information Commissioner. The decision given by Commission is final and binding on the Public Authority, unless the Public Authority challenges it before in High court.

Ever since it came into being, the CIC has given a number of landmark decisions which have clarified numerous issues relating to implementation of various provisions of the RTI Act. In this section an attempt has been made to compile important decisions of the Central Information Commission, India and Haryana State Information Commission to facilitate better appreciation of the provisions of the RTI Act. The decisions relating to Haryana have been dealt in detail for proper understanding of the issues involved. For details of the relevant decision, readers may like to peruse them on the website of the Commission www.cic.gov.in and http//cicharyana.gov.in

Decision of Central Information Commission

Right to information available to the Citizen under Section 3

PIO can decline information under section 3, if the applicant applies as a Managing Director of a company and not a citizen of India. (CIC/OK/A/2006/00121 – 27 June 2006).

The applicant had asked a number of information as Pradesh Adhyaksha of Rajasthan Pradesh Congress Committee. The information was denied to him quoting sec 3 of the RTI Act. The Commission upheld the contention of the public authority and also observed that it was a case similar in nature to an earlier case (NOCK/OK/A/2006/00268-case of S.K. Lal *vs* Railway Board). The Commission observed that "...It must be remembered that though the respondents are duty bound to supply the information asked for by the appellants, the appellants are also required to keep in mind the objective of RTI Act as outlined in the preamble to the act and that is to introduce the elements of accountability and transparency in the functioning of the public authority and to contain corruption. The Commission failed to appreciate how these objectives would be met if appellants asked for such diversified information which seemed to be designed to put the public authority under undue and uncalled pressure......and it therefore dismissed the case as frivolous and inconsequential (Decision No. CIC/OK./A/2006/00605 dated 30 April 2007).

While deciding complaint CIC/WB/C/2007/00104/105 dated 30 March 2007, the Commission had an occasion to examine whether a company or its directors will fall under the term citizen under the RTI Act 2005. A company or a corporation is a "legal person" and as such it has a legal entity. This legal entity is different from its share holders, managers or directors. This is a settled legal position in law sine the Solomon's case decided long back by the House of Lords. They have legal obligations. They can sue and can be sued in a court of law. RTI Act, 2005 confers right to information on all 'citizens'. A citizen under part II of the constitution that deals with "citizenship" can only be a natural born person and it does not even by implication include a legal or juristic person. Section 2(f) of the Citizenship Act defines a person under:

> "Person does not include a company, an association or body of individuals whether incorporated or not."

The objective of Right to Information Act is to secure access to information to all citizens in order to promote transparency and accountability. After discussing decision of the Supreme Court in Bennet Coleman Co and others *vs* UOI (1973) and Delhi Cloth Mills case (1983), the Commission observed that even though, companies and corporations have not been held to be a citizen, there are a number of cases where the Apex Court has granted relief to petitioner companies. In conclusion, the Commission directed that an application/appeal from an Association or a partnership firm or Hindu Undivided Family or from some other group of individuals constituted body or otherwise should be accepted.

Address of the applicant need not be personal

The applicant had provided the address of a Non-Governmental Organization (NGO) he was associated with, for the purpose of correct delivery of replies in response to his application.

The Commission (Case No. CIC/OK/A/2006/00050, Dated 3/7/2006) noted that the appellant has applied in his own name as a citizen as per the requirement of Section 3 of the RTI Act and had given the address of an NGO for the purpose of correct delivery by post.

It was accordingly held that merely giving the address of some organization does not imply that the institution was asking the information, and an RTI application could not be rejected on this ground alone, therefore, the concerned public authority was directed to immediately provide the information sought and the PIO was penalized according to provisions of Section 7 and 20 of the RTI Act.

Application fee is a must

Applicant paid a fee of Rs 50 CPIO rejected the application on the plea that exact fee was not paid. While considering the appeal, CIC held that, the PIO was not right in concluding that the appellant's application for information could be returned at the admission stage itself for her failure to enclose the exact fee amount instead of remitting a larger sum which she apparently did. The PIO interpreted the rules rather narrowly and literally, whereas what was needed was to inform the interpretation with a clearer understanding of the purpose and the intent of the Act, which is to facilitate easy transmission of information to those who seek it. In this context, Section 5(3) is the key to the understanding of the approach to be adopted by the Information Officers. This Section states that the CPIO "*...... shall deal with requests from persons seeking information and render reasonable assistance to the persons seeking such information.*" Thus, the PIO is required to assist the information-seeker to obtain the information sought by him and to help him comply with the procedures. A highly restrictive interpretation of the modalities of fee remittance surely goes counter to the spirit of Section 5(3) of the Act.

Information sought should be clearly specified

The applicant had asked for inspection of all Dak registers of the Corporation from 1.1.2003 onwards, pertaining to various departments, i.e., HRD, Vigilance MD's office, as well as the General Dak Regiser.

CIC in the appeal No. CIC/OK/A/2006/00260, dated

2.1.2007 noted that the information asked by the appellant from the public authority was vague. The Commission held that the applicant under the RTI Act should clearly specify the information sought in terms of Section 2(f) of the RTI Act. The appellant was directed to specify the information he seeks to inspect from the records.

No additional information can be sought at the appellate level

The appellant had filed an appeal against the order of the public authority, which had refused to provide him with the information sought. The appeal, however, was very lengthy with several repetitions and use of highly technical legal language. The appellant had also asked for information on some new points during the appeal.

The CIC in the appeal No. CIC/OK/A/2006/00069, dated 18/5/2006 held that an appeal should be drafted in a simple and direct manner and must be brief. It should not be unnecessarily long, too detailed and contain technical language with several repetitions.

The CIC further held that no fresh grounds for seeking additional information can be allowed at the appellate level under Section 19 of the RTI Act, unless found to be of a nature that would require their admittance, if the same has not been brought up in the application to the public authority.

PIO is provide all reasonable assistance to the RTI applicants

The complainant had applied for certain information from Food & Civil Supplies Department of Delhi Government, but the staff of the department misbehaved with her and did not provide her with the required information.

The Commission (Complaint No.CIC/WB/C/2006/00145, dated 10/8/2006) in its order held that misbehaviour with the applicant approaching public authorities under the RTI is not acceptable, and is violative of Section 5(3) of the Act. It held that the public authority would pay compensation to the applicant.

Due diligence under Section 20 (1)

If the time limit could not be adhered to by CPIO, then applicant should be taken in to confidence and periodical progress be apprised to him. (CIC/AT/A/2006/00031 of 10/07/2006.)

It may have been lot better if the CPIO had kept the complainant periodically informed about the stages of the processing of his case and taken him into confidence about the possibility of some delay. (CIC/AT/A/2006/00066 of 4 July 2006).

Reasons for Rejection of Requests

Through this order the Commission now wants to send the message loud and clear that quoting provisions of Section 8 (1) of the RTI Act ad-libitum to deny the information without giving any justification or grounds as to how these provisions are applicable is simply not acceptable and clearly amounts to malafied denial of legitimate information attracting penalties under section 20(1) of the Act. (CIC/Ok/A/2006/00163 of 07/07/2006.).

File Notings not exempt for disclosure

An appellant had sought information related to file notings. The information was refused to the appellant by the CPIO as the Department of Personnel and Training of the Government of India had in its website, declared that file notings are covered under the exempted category. The Appellate Authority also rejected his application for information on the same grounds.

In appeal No. CIC/OK/A/2006/00154, dated 29/1/2007 CIC held that file notings were not exempted from disclosure. The CIC cited its earlier decision in the case of *Satyapal vis-a vis. TCIO* (Appeal No. ICPB/A-1/CIC/2006), in which the IC had expressly ruled that file notings were information in terms of Sections 2(i) and 2(j) of the RIT Act, and have to be disclosed. The IC also issued a notice to the Department of Personnel, for propagating wrongful information on the status of the file notings and ordered department to remove such misleading information from its website.

Creating/Generating Information

In its oft-repeated decisions, the Commission has advised the information seekers that they ought not seek the views and comments of the CPIO on the questions asked by them. Yet, in the garb of seeking information mainly for redressal of their grievances, applications from requesters are filed. The CPIO's in turn, have also ventured to answer them. Thus, the information seekers as well as providers have erred in interpreting the definition of information. A CPIO of any public authority is not expected to create and generate a fresh, information because it has been sought by an appellant. The appellant is, therefore, advised to specify the required information, which may be provided, if it exists, in the form in which it is sought by him. (278/IC/(A)2006 of 18/09/2006).

Information can be supplied only in the form available

The applicant had sought certain information in a particular format, the PIO of a public authority.

The Commission (Case No.10/01/2005-CIC, dated 25/2/2006) held that if the information is not available in the particular format requested, it does not have to be created in the format sought by the applicant, and information under Section 2(f) includes information in any form available with a public authority and accessible. The Commission held that the applicant may be allowed, if he desires to inspect the original records at the office (10/0/2005-CIC, dated 25/2/2006).

Information specifically asked may be provided in the form of printouts and certified photocopies of original documents and records.

Applicant Seeking Opinions of the Authorities

The PIO is required to 'provide information' which is available in any form with his/her office rather than giving his/her personal opinions on the questions asked by the requester. (CIC/MA/A/2006/00150, dated 19 June 2006).

Language for providing information under RTI Act

The appellant had applied for some information from, Delhi Development Authority (DDA), regarding certain shops leased by the Authority. The appellant had sought this information in the Hindi language.

The CIC in the appeal No. CIC/WB/A/2006/00117, dated 7.3.2006 while interpreting Section 2(f) of the RTI Act, directed the DDA to provide the requested information by translating it in Hindi within 25 days of the issue of its decision.

Personal Discussion with the Requester

If there was general confusion regarding the kind of information that has been called for and that could have been supplied, it could have been easily resolved by a personal sitting between the appellant and the respondents. (CIC/WB/A/2006/00180, dated 5 July 2006).

Seeking Interpretation of Rule/Law

Before parting with this appeal, it must be pointed out that this is the first time a party has come up to the Commission asking for interpretation of a given law / rules as well as the interpretation of the powers of a quasi-judicial body. As I stated in the first appeal, the proper Forum to test the order of a Tribunal is as laid down under the appropriate Act or as provided in the Constitution. It would be wholly inappropriate to invoke the provisions of the RTI Act for the interpretation of laws and rules. It should be made clear that the laws and rules are themselves 'information' and being in public domain are accessible to the public.

Responsibility of PIO

The appellant complained to the Commission that his request for information has not been responded to. The Commission treated the appeal as complaint and directed CPIO (US, Home Department, Chandigarh Administration) to provide information within 10 working days. PIO was also directed to show cause why a penalty of Rs. 250 from the date information was to be provided subject to maximum of Rs. 25000 should not be imposed under Sec. 20(1) of the RTI Act (complaint No. CIC/WB/C/2007/00016 dated 24 February 07).

Information which relates to expired records cannot be provided

The applicant had sought certain information regarding the copy of an order pertaining to the appointment and charge sheeting of an army personnel. This order was supposed to be more than 20 years old.

The army, refused to provide the appellant with the required information and said that they could not provide such old information as according to their departmental rules for preservation of records, the maximum period for preservation of records was only 10 years.

The CIC held that, in this case records of the court martial trial was destroyed after a retention period of 10 years under the Army Rules (Appeal No. CIC/AT/2006/20, dated 23.3.2009). It held that there was no obligation on the part of the any public authority to provide non-existent information in terms of Section 2(j) of the RTI Act if that information is no longer available due to the fact that the records were not available, i.e., they have been destroyed after a maximum period of preservation, as per the departmental rules for destruction of old records.

Record Management under Section 4 (1) (a)

Record management system ought to be improved such that information which are to be disclosed could be easily provided after delineating those that is exempted. (CIC/OK/A/2006/00016 dated 15.6.06).

Videography

There is no provision in the Act disallowing videography (if an applicant wishes to meet the expenses at his own) and therefore cannot be excluded unless it violates the parameters of any information sought and agreed to be provided. (CIC/WB/A/2006/00051dated 04.07.2006).

Information held under Section 2 (j)

In this case records of the court martial trial were destroyed after a retention period of 10 years under the Army Rule 146. Information did not exist, it was physically impossible to provide it. There is no liability under the RTI Act on a public authority to supply non-existent information. (CIC/AT/A/2006/20 dated 23 March 2006)

As per RTI Act, a citizen can seek only that information which is available in material form. The public authority is not bound to answer queries like why and what and under what circumstances to the applicant. (Appeal No. 352/ ICPB)/2006 dated 10 May 2007).

The appellant sought information regarding stepping up of her pay with reference to her junior. While considering the appeal, the commission was of the opinion that this kind of information cannot be solicited under RTI Act. She has a grievance that she has not been granted stepping up of her pay along with her junior. This is purely a grievance which has to be taken up by concerned authority. As far as the RTI Act is concerned, the citizen can seek information which is available with the public authority in any material form. Appeal dismissed. (Appeal No. 484/ICPB/2007 dated 15 May 2007).

The appellant approached CPIO to inform him – "Who is the appointing authority and disciplinary authority for Judges and Chief Justices of High Courts and Supreme Court?" CPIO provided information about appointing authority. He attempted an explanation about disciplinary. Not satisfied with the reply the appellant approached the Commission. While considering the appeal, the Commission observed that appellants right under the RTI Act is defined by Sec. 2(f). Another Section 2(j) stipulates that an information as in Sec. 2(f) is to be held or be in control of a public authority before its disclosure can be authorized. The present request fails both these tests. What he is asking is neither a 'material' as stipulated in Sec. 2(f) nor is held by respondents as in Sec. 2(j).What one understands is that the appellant wants to provide him explanation for the surmise he has made about the "disciplinary authority" for the Chief Justice of India and to explain to him if the law is silent on the point. RTI Act does not caste any such obligation on the respondents. Appeal rejected. (Decision No. CIC/AT/A/2007/00155 dated 10 May 2007).

It is incorrect to state that the information sought does not fall within the definition of information under sec 2(f) merely because it needs to be "compiled and processed". ...There may be separate public authorities who can be asked to provide the information sought under sec 6(3) and if on the other hand no such information is available with Ministry or any of its attached and subordinate offices, the public authority may say so. But on no account information be denied because it will be required to be collected, since collecting information is indeed the primary task of a CPIO. (Decision in appeal No. CIC/WB/A/2006/00640 dated 16 September 06).

Information to be provided free if there is delay/ reimbursement to be provided in cases of delay

The applicant had applied for certain information regarding slum clearance from Urban Development Department of Delhi Government. She was not provided any information within the time limit, as the pubic authority could not ascertain the information asked by the applicant.

The CIC in the appeal No. CIC/WB/C/2006/00182, dated 29.6.2006 held that since there was a delay in replying to the information sought, the appellant should be provided information without costs as per the stipulation under Section 7(6).

The appellant was held entitled to reimbursement under Section 19(8)(b) of the Act. Further more, the CIC in this appeal also issued a show cause notice to the State Public Information Officer (SPIO) as to why the penalties prescribed under Section 20(1) of the Act be not imposed on him.

Pro-active disclosure information to be provided free

The applicant had applied to the public authority for sanctioned posts of engineers and other related information. The information was in any case required to be compulsorily declared under Section 4 of RTI Act, 2005 as pro-active disclosure information.

It was held by the Commission (Appeal No. CIC/WB/A/2006/00377, dated 20/11/2006) that the nature of information sought by the appellant was such that it was required to be furnished as *suo moto* information by a public authority, under pro-active disclosure requirements of Section 4(1)(b) of the Act.

The Commission also ordered that such information should be provided free of costs as mandated under Section 4(6) of the Act (Appeal No.CIC/WBA/2006/00377).

No Direct Appeal to the Commision

Appeal to CIC cannot be filed directly without filing first appeal before Appellate authority (order dated 18 Jan 06 in Appeal no CIC/A/1/2006), (order dated 20 Jan 06 in appeal No. CIC/A/4/2006) and (order dated 13 pr 06 in Appeal No. ICPB/A-16/CIC/2006).

Appeal by CPIO

CPIO is only information provider and not information seeker. There is no provision in the RTI Act to entertain appeal from CPIO. Such appeal is not maintainable (order dated 3 March 06 in appeal No. 06/IC(A)/CIC/2006).

Third Party has no absolute right to refuse information disclosure about it

The appellant, an employee of a public authority, had applied for some information relating to the prosecution of another employee (third party), because under similar circumstances the appellant was convicted while the other employee was exonerated.

The public authority refused to provide him the information on the grounds that the third party had refused the disclosure of information to the applicant.

The CIC in appeal No. CIC/AT/A/2006/00014, dated 22.5.2006 held that the RTI Act does not give third party an automatic right to order the Public Information Officer (PIO) of a public authority, not to disclose information pertaining to it. The CIC further held that the public authority is required to evaluate the third party's case in terms of the provisions of Section 8(1) (j) and Section 11(1) of the Right Act, 2005, and find out the information asked is not barred from disclosure.

Even if the information is barred from disclosure then the public authority is to examine if it would be in the public interest to disclose the information sought and its disclosure will outweigh harm if any to the individual third party. The public authority has to arrive at the findings by properly assessing the facts and circumstances of the case. A speaking order should thereafter be passed accordingly.

Life and liberty under Section 7 (1)

Matter to be treated as one of life and liberty would require the following:

- The application be accompanied with substantive evidence that a threat to life and liberty exists.
- Agitation with use of Ahimsa must be recognized as a bonafied form of protest, and therefore even if the claim of concern for life and liberty is not accepted, in a particular case by the public authority, the reasons for not doing so must be given in writing in disposing the application. (CIC/WB/C/2006/00066 dated 19.04.2006.).

Ministerial staff also liable of penalty

It is clear from the above that the errant officials are functioning at the clerical level in the office of the PIO, Shri

Meena. Whereas under Section 5(5), an officer does not himself have to be designated as a PIO/APIO to be liable for penalty for contravention of the provisions of this Act, officials functioning even at the clerical level and above category of Class-IV will be deemed to be "officers" in the application of this Act. In the normal course, therefore, they would be liable to penalty under Section 5(5) if their assistance had been sought under Section 5(4) of the Act. In this case, therefore, as already held, they cannot plead exemption from application of this provision. (Adjunct to CIC/ WB/C/2006/00018, dated 28.9.2006).

Period prior to Twenty Years under Section 8 (3)

Section 8 (3) is part of section 8, which deals with 'exemption from disclosure of information'. Section 8 (1) specifies classes of information which are exempted from disclosure. What section 8 (3) stipulates is that the exemption under section 8 (1) can not be applied if the information sought related to a period prior to 20 years except those covered in section clauses (a), (c) and (i) of sub-section 8 (1). In other words, even if the information sought is exempt in terms of other sub-section (1) of section 8, and if the same relates to a period 20 years prior to the date of application, then the same shall be provided. (37/ICPB/2006, dated 26 June 2006).

Presence of Respondents before CIC

The appellant had filed an application before CPIO, Ministry of Information and Broadcasting to seek information on five counts regarding provisions of Cable Network Act and registration and renewal of cable networks and cable networking operations in Chhattisgarh. The CPIO returned the application along with postal orders stating that the application be resubmitted along with fee in cash/bank draft. The applicant preferred an appeal before CIC.

On the date of hearing neither appellants nor the respondents was present. The Commission took a serious view that while absence of the appellant is acceptable but that of PIO is not. Any absence without reasonable cause and prior communication would be looked upon seriously (Decision No. CIC/OK/C/2006/00152 dated 23 March 2007).

Public Activity

The information asked for should be an outcome of a public activity. A copy of petition filed by another person can be denied under Section 8(1)(j) of the Act as it is not an outcome of any public activity (Decision No. 604/IC(A)/2007 dated 2 April 2007).

Travel Expenses

Travel expenses were charged to the public account. Disclosure of information cannot be denied on the ground of this being personal information and not a public activity and serves no public interest, etc. Travel has been performed as a part and in discharge of official duties and the records related to same are public records and therefore, a citizen has the right to seek disclosure of the same. (63/IC (A)/2006, dated 30 March 2006).

Security, Sovereignty and Integrity

The applicant asked for a copy of the order through which the Ministry of Home Affairs had authorized the CBI to intercept telephone calls under the Indian Telegraph Act, 1885 — Both the PIO and the Appellate Authority held that the requested information could not be supplied to the applicant as it attracted the exemptions under Section 8(1)(a)(g) and (h). While considering the appeal, the Commission held that quite clearly, the specific cases of interception and surveillance by the authorized agency has to be kept highly confidential because of the very nature of the surveillance operation. Its security implications are undisputed — But to say the same about the authorization of the Union Home Ministry to select intelligence and law enforcement agencies, investing them with general power of surveillance, won't be correct. To say that the matter which is already in common domain should be formally denied to a requester for information on grounds of state security will mean stretching the exemption under Section 8(1)(a) of the RTI Act a bit too far. It cannot be open to a governmental agency to wrongly classify its document as Secret or Top Secret and, then claim the privilege or the exemption provided under Section 8, especially Section 8(1)(a). (Order dated 21-02-2006 in Appeal CIC/A/12/2006).

Income Tax Returns

Income Tax Returns filed by an assessee are confidential information, which include details of commercial activities and that it relates to the third person. These are submitted in fiduciary capacities. There is no public action involved in the matter. Disclosure is exempted under section 8 (1) (j). (22/IC (A)/2006, dated 30 March 2006).

Annual Property Returns

CIC held that the Annual Property Return is in the nature of personal information given to the Public Authority in confidence by an employee. The Government has set in place an elaborate system of dealing with this information while maintaining its confidentiality. Generally, the information in the annual property returns is retained by the public authority in sealed covers/or in some other mode under proper "secrecy" classification and used only when the public servant, whose return it may be, faces a charge or an enquiry. It is not held as a public information, but rather a safety valve

– a deterrent to public servants that investments or transactions etc. in properties should not be done without the knowledge of the public authority. While there may be an arguable case for disclosing all such information furnished to the various Public Authorities by the public servants, till such time the nature of this information remains a confidential entrustment by the public servant to the Public Authority, it shall be covered by section 8 (1) (j) and cannot be routinely disclosed. It will also attract the exemption under Section 8 (1) (e) and in certain cases the provisions of Section 11 (1), being an information entrusted to the public authority by a third person, i.e. the public servant filing property return. On the whole, property returns of public servants, which are required to be compulsorily filed by a set date annually by all public servants with their respective public authorities, being an information to be used exceptionally, must be held to serve no general public purpose whose disclosure the RTI Act must compel. However, all public authorities are urged that in order to open the property returns of all public servants to public scrutiny, the public authorities may contemplate a new and open system of filing and retention of such returns. he public servants may be advised in advance that their property returns shall be open and no more confidential. The property return forms may be so designed as to give only such transactions and assets related details, which may not violate civil servants' right to privacy. These steps may bring the curtain down on the rather vexed question of how private is the information given in "property returns" or that it is a public information, which is not private at all. (order dated 10 July 06 in appeal Mo. CIC/AT/A/2006/00134).

Biodata and Medical Records under Section 8 (1) (j)

The appellant asked for copies of the biodata submitted by four candidates at the time of their appointment as Assistant

Directors and also copies of their medical reports submitted by the medical authorities declaring these candidates fit or unfit.

The CIC held that when a candidate submits his application for appointment to a post in a public authority, the same becomes public document and he can not object to the disclosure on the ground of invasion of privacy and directed the PIO to provide copies of the biodata.

As far as medical reports are concerned, they are purely personal to the individuals and furnishing of the copies of medical reports would amount to invasion of privacy of the individuals and need not be furnished. However, the PIO will disclose to the requester the information whether all four candidates had been declared medically fit or not. (ICPB/A-9/CIC/2006, dated 3 April 2006).

Certified copies of letters written by appellant himself

The appellant approached CPIO for inspection of all files relating to certain search and seizure operation carried out by the public authority against appellant's group of concerns and correspondence he addressed to the officers of the public authority in connection with search and seizure operation.

While considering the appeal the Commission observed that it was not open to the appellant to seek copies of the very letters he had written to public authority as this information was already accessible to the appellant himself. As regards file notings, the CPIO had denied these based on exemption provided in section 8(1)(g) of the RTI Act. It was mentioned that information was personal to the applicant and his group of concerns and it did not involve any public purpose. It was also contended by them that notings contained information relating to the sources of information of the public authority whose disclosure would be dangerous to life and physical safety of such persons and sources.

While considering this appeal, the Commission quoted

with approval their decision CIC/AT/A/2007/00018 dated 26 February 2007 wherein the following observations were made:

> "The Commission in normal course allows information about action on the petition made by the citizen to the public authority. But it also takes the precaution to ensure that these petitions are not without an element of public purpose in them. The case of appellant does not fall in that category. He is admittedly at the receiving end of the law enforcement function of the public authority and has retaliated by writing a spate of letters to them. The PIO has thus rightly declined this information to the applicant. The Commission also upheld the contention of the respondent in denying the file noting which contained details of informants/sources. The Commission observed that it would undoubtedly protect the right of every citizen to access information admissible under RTI Act, but this rule will have to be modified when a person at the receiving end of the enforcement seeks to subvert the process by invoking the freedom granted under RTI Act to contrive to access vital information critical to that process. In such cases the provisions of the law have to be interpreted strictly to make sure that the larger public interest is not allowed to suffer. (Decision CIC/AT/2007/00017, dated 28 March 07).

Consultation between the President and the Supreme Court cannot be disclosed

The applicant filed an RTI application with the Supreme Court of India. He wanted information regarding the exchange of communication between the Chief Justice of India and the President of India regarding the appointment of Supreme Court and High Court judges. The information sought by the applicant was refused by the Supreme Court.

The CIC in the appeal No. CIC/AT/A/2006/00113, dated 10.7.2006 held that the entire process of consultation between the President of India and the Supreme Court of India cannot be disclosed as the process of consultation is exempted under Section 8(1) (e) and 11(1) of the RTI Act, 2005. Moreover, under Article 124(2) of the Constitution of India, this is barred from disclosure.

Information on ongoing Investigation

The applicant had sought details regarding the progress of an investigation of a case by the police.

The CIC dismissed the appeal relating to the disclosure of information appeal in No. CIC/AT/A/2006/00004, dated 30.6.2006. It ruled that the disclosure of information, in cases under investigation by the police was exempted, according to the provisions of Section 8(1)(g) and 8(1)(h), of the Act. The Commission justified not to disclose information in cases of ongoing police investigations, because it could hamper the investigation process.

Information on an ongoing investigation can be given in special circumstances

The appellant wanted information on the ongoing investigation into the death of daughter under mysterious circumstances.

The CIC in appeal No. CIC/AT/A/2006/00355, dated 26.12.2006 held that this case was an exception to the general rule laid down in Section 8(1)(h) of the Act, which prohibits the disclosure of information, as the supply of information to the victim's family would not put any obstacles or impede the process of investigation.

The Commission further noted that, "Far from impeding the investigation, taking the appellant into confidence will give a positive direction to the investigation and enable the authorities to swiftly reach the truth". The commission ordered the police to provide the status of the investigation to the appellant within three weeks.

Contents of a departmental enquiry can be disclosed, if no bar from the Court

The appellant, a retired employee sought some information from the public authority about the denial of promotion to him while he was in service.

The matter was pending in a judicial body (Central Administrative Tribunal). The public authority refused to provide him the information on the grounds that the matter is pending in a judicial forum.

The Commission held that if a matter is sub-judice the same is not prohibited from disclosure as per the law in Section 8(1) (b), which prohibits the disclosure of any information which has been banned from disclosure by a court of law. As it is applicable only in cases where there is an express order from the court that information sought should not be disclosed, which was not the position in the present case, therefore such information should be supplied to the appellant (Appeal No.267/ICPB/2006, dated 10 January 2007).

Commercial Confidence

Appellant sought details of loans sanctioned and disbursed to a particular company – without indicating the bonafide public interest in seeking the information. CPIO denied the information. While considering the appeal, the CIC upheld the view that details of properties and securities submitted by the borrowers are in the nature of commercial confidence, the disclosure of which is exempted under Section 8(d) of the RTI Act - Also, the information sought relate to collateral and securities taken by the concerned company and its directors, which are personal information. This has no relationship with any public activity or interest. Disclosure of such information would cause unwarranted invasion of privacy of individual/third party, as per Section 8(1) (j). (order dated 29 March 06 in Appeal No. 19/IC(A)/2006).

Commercial Secrets Protected by Law under Section 8(1) (d) and 11(1)

A request was received by the Chief Commissioner of Customs for the names of importers and exporters in daily list of import and export which are being published from the custom houses. But a notification No. 128/2004-Cus (NT) dated 19 November 2004 forbids the disclosure of the names requested.

The CIC held that the notification containing rules are in the nature of subordinate legislation is appropriate under Section 8(1) (d) of the RTI Act. CIC/MA/A/2006/00012, dated 10 March 2006.

Contract Under Section 8(1)) (d)

Ramesh Chand applied to National Institute of Science Communication and Information and sought information on terms of the conditions and their implementation regarding a contract with another firm. The CIC held that a contract with a public authority is not confidential. Offer, completion, quotations, bid, tender, prior to conclusion of a contract can be categorized as trade secret, but once concluded, the confidentiality of such transactions connot be claimed. Any public authority claiming exemption must be put to strictest proof that exemption is justifiably claimed. Therefore, this public authority was directed to disclose the list of employees.(CIC/WB/C/2006/00176, dated 18 April 2006).

Cut-Off Marks

The Commission has directed the Staff Selection Commission to furnish the mark sheets (for written examination as well as interview) to the candidates along with cut-off marks for different categories of candidates. (180/IC (A)/2006, dated 17.08.2006).

DPC Minutes

DPC minutes and proceeding connected with the same are not exempt from disclosure. (Full Bench decision of Commission in CIC/WB/C2006/233, dated 23 April 2007).

Drafting an Application

Appeal should be drafted in a simple and direct manner and must be brief. It must not be unnecessarily long, too details and couched in legalese with several repetitions.

No fresh grounds for information can be allowed to be urged at appellate levels unless found to be of a nature that would warrant their admittance, if the same has not been brought up at the primary level i.e. PIO level. (CIC/Ok/A/2006/00069 of 18.05.2006 & CIC/AT/A/2006/00128, dated 13.07.2006).

Invasion of Privacy

The applicant had asked for a copy of the leave application together with enclosures and also grounds cited by an employee in her application for transfer from Dehradun to Delhi. The information was denied on the plea that its disclosure would invade the privacy of an individual, even though a public servant, and information available with the public authority. The contention of the public authority was upheld by the CIC. (Appeal No. 448/ICPB/2006 dated 9 May 2007)

The appellant had asked for 16 information including nature of illness of a staff member. While other information were provided, information about nature of illness was denied by the CPIO on the plea that it relates to the personal information of third party the disclosure of which has no relationship to any public interest or activity and it would cause invasion of privacy of the individual. The Commission declared that the CPIO had correctly denied the information section 8(1) (j) of the RTI Act (Decision No. 422/ICPB/2006 dated 26 April 2007).

Investigating Officer and Privacy

A citizen requested from the RBI certain information relating to the findings of an inspection of the Memon Cooperative Bank Limited, Mumbai, which was conducted on the basis of a complaint filed by him and a copy of the inspection report along with the name(s) of the investigating officers.

The CIC directed the RBI to furnish a copy of the inspection report after the due application of section 10(1) of the Act. Alternatively, the appellant should be provided a substantive response, incorporating major findings of the inspection report and indicating the action taken on the findings of the report. However, the names of the investigating officers may not be revealed as it would not serve any public interest. (177/IC (A)/2006, dated 17 August 2006).

Order Appointing the Examiners

PIO of the Delhi University was directed to supply the certified copies of the orders appointing the examiners and of the files dealing with his application re-totaling of marks of the applicant. (CIC/OK/A/2006/00051, dated 04.07.2006.)

Public authority to disclose information if public interest outweighs the harm to the protected interests

The appellant had sought a copy of the letter received by the public authority regarding his suspension, from CBI, which was investigating the case. The public authority replied that the information requested by the applicant was exempted from disclosure by virtue of Section 8)1)(g) and 8(1)(h) of the RTI Act.

The Commission (Appeal No.CIC/WB/A/20060523, dated 26/3/2007) while rejecting the appeal of the applicant, held that the exemptions from disclosing information, under Section 8(1)(h) of the RTI Act as well as under the relevant provisions of the Official Secretes Act, would apply. The Commission further said that if the public authority, decides that public interest in the disclosure would outweigh the harm to the protected interests, it can disclose the information which was not the position in this case.

Public Interest and Consumer Protection

Appellant has made the case of public interest on the grounds of adulteration in distribution of diesel and petrol. He has however not substantiated his point as to how he would prove his allegations on the basis of disclosure of income tax returns filed by the third party. Apparently there is no direct relationship between malpractices of petrol and diesel and income tax returns, which is mainly the basis for seeking information. (37/IC (A)/2006, dated 12 May 2006).

Public Interest and Environmental Protection

Shri Piyush Mahapatra made two applications on 5 December 2005 at the reception of the Ministry of Environment and Forests seeking information relation to research and testing of a number of GM Crops and studies and allergy/toxicity tests conducted on some GM crops.

The CIC held that the CPIOs of Ministry of Environment and Forests and Department of Biotechnology, both public authorities being part of the regulatory regime are directed to cooperate to supply information sought by the applicant. Both the Ministry of Environment and Forests and Department of Biotechnology have an informative website. Information on research, testing and studies being of public interest may be placed on these as available in conformity with section 4 (1) to ensure ease of access. (CIC/WB/C/2006/00063 and CIC/WB/C/2006/00064, dated 30 May 2006).

CPIO informed that delay arose because information was to be obtained from different branches of the secretariat which was rejected on 23 January 2007 being exempted under sec 8(1)(g) of the RTI Act. However, during first appeal the appellant was allowed inspection and copies of specified documents were provided to him. In appeal before the Commission, the appellant alleged that only a part of the information was provided and that the PIO, Chandigarh administration had tried to mislead the Commission. He also submitted that reply received from the appellate authority indicated the information asked for by the appellant was not available with the public authority. Also whatever information was available with the public authority has been provided as specified by the appellant after inspection of the records.

The Commission agreed with the Appellate Authority that only such information as available with the public authority can be provided. However, this does not exempt the public authority in a case concerning information of which it is custodian being inexplicably unaccounted for, from making every effort to trace it, identify the person responsible for its misplacement and take disciplinary action against the defaulting employee(s). As regards attribution of delay to late receipt of information from other branches, the Commission observed that the CPIO has failed to identify the officials from whom she had sought information under Section 5(4) of the Act or even plead imposition of penalty under Section 5(5). The Commission therefore directed that a penalty of Rs. 250 per day be recovered from the salary of the PIO.

The applicant sought copy of *Lal Dora certificate* issued in respect of property lease of petrol pump at Bawana. The SDM concerned replied that *Lal Dora certificate* of land on which the petrol pump is operated has not been issued from this sub division, particulars/details asked for cannot be provided. The applicant made two more reminders wherein he pointed out that certificate might have been issued prior to 1997 but records must have been transferred when the sub division was created. He did not receive any response and approached the Commission. While taking note of the complaint, CIC observed that the applicant has not taken recourse to first appeal under Section 19(1) nor has it pleaded before the Commission that it should be treated as a complaint 18(1)(e). They also observed that the SDM has only pointed that they did not have the information without advising his own DC where this information would be available. It is the duty of the PIO to obtain this information under Section 5(4) so that it could be provided to the applicant. The Commission ordered that the next senior officer would hear the applicant, will determine where the information sought by the applicant was held and ensure that information is provided to the applicant within 20 days. (Decision dated 23 May 07 in Appeal No. CIC/WB/2007/ 00113).

Scope of Remedy by CIC

In an appeal under RTI Act, the Commission is only concerned with whether timely and full information sought by a citizen has been furnished by the public authority. However it cannot examine the merit of the decision of the public authority. (Appeal No. 449/ICPB/2007, dated. 9 May 2007)

The applicant in this case has attempted to use RTI route in order to force Income Tax authorities to issue notice to the third party viz Tata Motors, a tax notice for allegedly filing faulty form 16 under income tax laws. He did not receive a favourable response from the CPIO. He made an appeal. Based on the order of the appellate authority, income tax authorities made inquiries with Tata Motors and came to conclusion that forms 16AA and 12BA issued to the appellant were correct in all respect. It was also found that there was a pending industrial dispute between appellant and the third party. While considering the Appeal, the Commission observed that information solicited by the appellant is more in nature of a complaint against his former employer. It is not possible to settle for the applicant, through the instrumentality of the RTI Act, an industrial dispute which he had with the third party. Appeal rejected. (Decision No. CIC/AT/A/2007/00251 dated 14 May 2007).

Penalty Under Section 20(1)

For the first time, Shri Wajahat Habibullah, Chief Information Commissioner imposed a penalty of Rs. 25,000 on a PIO for a complaint number CIC/WB/C/2006/00040, 5 June, 2006. PIO has failed to appear before the Commission on due date and time despite a telephone reminder. Because the burden of proving that he acted reasonably and diligently is on the PIO under Provision II to Sec 20(1), it is assumed that he has no reasonable cause to show why penalty should not be imposed. Under the aforementioned section of the Act, penalty shall be imposed on any of the following grounds, if the PIO has—

- refused to receive an application
- not furnished the information within the time frame specified in section 7 (1)
- malafidely denied the request for information or knowingly given incorrect information
- obstructed in any manner in furnishing the information by not supplying some of the information sought by the applicant as found by us in the Decision Notice of 23 May 2006, the PIO is in violation of (b) above, and by evading his responsibility to provide the information sought also obstructed the complainant's. He will therefore pay a penalty of Rs. 250 for every day subject to a maximum of Rs. 25,000.
- CIC/WB/C/2006/00040, 5 June 2006.

Disciplinary action against Appellate Authority

The appellant had asked for certain information from the PIO of the CSIR (public authority). The information was refused by the PIO stating that it was exempted under the RTI Act and was informed about the appellate authority with which he could file the first appeal.

The Appellate Authority, however, without filing a formal appeal by the applicant/appellant, sent a letter to the applicant that the information asked by the applicant could not be supplied.

The CIC in the appeal No. CIC/EB/C/2006/00040, dated 24.4.2006 recommended disciplinary action against the Appellate Officer by extending the meaning of Section 20(2) of the RTI Act. The Commission held that though an appellate authority is not covered under the penal provisions of the Act but in this case, if clearly failed to uphold the Act in public interest. It was observed that this decision might be sent to the public authority to consider disciplinary action against the Appellate Authority, under their service rules.

Compensation to the Applicants

Misbehaviour with applicants approaching public authorities under the RTI is not acceptable and is violative of section 5 (3). In this case the PIO will invite the appellant to visit his office and identify members of his staff who refused to provide her the information. Under section 19 (8) (b) the public authority will pay Rs. 100 as damages suffered to the applicant. This may be either directly or through recovery from the erring officials, as deemed appropriate by the PIO. (CIC/WB/C/2006/00145, dated 10 August 2006).

Compensation under Section 19(8) (b)

For the first time, the CIC in its decision directed the Central Government Health Scheme, Pune to pay a sum of Rs. 5,000 to the appellant Ms. M. N. Trival as compensation and refund her the sum of Rs.60 paid by her as fee for non-application of mind by both the PIO and AA resulted in the appellant's having to interact with PIO and CIC repeatedly causing mental harassment to her. (Decision number 30/ICPB/2006, dated 13 June 2006).

HOD's failure to assist the Commission

The Commissioner of Municipal Corporation Delhi has failed to assist the Commission, which he was legally bound to do, and he also failed to explain as to why the orders of this Commission were not executed. It also appears that he has thereby caused an interruption to the proceedings. He has, therefore, committed offences punishable under Section 176, 187, 188 and 228 of Indian Panel Code. Now therefore, it is ordered as follows:

> That the Commissioner, MCD shall appear in person on 18 August 2006 at 10:30 am and show cause (a) as to why he be not prosecuted for committing the said offences and (b) as to why appropriate action be not recommended against him under section 20(2) of the Right to Information Act; and (c) as to why such further action or actions be not taken as this Commission may deem fit and proper.

He further directed to furnish the names and address of the concerned CPIO(s) who were responsible for not furnishing the information to the appellant so as to enable initiation of appropriate proceedings against them. (CIC/WB/C/2006/00040, 9 August 2006).

Review of a Decision

A review is permissible only if—

- There is a technical error in the decision

- There was an omission to consider certain material facts relevant for the decision
- Appellant was not given opportunity to be heard
- PIO has not enclosed relevant supporting documents in his comments to CIC. (1/2006, dated 16.5.06).

Medical treatment and Postmortam Report of School Student to the Parents

Shanno Khatun the 11 years old student, who died on April 17, 2009 after being allegedly subjected to to corporal punishment by her class teacher in her MCD school in Bawana, Delhi, the Central Information Commission has directed the dean of Maulana Azad Medical College, where her postmortam was conducted and Lok Nayak Jai Parkash Hospital, where Shanno underwent treatment before death to give the copy of the postmortam and treatment reports respectively to appellant.

The Commission however, accepted MAMC's submission that the matter cannot be covered under Section 7(1), life and liberty. But the Commission questioned how the PIO could deny information under clause 8 (1)(J) and how the medical records of a dead person would be covered under clause 8 (1)(J).

Source:The Times of India, May 27, 2009.

Decisions of Haryana State Information Commission

Apart from these brief analysis of the decisions of the Central Information Commission select decisions of the Haryana Information Commission are also included. The objective is to enable various stakeholders to understand the issues and the interpretation of the RTI Act by the appellate authorities. This will help in better application of the provisions of the RTI Act by the stakeholders. Moreover, the decisions of the Haryana Information Commission give a deep insight on various administrative issues relating to governance in the state.

Details of the Selection of Excise Inspectors and Auditors by Staff Selection Commission, Haryana (HSSC) *(Case No.1118 & 1119 of 2006* dated 25.01.200)

The appellant had asked for information pertaining to :

(i) Marks obtained by him in the written test as well as interview.
(ii) Names of the selected candidates.
(iii) The marks secured by the selected candidates both in the written examination and in interview.
(iv) The criteria adopted by the HSSC for viva voce.
(v) The details of educational qualifications and other qualifications of the selected candidates for which they have been given preference in selection.

The HSSC has provided the marks obtained in the written examination as well as in the interview by the appellant. The PIO informed the SIC that HSSC has not adopted any specific criteria for giving marks for specific attributes and the selection is based on an overall assessment of the abilities of the candidates at the time of interview. The IC held that HSSC is bound to provide information as none of the grounds put forward in the written reply for denying this information has any justification.

Latter on after a month the appellant had asked for additional information namely :

(i) Photo copy of the answer sheets of the written examination.
(ii) Photo copy of the question paper.
(iii) The key of right answers as calculated by the Commission.

It has been argued by the respondent department that it is not possible to furnish this information since the answer sheets have been destroyed as per the procedure and policy of the Commission. A photo copy of the proceedings signed by one of the members and Supdt. Confidential, Supdt Scrutiny, Confidential Assistant and Storekeeper has also been placed on record which shows that used/unused question booklets, answersheets, admitcards and application forms pertaining to the posts of Excise Inspectors and Auditors where results were declared on 6.6.2006 have been destroyed on 30.10.2006 as per policy approved by the Commission and no litigation of any kind was pending before the Commission. The IC asked to show the actual system of destruction of record relating to written examination which was being followed in the Commission. In response to this direction the Secretary-cum-Ist Appellate Authority informing that in accordance with the resolution dated 27.7.1992 read with resolution dated 1.10.1994 the necessary papers namely answer sheets except (Written Examination Results, Award List, Key book) will be destroyed after 3 months from the date of declaration of the result of the selection. A copy of the resolution dated 1.10.1994 signed by the Chairman as well as Members of the HSSC (Then called the Subordinate Services Selection Board, Haryana) has also been annexed to the reply. The appellant maintained that since he had already made a request for these records within the three months, it was improper and malafide on the part of the respondent department to destroy the record. However, denying any malafide the respondent department argued that in view of the fact that a reply had already been furnished vide letter dated 18.10.2006 to the appellant and since there was no pending litigation before the SSC in connection with this selection the record was destroyed as per the prevailing policy of the SSC. There was no malafide of any kind as this is the policy which is being uniformaly followed in all the cases by the respondent departnment.

Information Commission said that as per the factual position and the arguments advanced by both the parties it is clear that while destroying the record in this case the HSSC acted as per the accepted policy with regard to destruction of record and no particular exception was made in this case. The application filed by the appellant had already been disposed off by the HSSC and at the time of destruction of record there was no matter pertaining to the subject pending before the respondent department and even the appeal filed before the Information Commission. Therefore does not seem to be any malafide on the part of the respondent department in destroying the record pertaining to these cases. In view of the fact that the relevant record for which a demand has been made by the appellant has already been destroyed by the HSSC any finding with regard to the right of the appellant for access to this record will be purely of an academic nature. Some of the judgements of the Central Information Commission quotted by the appellant involving the UPSC decided on 15.12.2006 and 13.11.2006 are not relevant to the facts of this case, since they do not pertain to the subject of furnishing photocopies of the answer sheets as is being requested by the appellant. These decisions therefore do not help the case of the appellant.

Chief Information Commissioner gave the following directions:-

1. The HSSC shall furnish the information requested by the appellant except marks obtained by him both in written test and interview which has already been communicated to him. A compliance report in this regard shall be sent to the Information Commission..
2. It is not possible to furnish the additional information requested by the appellant since the relevant record already stands destroyed as per the accepted procedure prevailing in the SSC, Haryana.
3. Keeping in view the provisions of the RTI Act, 2005

the respondent department should consider reviewing their practices with regard to destruction of records to ensure that they are in tune with the provisions of the RTI Act in future.

Deemed Refusal of Information *Case No.1111 of 2006 Dated 25.01.2007*

The appellant finding no response from the SPIO within the time limit despite depositing the application fee and additional fee and treating it as a case of deemed refusal, he filed the first appeal with the First Appellate Authority. Alleging that incomplete information was supplied in response to his appeal with the First Appellate Authority, he filed second appeal before the Commission.

The PIO sent a written statement according to which information has been supplied to the appellant. Since, the appellant alleged that this was not received by him that information was given vide registered letter and the appellant was further advised in the same letter to inspect the record to which he has not responded.

However, the appellant contends that the information is incomplete. However, the department says that they would locate the remaining documents. Chief Information Commissioner, issued the following directions :

1. The department should locate copies of the documents and furnish to the appellant within a period of 20 days.
2. In view of the delay which has taken place no further charges shall be recovered from the appellant.
3. The names of the APIO/PIO/First Appellate Authority and the person who is authorized to accept cash shall be prominently displayed on the notice board of the Public Authority.
4. Registers giving information about the applications

received under the Right to Information Act and their disposal have to be maintained in the formats supplied during the hearing.

5. The compliance report on all the above points should be sent to the Commission within 20 days.

Give Acknowledgement of the receipt of Application — Casual Approach by PIO and first Appellate Authoirity Case No. 1084 of 2006, Dated: 11.01.2007

The applicant had submitted two separate applications ASPIO o/o DFO, Pinjore. But he did not receive any response from the ASPIOs. The applicant submitted his first appeal before the First Appellate Authority. The First Appellate Authority directed the DFO, Pinjore to supply the information to the applicant after receiving the prescribed fee and additional fee under the Act. At the time of second appeal, APIO submitted that information has been given to the appellant.

The appellant, however, said that he has received the communication sent by the respondents but information is incomplete. Further, this information relates to only two of his applications addressed to ASPIO o/o DFO (R&T), Pinjore. His letter addressed to ASPIO o/o the DFO, Pinjore has not been responded till date. He also submits that the First Appellate Authority instead of passing an order, forwarded his application to the office of DFO, Pinjore for giving information to the appellant.

The respondents submit that the appellant had been asked to deposit the necessary additional fee with the office of DFO (R&T), Pinjore and obtain the information. It is further stated that the information sought was voluminous and the appellant is expected to deposit about Rs. 70,000 as additional fee.

A perusal of record on file shows that the respondents have not acknowledged the receipt of the two applications till date. This is inspite of the fact that the copies of these applications show their receipt by the office. It was only when appellant sent his appeal to the Respondent No. 1 that directions to DFO, Pinjore were issued to provide information expeditiously to the appellant. Again, the second application addressed to ASPIO o/o DFO, Pinjore has still not been responded to. It is further submitted that applicant did not come to receive the information though he was asked to collect the information after depositing the additional fee in terms of his application where he had indicated his desire to collect the information personally.

The State Information Commissioner, pointed out that the manner in which this matter has been dealt with by the Forests Department is highly regrettable. No serious effort was made to trace the applications and furnish information till a notice was received from the Commission. Even after the receipt of the notice from the Commission containing copies of the two applications submitted by appellant , the respondents are not even aware of application addressed to ASPIO o/o DFO, Pinjore. The information given in response to application addressed to DFO (R&T), Pinjore is also incomplete. The appellant has not been informed till date the exact amount of additional fee, he is expected to deposit. The estimate for additional fee approximate of Rs. 70,000 mentioned today during the hearing does not seem correct in view of the fact that appellant in his application addressed to ASPIO, DFO (R&T) does not seek any documents. The First Appellate Authority dealt with the application for appeal without even calling the applicant and in a very casual manner. The information furnished in response to this application is also held to be incomplete. Even the notices issued by the Commission have not been properly and promptly responded. Accordingly, following directions are hereby given.

1. SPIO-cum-Conservator of Forests shall provide

complete information, duly attested, within 15 days of receipt of this order to the appellant in response to both of his letters which were enclosed with the notice issued by the Commission. In case certain documents are to be provided, they would be provided free of cost in view of delay in providing the information.

2. The appellant shall have the option to approach the First Appellate Authority, if he is not satisfied with the contents furnished to him.
3. The respondents shall submit a report to the Commission as to what happened to two applications.
4. A notice shall be issued to respondents as well as SPIO-cum-Conservator of Forests asking them to show cause as to why penalty at the rate of Rs. 250 for each day of delay in supplying the information to the appellant in each case be not imposed upon them.

Penalty on Complaint: *Case No. 139 of 2006,* Dated 4.1.2007

Receiving no response from the SPIO, the complainant filed an appeal with the Divisional Commissioner, Gurgaon who referred the matter to the Deputy Commissioner, Faridabad with the direction to provide him the requisite information as per the provisions of the Act. Finding no response the present complaint has been filed before the Commission.

The complainant is asking for certified copies of all letters and their enclosures addressed to the Director Town & Country Planning Haryana by the Deputy Commissioner, Faridabad in response to the letter of the Director TCP Haryana dated 10.5.1999 regarding verification of revenue documents along with file notings. A copy of the communication dated 10.5.1999 from the Director Town & Country Planning Haryana addressed to the Deputy Commissioner, Faridabad has also been annexed to the application. A perusal of the documents shows that the matter was referred by the Director TCP to the D.C.Faridabad to verify the ownership of certain land with respect to which licence was granted to Ms Durga Builders Pvt. Ltd. and its associate companies. More than a period of 7 years has elapsed and some reply must have been sent in response to this communication. The SPIO o/o DC Faridabad has neither responded to the notice issued by the Commission nor has any body appeared on his behalf in the hearing today. Under these circumstances these directions are hereby given :

1. The information requested by the complainant shall be furnished to him before 31.1.2007 and no further charges shall be levied from him for this purpose.
2. A notice under Section 20(1) of the RTI Act shall be issued to the SPIO o/o DC Faridabad asking him to show cause as to why a penalty of Rs.250/- for each day of delay should not be imposed on him for not supplying the information to the complainant. The reply should reach the Commission by 31.1.2007 and the SPIO shall be present personally before the Commission on 8.2.2007 at 1.00 pm.

Compensation fo Harassment, case No.1681 of 2007, Dated: 1.4.2008

This matter has arisen in pursuance of the earlier orders passed by the Commission in this case on10.1.2008.In response to the notice issued by the Commission a detailed reply has been filed by the Estate Officer–I, HUDA, Gurgaon (Respondent). As per record submitted by the HUDA office, the information has already been furnished. However, keeping in view the Commission's directions a photocopy of the complete file pages (1 to 165) including correspondence and noting portion has been sent to the appellant free of cost. It has been pointed out that due to heavy load of work and the transfer of assistants from one office to another the delay took place which has been regretted during the hearing. It was pointed out that certain administrative changes took place in the Estate Office during the months of August to October and with creation of another office work was bifurcated and record had to be transferred. The delay was mainly attributable to this fact and pointed out that due to heavy load of work and the transfer of assistants from one office to another the delay took place which has been regretted during the hearing. It was pointed out that certain administrative changes took place in the Estate Office during the months of August to October and with creation of another office work was bifurcated and record had to be transferred. The delay was mainly attributable to this fact and was not intentional. The SPIO during the hearing also pointed out that information is being furnished to all the applicants as per the provisions of the Act and such cases of delay will not be repeated.

The Commission keeping in view the reasons cited by the SPIO and the assurance of better performance in future the Commission is of the view that penal proceedings need not be was not intentional. The SPIO during the hearing also pointed out that information is being furnished to all the applicants as per the provisions of the Act and such cases of delay will not be repeated.

The Commission keeping in view the reasons cited by the SPIO and the assurance of better performance in future the Commission is of the view that penal proceedings need not be continued in this case. However, it can not be denied that avoidable harassment has been caused to the appellant in getting a simple piece of information to which he was entitled as an allottee. The following directions are therefore hereby given in this case :

1. The penal proceedings initiated against the Estate Officer-1, HUDA, Gurgaon are hereby dropped.
2. A sum of Rupees 5000 is awarded as compensation to the appellant for the harassment and detriment

caused to him in obtaining information in this case. This amount shall be paid by the Respondent Department by the 20 April, 2008 under intimation to the Commission.

Issuing Public Notice for Change of Designation of PIO as well as Collecting Information from Other Departments for the Applicant *in Case No.24 of 2008* Dated: 24.4.2008.

The complainant had applied with the office of Chief Secretary to Government of Haryana, Chandigarh requesting for detailed information with regard to implementation of the reservation policy in Haryana State. In particular he desired to have information pertaining to the progress achieved in filling up the back-log of posts reserved for them and also action in the context of the 85th Constitutional amendment made applicable by the State of Haryana w.e.f. 16.3.2006. The SPIO responded vide letter dated 13.9.2007 advising the complainant to send the Postal Order in favour of Under Secretary (General), Government of Haryana and the earlier one sent in favour of Under Secretary General Administration was returned. Subsequently, vide letter dated 15.10.2007 the respondent-department took the plea that the information requested vide the application is not covered under Section 2(f) of the Act. The complainant was further asked to deposit a sum of Rs.100 for obtaining copies of various instructions. Dissatisfied with the response an appeal was filed with the First Appellate Authority on 25.11.2007. Alleging that no worthwhile information was provided by the First Appellate Authority, the complainant sent a representation to the Commission which was entertained as a complaint under Section 18(2) of the Act.

In response to the notice issued by the Commission, a reply has been filed by the respondent-department vide letter dated 18.3.2008. It has been mentioned in the reply that the reason for sending the Postal Order was because the Under Secretary General has been designated as Drawing & Disbursing Officer in the Secretariat and payments are to be made in favour of Draft/Postal Orders drawn in his name and not in favour of any other authority. It has also been mentioned that vide letter dated 15.11.2007 the requisite information has been sent to the complainant by the Deputy Secretary, General Administration. The complainant, however, pointed out that full information has not been furnished to him as per his application dated 22.8.2007. The contention of the office of Chief Secretary that he should obtain this information by approaching different departments was incorrect. No information has been furnished on the posts which have been filled up out of the back-log of reserved posts by the various departments. His specific query about the seniority of persons promoted before 1.3.1996 in the context of 85th Amendment of the Constitution made applicable from 16.3.2006 has also not been specifically answered. He desired that information requested by him should be specifically furnished on these points.

The contention of the office of Chief Secretary that information about the back-log of the posts which have been filled up should be obtained by the complainant by approaching various departments is not acceptable. It is the responsibility of the office of Chief Secretary to provide this information by obtaining it from whatever source it has to be obtained. It was admitted during the hearing that the Welfare of Scheduled Castes and Backward Classes Department, Haryana monitors the progress of filled up of posts reserved for various categories and information on posts is colleted by this department from all Heads of Departments, Boards and Corporations. It should not be difficult for the office of Chief Secretary to Government Haryana to obtain this information since this information is also provided to the concerned Committee of the Haryana Vidhan Sabha as well as the National Commission for SCs & STs on a periodical basis. The department, however, requested for sometime to collect this information and furnish it to the complainant. It was pointed out by the Commission that publicity should be given about the fact that all applications addressed to the various Public Information Officers of the Chief Secretary's Office should be accompanied by Demand Draft/Indian Postal Order drawn only in favour of Under Secretary General, Government of Haryana. The following directions are hereby given in this case :

1. A brief public notice shall be issued by the office of Chief Secretary to Government of Haryana for the information of the general public that all applications under the RTI to be filed with the office of Chief Secretary if accompanied with the requisite fee in the shape of Demand Draft/Indian Postal Order shall be drawn in favour of Under Secretary General, Government of Haryana, Chandigarh. This notice should be published by the 15th of May, 2008 under intimation to the Commission.
2. Information on the progress achieved in filling up the back-log of posts mainly for the reserved categories up to the period ending 31.12.2007 from the date of issue of instructions dated 8.3.2006 shall be furnished to the complainant. Similarly information regarding the policy applicable for determination of seniority of persons promoted before 1.3.1996 in the context of 85th Amendment of the Constitution made applicable w.e.f. 16.3.2006 by the Haryana Government shall also be intimated to the complainant.
3. Keeping in view the request of the respondent-department the above information shall be furnished to the complainant before the 31st of May, 2008 and a compliance report sent to the Commission by 10th of June, 2008.

Ministers' Asset to Remain Secret: PM Office

At a time when pressure is mounting on the judiciary to disclose its assets, the executive wings of the government has come into the limelight for its reluctant commitment towards transparency.

In a decision that could have far reaching impact on administrative accountability, the PM's office, seen as leading the government towards transparency, has decided to withhold information related to assets of ministersand their relatives.

Responding to a query by applicant, the PM office termed the information as exempt under sub-clauses (e) and (J) of Section 8 (i) which relate to the immunity granted to "ducuments fiduciary relationship" and Cabinet documents"under the RTI Act. The appellant has now filed an appeal with the CIC.

The PMO had initially agreed to part with the information had by a letter on 19 May, 2008, made all the details available to the cabinet secretariat to deal with similar RTI applications in future. In a curious U-turn on 17 December, 2008, the PMO, which has often been credited with guiding the government towards transparency, held that details sought by the applicant were exempt from disclosure. The 'no' was repeated on 27 January, 2009, when the appellant persited with his effort.

It was last year that the appellant had filed the RTI application seeking details of assets of the Union Ministers and their relatives for the last two years from the Cabinet Secretariat. The letter was forwarded to the PMO for necessary action. In his appeal, appellant points to the PMO's reversal of stance. "The PMO was ready to divulge the information but there has been a change in decision, appellant said.

Source:The Times of India, February 22, 2009.

Judges Can't Reveal Assets like Netas : High Court

The Delhi High Court on 24.3.2009 observed that judges couldn't be put on the same footing as MPs and MLAs on the issue of asset declaration since such information may be misused. "Public interest standard for the judiciary has to be different from other institutions. So judges have to be treated differently from people's representatives on the issue", judge while hearing an RTI applicant who argued that judges, like MPs and MLAs should declare their assets. High Court while hearing a petition filed by the Supreme Court challenging the January, 2006 order of the CIC directing the apex court to reveal information pertaining to assets declared by its judges bebore the Chief Justice. The HC had on January 19 stayed CIC's order in which the CIC had held that the office of Chief Justice of India comes within the ambit of the RTI Act and information given to CJI has to be revealed to the RTI applicant. The court opined that judiciary should be liberated from all kinds of fear that personal information of judges might be misused if divulged under RTI Act, echoing the argument put forward by the SC in the submissions before HC. "Judges have to work according to law and without fear. For the proper functioning of judiciary it has to be liberated from all kinds of fear. Election Commission and other such institutions are vibrant because thay are independent," court also pointed out that if judge refused to disclose his assets there is no law that can force him to do so.

Source: *The Times of India*, March 25, 2009.

Bill Related to the Disclosure of Judges' Properties

Due to the protest of Members of Upper House of Parliament Law Minister, Veerappa Moily, deferred the introduction of "The Judges declaration of Assets and Liabilities Bill, 2009" in Rajya Sabha on August 3, 2009. Most likely, after some amendments this Bill will be introduced again in the coming winter session of the Parliament. As per the provision of the

Bill, High Court and Supreme Court Judges were to disclose their assets to the President. The opposition to the Bill was mainly due to Clause 6 of the Bill, according to which the assets disclosed to the President would be kept confidential in normal circumstances but it can be accessed in case of any probe into judicial misconduct or impropriety against a judge and be made public in such situations. Details of assets declared were kept out of the bounds of press as well as provisions of the RTI Act, so that disclosures are not used to harass judges by the frustrated litigants who are aggrieved by the ruling of the judicial officers. However, Members were of the view that provision was against the spirit of Article 19(1)(a) of the Constitution. They were saying that on the one hand Supreme Court order asks citizen contesting election not only to declare their assets, liabilities, education backgrond and criminal antecedents. This order further says that these disclosures would also be made public. Therefore, there can't be two sets of interpretation of article 19(1)(a).

REFERENCES

—— http :// cic. gov. in

—— http :// cicharyana.gov.in

—— PRIA, Analysis of Judgements of the CIC on RTI Act, 2005, New Delhi, October, 2007.

7 Act and Rules : Issues and Concerns

The Right to Information Act has completed four years of its implementation. The response of this Act has been very positive and it has received very wide and warm welcome from the people. People are learning the importance of the power of information.That is why, the people of every section have been seeking information from the different authorities.This is increasingly contributing to the accounability and transparency in administration. Public Authorities and Public Information Officers are becoming increasingly aware of their full responsibilities. Beside it is providing learning experience for each entity involved in the working of the law. However, the Act still being in infancy, there are many questions in the minds of the information providers and seekers both. To overcome this problem, in this chapter most of the basic questions relating to the better understanding of the different provisions of the Act and Haryana RTI Rules have been explained.

Q.1. What is RTI ?

Ans. RTI stands for Right to Information. Right to Information is a part of fundamental rights under Article 19(1) of the Constitution. Article 19 (1) says that every citizen has freedom of speech and expression. As early as in 1976, the Supreme Court said in the case of Raj Narain *vs* State of UP, that people cannot speak or express themselves unless they know. Therefore, right to information is embedded in Article 19. In the same case, Supreme Court further said that India is a democracy. People are the masters. Therefore, the masters have a right to know how the governments, meant to serve them, are functioning. Further, every citizen pays taxes. Even a beggar on the street pays tax (in the form of sales tax, excise duty, etc) when he buys a piece of soap from the market. The citizens therefore, have a right to know how their money was being spent. These three principles were laid down by the Supreme Court while saying that RTI is a part of our fundamental rights.

Q.2. If RTI is a fundamental right, then why do we need an Act to give us this right ?

Ans. This is because if you went to any Government Department and told the officer there, "RTI is my fundamental right, and that I am the master of this country. Therefore, please show me all your files", he would not do that. In all probability, he would throw you out of his room. Therefore, we need a machinery or a process through which we can exercise this fundamental right. Right to Information Act 2005, which became effective on 12th October, 2005, provides that machinery. Therefore, Right to Information Act does not give us any new right. It simply lays down the process on how to apply for information, where to apply, how much fees etc.

Q.3. What are objectives of RTI Act?

Ans. (a) to provide for setting out practical regime of right to infomation for citizens to secure access to information under the control of public authorities;

(b) to promote transparency and accountability in the working of every public authority;

(c) to set up Central Information Commission and State Information Commission and for matters connected therewith;

(d) to contain corruption and to hold governments and their instrumentalities accountable to the people; and

(e) to harmonise revelation of information with public

interests, including efficient operations of the governments, optimum use of limited fiscal resources and the preservation of confidentiality of sensitized information.

Q.4. When did RTI Act come into force?

Ans. RTI Act came into force on the 12th October, 2005.

Q.5. Who is covered under the RTI Act?

Ans. The Act extends to the whole of India, except the State of Jammu and Kashmir .

Q.6. What does information mean?

Ans. Information means any material in any form including records, documents, memos, e-mails, opinions, advices, press releases, circulars, orders, logbooks, contracts, reports, papers, samples, models, data material held in any electronic form and information relating to any private body which can be accessed by a public authority under any other law for the time being in force.

Q. 7. Can information be sought pertaining to oral advice given by experts to the Public Authority?

Ans. No, the RTI Act covers only recorded information which is recorded on paper or in electronic form. However, the definition of information as per Section 2 (f) of the Act is as under " Information means any material in any form, including records, documents, memos, e-mails, *opinions, advices,* circulars, orders, logbooks, contracts, reports, papers, samples, models, data material held in any electronic form and information relating to any private body which can be accessed by a public authority under any other law for the time being in force ". Appearance of the word 'advice and opinion' create confusion in the minds of information seekers. Therefore, this issue needs to be clarified by the Information Commissions and the Courts.

Q. 8. If the process of taking samples results in substantial damage to the public work concerned, can the PIO issue a rejection order?

Ans. This is another area where detailed guidelines are required for the PIO to take action. If taking samples from a public work results in damaging the structure, the PIO may mention the same in his rejection order. The SIC will give the PIO a reasonable opportunity to justify denial of the sample. If action is taken in good faith the PIO will not attract any penalty.

Q.9. What does record mean?

Ans. Record means: (a) any document, manuscript and file; (b) any microfilm, microfiche and facsimile copy of a document; (c) any reproduction of images embodied in such microfilm; and d) any other material produced by a computer or any other device.

Q.10. Some applicants ask questions 'why something was not done? Who is responsible?' Are such types of questions answerable under RTI Act?

Ans. If it is covered under the definition of 'Information'/ 'Record' then only it can be given, otherwise, it would be considered as creating the Information which is not required under the RTI Act.

Q.11. In office procedure rules records are to be destroyed within some stipulated period. If such

outdated records still exist in office and an applicant asks for these documents. Is it necessary to provide such information?

Ans. Yes, before destroying the record, public authority should ensure that there is no pending RTI application.

Q.12. What does Right to Information under the RTI Act mean?

Ans. Right to Information means the right to : (a) inspect works, documents and records; (b) take notes, extracts or certified copies of documents or records; (c) take certified samples of material; (d) and obtain information in form of printouts, diskettes, floppies, tapes, video cassettes or in any other electronic mode.

Q.13. What does "public authority" mean?

Ans. Public authority means any authority or body or institution of self-government which is established by:

(a) the Constitution; (b) any other law made by Parliament or State Legislature; (c) by notification or order made by the appropriate Government and including any body or NGO substantially financed by the Cente, State and Local Governments.

Q.14. Who is 'Third Party'?

Ans. The person whose information has been sought is the third party. The person applying for information is the first party; the public authorty to whom application has been addressed is the second party.

Q.15. What are the obligations of public authority?

Ans. Public authority is obliged to maintain its record in indexed and cataloged form. It should also try to ensure that record is computerized and ultimately connected through a network all through the country. Public authority is further supposed to publish the following details about itself:

(i) the particulars of its organization, functions and duties;

(ii) the powers and duties of its officers and employees;

(iii) the procedure followed in its decision-making process, including channels of supervision and accountability;

(iv) the norms set by it for the discharge of its functions;

(v) the rules, regulations, instructions, manuals and records used by its employees for discharging its functions;

(vi) a statement of the categories of the documents held by it or under its control;

(vii) the particulars of any arrangement that exists for consultation with, or representation by the members of the public, in relation to the formulation of policy or implementation thereof;

(viii) a statement of the boards, councils, committees and other bodies consisting of two or more persons constituted by it. Additionally, information as to whether the meetings of these are open to the public, or the minutes' of such meetings are accessible to the public;

(ix) a directory of its officers and employees;

(x) the monthly remuneration received by each of its officers and employees, including the system of compensation as provided in its regulations;

(xi) the budget allocated to each of its agency, indicating the particulars of all plans, proposed expenditures and reports on disbursements made;

(xii) the manner of execution of subsidy programmes, including the amounts allocated and the details and beneficiaries of such programmes;

(xiii) particulars of recipients of concessions, permits or authorizations granted by it;

(xiv) details of the information available to, or held by it, reduced in an electronic form;

(xv) the particulars of facilities available to citizens for obtaining information, including the working hours of a library or reading room, if maintained for public use; and

(xvi) the names, designations and other particulars of the Public Information Officers.

Q. 16. Is it enough to publish information under Sec. 4 only once at the time of the commencement of the RTI Act?

Ans. Updating of information is under Sec. 4 of the RTI Act is a statutory requirement. The State Government has to come out with general instructions for time bound updating of all categories of information. Every public authority may in turn issue detailed instructions for updating information specific to its functions.

Q. 17. How much is the penalty, in case a department is not able to meet deadline for proactive disclosure?

Ans. There is no penalty for not meeting this deadline. However, it is advisable to publish maximum information within the deadline and give it wide media publicity. This will reduce criticism from media and other quarters, as they will understand the sincerity of the Government in this regard.

The Information Commission also has powers {Sec. 19(8) (a) (vi) } to receive from a public authority, an annual compliance report in relation to Sec. 4. This reporting mechanism makes a public authority answerable to the Information Commission for all acts of commission and omission in relation to proactive disclosure.

Q. 18. If the information requested by a citizen has already been proactively disclosed, can a PIO refuse to accept the request?

Ans. There is nothing in the RTI Act that states that information disclosed proactively should not be provided to a citizen on request. Sec. 4 (4) requires that all material disseminated under this Act should be available with the PIO and as far as possible in electronic format. The objective behind this is that the citizen need not wait for 30 days to get access to information that is already being proactively disseminated. If it is available in printed format the PIO can make copies of the same or provide photocopies of the relevant pages to the citizen. If such information is available only in electronic format the same may be provided on floppies, diskettes, CDs or in the form of printouts upon payment of fees at rates prescribed by the Government.

Q.19. Who is Assistant Public Information Officer (APIO) and what are his duties?

Ans. Public authority designates an officer as APIO at each sub-divisional or other sub-district levels. The duties of APIO are to receive the application for information/ appeal from the applicant and to transfer the same to the PIO/First Applellate Authority/Infomation Commission .

Q.20. Who is Public Information Officer (PIO)?

Ans. PIO is an officer designated by the public authority in all administrative units or offices under it to provide information to the applicants. For providing information PIO may seek the assistance of any officer, who is having the custody of records and documents In case of contraventions of the provisions of this Act, such officer shall be treated as a PIO.

Q.21. In Information Officer is on long leave then who provides the information?

Ans. The person handling his charge will have to provide such information.

Q. 22. Whether the Assistant Public Information Officer (APIO) is an assistant to the Public Information Officer (PIO)?

Ans. No, the APIO is not an assistant to the PIO. Like PIO, he is also a functioning under the Act. Instead, he has the duty just to receive applications and appeals and transfer them to the PIO and appellate authority respectively.

Q.23. What is the Application Procedure for requesting information?

Ans. Application can be made to the PIO or APIO in writing or through electronic means. Reasons for seeking information are not to be given. Applicant should attach the prescribed application fee also.

Q. 24. Should a format of RTI application be prescribed by government?

Ans. The RTI Act does not specify any such format. Sec.

6(2) states that the applicant need give only enabling information to contact him/her by the PIO. A format may be developed in the Rules that Central/State Governments are required to frame for implementing this Act for the convenience of the public. But insistence upon using a prescribed Performa may result in illegal profiteering by unscrupulous elements through the sale of application forms. Citizens are allowed to apply on plain paper giving their contact details and nature of information requested as per guidelines. An application whether made on plain paper or in a prescribed format may contain the following points:

(i) name of the applicant.
(ii) name of the father/husband (as the case may be) of the applicant.
(iii) contact details of the applicant including complete postal address, telephone numbers and email address (if any).
(iv) name of the public authority from whom the information is being requested.
(v) nature and details of the information requested
(vi) whether proof of payment of application fee is attached or not.
(vii) if the applicant claims fee waiver whether proof of BPL status is attached or not.
(viii) whether the applicant wishes to received the information by post?

Q.25. If the same kind of information is sought by more than one person should it be made available to all such applicant?

Ans. Every public authority should assess the information needs of people who contact it from time to time. This will help the public authority ascertain what kind of information is requested by people frequently. All such information which has been requested by several applicants should be uploaded on the Internet and updated from time to time. Applicants who have access to Internet facilities may be directed to access the information on the concerned website thereby saving PIOs valuable time. If such frequently requested information can be made available to the PIO in the Public Information Directory/Handbook required to be published under Sec. 4, a lot of time, energy and resources can be saved.

Q.26. What are the duties of a PIO?

Ans. PIO deals with RTI applications. In case of the inability in writing the application, PIO helps to write the application for the information seeker.

If the demanded information is with some other public authority, the PIO transfers the application to the same within 5 days and inform the applicant immediately.

PIO, on receipt of an application, either provides the information within the stipulated period or rejects it. In case of acceptance of application PIO , the SPIO/ ASPIO will assess the requisite additional fee and inform the applicant in within a period of seven days. In Haryana, PIO has to give a notice of 15 days for depositing the additional fee which is not the case at the Centre level and in any other State. After getting the additional fee, he provides the information within the stipulated period. If additional is not received within 15 days, it is costrued that the applicant is not interested in the information, therefore, PIO may file the application. In case of rejection, PIO is to communicate to the applicant — (i) the reasons for such rejection, (ii) the 30 day appeal period within which an appeal against such rejection may be preferred, and

(iii) the particulars of the Appellate Authority .

If information sought is of third party, the PIO within 5 days from the receipt of the request has to give a 10 days written notice to the third party. He will take third party's representation into consideration before giving third party information. Third party may make a representation in writing or orally before the PIO within 10 days from the date of receipt of such notice .Furthermore, the third party has a right to be heard in respect of application and appeal .

Q.27. What is the time limit to get the information?

Ans. Time limits are the followings :

(a) Normally 30 days for information from the date of application; (b) 48 hours for information concerning the life and liberty of a person; (d) 40 days in case of information pertaining to third party ; (e) 45 days if information relates to allegation of human rights violation against, the listed intelligence and security organisations. * 5 days shall be added to the application received by APIO, provided APIO's office is at the regional level and PIO's at the headquarter level.

** Failure to provide information within the specified period is a deemed refusal.

*** If the information is provided after the specified time, it shall be given free.

Q.28. Can Public Information Officer, his assistant or subordinate staff can be punished for delay in providing information? What if the situation is beyond his control?

Ans. Under Section 5(5) of the Act any officer whose

assistance has been sought by PIO is equally liable under the act as the PIO?

Under Section 21 of the Act action taken in good faith is protected, but it must be proved based on documentary evidence.

Q. 29. How does a PIO decide whether the information requested relates to the life and liberty of the individual?

Ans. The Act does not define Life and Liberty related information, therefore, this category of information usually relates to the work of law enforcement and security agencies. Till Life and Liberty related information is defined in the Act, it should be defined in the RTI rules. The Central and State Governments will have to come up with guidelines for treating such information requests with due diligence and urgency.

Q. 30. How can addition fees be collected for providing information regarding the life and liberty of a person considering the fact that such information should be provided within 48 hours?

Ans. The Government will have to issue clear guidelines regarding the procedure for providing information in such cases as there may not be enough time available for completing such procedures. It is advisable to provide such information immediately without charging any additional fees.

Q. 31. The RTI Act states that information must be provided free of cost if it is not given within specified the time limit. What is the process for refunding the money to the applicant?

Ans. Yes, the applicant is entitled to information free of cost if it is provided after the lapse of the deadline stipulated in the Act. The State Government should prescribe the process for refunding the additional fees paid by the applicant. It should also specify whether the application fee will also be refunded to the applicant in such cases. This process of refund must take the convenience of the applicant into consideration.

Q.32. Can Information be provided in the form, in which it is requested?

Ans. Information is provided in the form in which it is sought unless it disproportionately diverts the resources of the Public Authority or is detrimental to the safety or preservation of the record in question.

Q. 33. Is there a limit to the quantum of information sought ?

Ans. The Act does not permit rejection of an application simply because it relates to a large number of documents. In any case, officials should consider the processing of applications as a cooperative activity, thus the applicant in getting the information. If a large number of records are involved, the PIO can contact for clarification on the exact requirement of information without unnecessarily burdening the PIO.

If the applicant is not easily accessible except by post, then the PIO may give detailed reasons in writing for not being able to meet the information request. This will indicate to the DAA or the SIC that the PIO had take action in good faith and had done all that was possible to honour the citizen's right to seek information if the applicant files an appeal. No penalty will be imposed on the PIO if it is evident that he/she has taken action in good faith. (Sec. 21)

If some of the information requested relates to the work of other public authority within the same department or in other department, the PIO has the power to transfer those parts of the application to relevant public authority under Sec. 6(3)...

Q.34. Which information is not open to disclosure?

Ans. Following kinds of informations are not open to disclosure: (a) information relating to sovereignity & economic interest of the country ; (b) information forbidden by Courts and Tribunal; (c) information relating to privelege of Parliament and State Assemblies; (d) information relating to the commercial and trade secrets of the third party; (e) information available to a person in his trust relationship; (f) information shared with other country in confidence; (g) information endangering the life or physical safety of any person; (h) information impeding the the process of investigation; and (i) cabinet papers and deliberations; and (j) personal information of an individual, and etc.

* However, the above can be given if the public interest in disclosure is greater than the protected interests. At the sametime, information, the disclosure of which, violates the copy right of the individual and information of intellingence and security organizations given in Schedule 2 of the Act, also can not be given.

Q. 35. If a case is still under consideration (i.e. 'live' or 'current' file) for final decision can that file be made available to the a requestor before the decision has been taken?

Ans. Aspects of the file which are pending decision can be disclosed even if the matter is not complete. Information can be denied only if the file is having certain Information which are falling in the exempted category.

Q.36. What do cabinet papers mean?

Ans. Cabinet papers include the reasons, the material on the basis of which decision has been taken. They can be disclosed only after the cabinet decision has been taken and the matter is complete or over.

Q.37. How old information can be applied for?

Ans. It depends on the record retention schedule of the public authority. In case of exempted information, except the information falling in sub-clauses a, c and i of Section 8(1) an information relating to any occurence of an event which has taken place 20 years before the date on which a request is made, can be provided.

Q.38. What is the RTI fee structure in Centre and Haryana ?

Ans. Fee Structure is as under:

Both at Centre and State levels, no fee for inspection of record , if such an inspection is made for one hour only.

However, for more than one hour of inspection, Rs. 10/- shall be charged for every 15 minutes in Haryana and at the Central level it is Rs. 5/ every 15 minutes. Every fraction of period above 15 minutes shall be counted as a complete period of 15 minutes.

* There is no fee (Application or other additional fee

for xerox copy, CD and Floppy, etc.) for citizens Below Poverty Line.

Q.39. What are the modes of fee payment?

Ans. Fee is payable to PIO in Haryana through Cash, Treasury Challan, Indian Postal Order and Demand Draft.

* At the Central Government level, modes of paying fee are cash, demand draft/bankers cheque and Indian Postal Order.

Q.40. Who are the First and Second Appellate Authorities?

Ans. First appeal means an officer who is senior in rank to the PIO. An appeal can be made to him within 30 days from the expiry of the prescribed time limit or from the receipt of the decision. First Appeal has to be disposed of within 30 days from the date of its receipt. Period is extendable by 15 days if necessary.

Second Appeal means the Central or the State Information Commission as the case may be. There is no hierarchy of Information Commissions. An appeal to the Commission can be made within 90 days of the date on which the decision was given or should have been made by the First Appellate Authority. Delay may be condoned by the First and Second Applellate Authorities, if sufficient cause is shown.There is no time limit for the disposal of appeal by the Commission.

Q.41. How is Central Information Commission constituted?

Ans. 1. Central Information Commission is constituted

by the Central Government through a Gazette Notification.

2. Commission includes 1 Chief Information Commissioner (CIC) and not more than 10 Information Commissioners (IC) who is appointed by the President of India.
3. Oath of Office will be administered by the President of India according to the form set out in the First Schedule.
4. Commission has its Headquarters in Delhi. Other offices can be established in other parts of the country with the approval of the Central Government.
5. Commission exercises its powers without being subjected to directions by any other authority.

Q.42. What is the eligibility criteria and what is the process of appointment of Centre Information Commissioner (CIC) ?

Ans. 1. Candidates for CIC must be persons of eminence in public life with wide knowledge and experience in law, science and technology, social service, management, journalism, mass media or administration and governance.

2. Information Commissioner (IC) should not be a Member of Parliament or Member of the Legislature of any State or Union Territory. He shall not hold any other office of profit or connected with any political party or carrying on any business or pursuing any profession.
3. Appointment Committee includes Prime Minister (Chair), Leader of the Opposition in the Lok Sabha and one Union Cabinet Minister to be nominated by the Prime Minister.

Q.43. What is the term of office and other service conditions of Central Information Commissioner?

Ans. 1. Central Information Commissioner is appointed for a term of 5 years from date on which he enters upon his office or till he attains the age of 65 years, whichever is earlier.

2. Central Information Commissioner is not eligible for reappointment.

3. Salary is the same as that of the Chief Election Commissioner. This can be varied to the disadvantage of the Central Information Commissioner during service.

Q.44. What is the term of office and other service conditions of Central Information Commissioner?

Ans. 1. Central Information Commissioner holds office for a term of five years from the date on which he enters upon his office or till he attains the age of sixty-five years, whichever is earlier and can not be eligible for reappointment as Central Information Commissioner.

2. Salary will be the same as that of the Election Commissioner. This is not be varied to the disadvantage of the Central Information Commissioner during service.

3. Central Information Commissioner is eligible for appointment as Central Information Commissioner but can not hold office for more than a total of five years including his/her term as Central Information Commissioner.

Q.45. How is the State Information Commission constituted?

Ans. 1. The State Information Commission is constituted by the State Government through a Gazette

notification. It does have one State Chief Information Commissioner (SCIC) and not more than 10 State Information Commissioners (SIC) to be appointed by the Governor.
2. Oath of office is administered by the Governor according to the form set out in the First Schedule.
3. The headquarters of the State Information Commission is decided by the State Government. Other offices may be established in other parts of the State with the approval of the State Government.
4. The Commission exercises its powers without being subjected to any other authority.

Q.46. What is the eligibility criterion and what is the process of appointment of State Chief Information Commissioner/State Information Commissioners?

Ans. 1. The Appointments Committee is headed by the Chief Minister. Other members include the Leader of the Opposition in the Legislative Assembly and one Cabinet Minister nominated by the Chief Minister.
2. The qualifications for appointment as SCIC/SIC is the same as that for Central Commissioners.
3. The salary of the State Chief Information Commissioner is the same as that of an Election Commissioner. The salary of the State Information Commissioner is the same as that of the Chief Secretary of the State Government.

Q.47. What are the powers and functions of Information Commissions?

Ans. 1. The Central Information Commission/State Information Commission has a duty to receive complaints from any person —

(a) who has not been able to submit an information request because a PIO has not been appointed ;
(b) who has been refused information that was requested;
(c) who has received no response to his/her information request within the specified time limits;
(d) who thinks the fees charged are unreasonable;
(e) who thinks information given is incomplete or false or misleading ; and
(f) any other matter relating to obtaining information under this law.

2. Power to order inquiry if there are reasonable grounds.
3. CIC/SCICs have powers of Civil Court such as —

   (a) summoning and enforcing attendance of persons, compelling them to give oral or written evidence on oath and to produce documents or things;
   (b) requiring the discovery and inspection of documents;
   (c) receiving evidence on affidavit;
   (d) requisitioning public records or copies from any court or office;
   (e) issuing summons for examination of witnesses or documents;
   (f) any other matter which may be prescribed.

4. All records covered by this law (including those covered by exemptions) are to be given to CIC/SCIC during inquiry for examination.
5. Power to secure compliance of its decisions from the Public Authority includes—

(a) providing access to information in a particular form;
(b) directing the public authority to appoint a PIO/APIO where none exists;
(c) publishing information or categories of information;
(d) making necessary changes to the practices relating to management, maintenance and destruction of records ;
(e) enhancing training provision for officials on RTI;
(f) seeking an annual report from the public authority on compliance with this law;
(g) require it to compensate for any loss or other detriment suffered by the applicant;
(h) impose penalties under this law; and
(i) reject the application.

Q.48. What procedures are followed by the Information Commissions in deciding the appeal ?

Ans. ICs follows the following procedures while deciding the appeals:

1. Before deciding an appeal the Commission shall service notice to the concerned persons.
2. Entertain any evidence in support of appeal, which may be oral or in writing from the concerned persons.
3. Examine on oath or by having affidavits from the concerned persons.
4. Peruse or inspect the documents or any records or copies.
5. Inquire through the authorised officer the facts of an appeal or may require facts in detail, if so may hear the SPIO or any other senior officer who had decided the first appeal as the case may be.

6. Receive evidence on affidavits from the SPIO or any other senior officer who had decided the first appeal or from any other person from whom the evidence may be deemed necessary

Q.49. What is the mode of serving the notice by the Information Commission?

Ans. The Information Commission in Haryana may serve notice to the persons concerned in any of the following modes:

1. By hand through process server.
2. By registered post with acknowledgement due; or
3. By publication in the newspaper.

* CIC in addition to the above serves notice by speed post and Under Postal Certificate (UPC).

Q.50. Does the Haryana State Information Commission make order in writing?

Ans. Yes,

1. The Commission shall make order in writing and pronounce the same in the presence of the concerned parties.
2. The party concerned may obtain the copy of the order from the Commission.
3. The Commission shall make order in writing and pronounce the same in the presence of the concerned parties.
4. The party concerned may obtain the copy of the order from the Commission.

Q.51. What is the reporting procedure?

Ans. 1. Central Information Commission will send an annual report to the Central Government on the implementation of the provisions of this law at the end of the year. The State Information Commission will send a report to the State Government .

2. Each Ministry has a duty to compile reports from its Public Authorities and send them to the Central Information Commission and State Information Commission, as the case may be.
3. Each report will contain details of number of requests received by each Public Authority, number of rejections and appeals, particulars of any disciplinary action taken, amount of fees and charges collected, etc.
4. Central Government will table the Central Information Commission report before Parliament after the end of each year. The concerned State Government will table the report of the State Information Commission before the Vidhan Sabha (and the Vidhan Parishad wherever applicable).

Q.52. Can an applicant directly make a complaint to the Information Commission?

Ans. Yes, in case of the following grounds, applicant can directly make a complaint to the Information Commission; (a) if a PIO/APIO has not been appointed in any public authority; (b) if the PIO/APIO has refused to accept the application; (c) has not provided the information in time or has asked for unreasonable fee; (d) has provided misleading, false, incomplete information. And if the commission considers it appropriate the commission may accept the complaint and initiate an enquiry into the matter .

Q.53. What are the penalty and disciplinary action provisions in the Act?

Ans. The Information Commission can impose a panality

of Rs. 250 per day till the information is provided. The penality amount can be upto a maximum of Rs. 25000. The PIO is personally liable for the penality. Penalty amount is deposited in government. exchequer.

Penalty is imposed for the following reasons :

(a) not accepting an application;
(b) delaying information;
(c) rejecting application without reasonable cause;
(d) malafidely denying information;
(e) knowingly giving incomplete, incorrect, misleading information;
(f) destroying information that has been requested and obstructing furnishing of information in any manner. The Information Commission can also recommend disciplinary action under the service rules for violation of the Act against an erring PIO.
* Commission can also make provision of compensation for the applicant, which is to be born by the concerned public authority.

Q.54. Which organizations are not falling in the ambit of RTI Act?

Ans. The following 6 intelligence and security orgnizations are out of the Act:

(i) State Criminal Investigation Department (C.I.D.) including the Crime Branch;
(ii) Haryana Armed Police;
(iii) Security orgznizations of Police;
(iv) Haryana Police Telecommunication Organization;
(v) India Reserve Battalion;
(vi) Commando.

* Central Government has listed 18 such organizations.
** However, if there is any allegation of corruption and

human rights violations against the above organisations, then information of the above organizations will also have to be given.

Q.55. As a second appellate authority, whether Information Commissioners' decisions are binding and compulsory? Whether interpretation in one case can be quoted as a ruling in other case on lines of SC decisions?

Ans. According to Sec. 19 (7) of RTI Act 2005 the decisions by the second appellate authority (Central/State Information Commission) are final and binding. This will have to be dealt separately while framing the rules.

Q. 56. Can the absence of a time limit for disposing appeals by the Information Commission undermine the appeals regime?

Ans. It is a matter of concern that the RTI Act has no time limit for disposal of appeals by the Information Commission, whereas the DAA is required to dispose off appeals within 30 days. However, a time limit for Information Commission appeal could still be provided for under the RTI Rules framed by the State. However, in the followings two circumstances, it is understood that the IC is time bound, though not written in the RTI Act :—

- To issue stay order, within the days left out of the 30 days time given by the PIO, in case of appeal by third party against the decisions of PIO and First Appellate Authority to release information given by the third party to the public authority in confidence; and
- Approval to the PIO of notified agencies within 45 days in cases where information sought has to

do with allegations of corruption or human rights violation committed by any member of the intelligence or security organisations notified under Schedule 2 of the RTI Act (Sec. 24 (1)).

Q. 57. Will the APIO be punished for giving wrong or misleading information just as a PIO can be penalised under this Act?

Ans. The APIO is not duty bound to give information to the applicant. However, if the information sought is under his/her control then such information may be given upon payment of the prescribed fees (if any). However, APIO is liable for penalty for providing wrong or misleading information even under other laws like the Indian Evidence Act and he Indian Penal Code.

Q.58. What is the Jurisdiction of Courts?

Ans. Lower Courts are barred from entertaining suits or applications against any order made under this Act. However, the writ jurisdiction of the Supreme Court and High Courts under Articles 32 and 226 of the Constitution remains unaffected. Therefore, one can approach High Court and Supreme Court against the decision of the Information Commission.

Q.59. Whether the information relating to matters which are pending in court, can be provided under the act?

Ans. Yes, if it is not covered by any of the exemptions especially the ones related to contempt of court.

Q.60. What is the role of Central/State Governments?

Ans. 1. Develop educational programmes for the public

especially disadvantaged communities on RTI.

2. Encourage Public Authorities to participate in the development and organization of such programmes.
3. Promote timely dissemination of accurate information to the public.
4. Train officers and develop training materials.
5. Compile and disseminate a User Guide for the public in the respective official language.
6. Publish names, designation postal addresses and contact details of PIOs and other information such as notices regarding fees to be paid, remedies available in law if request is rejected, etc.

Q.61. Who has the Rule making power?

Ans. Central Government, State Governments and the Competent Authority are vested with powers to make rules to carry out the provisions of the Right to Information Act, 2005.

Q.62. Who has the power to deal with the difficulties while implementing this act?

Ans. If any difficulty arises in giving effect to the provisions in the Act, the Central Government may, by Order published in the Official Gazette, make provisions necessary/expedient for removing the difficulty.

Q.63. Can government officers get access to their Annual Confidential Reports (ACRs) under the RTI Act?

Ans. ACRs are confidential documents. Opinion is divided as to whether an officer should be given a copy of his/her ACR under the RTI Act. Some believe that ACRs are personal documents and therefore enjoy the protection of exemptions to RTI under Sec.8 (1) (j) unless it seems that public interest is better served by disclosing the ACR. Such cases are decided by the Information Commission on case to case basis.

Q. 64. Can students ask for copies or inspection of their answer sheets?

Ans. RTI Act does not prevent a student from accessing his/her answer sheets. Initially many ICs were of the views that answer sheets can not be disclosed, as, it was considered personal information and public authority being in fiduciary relation with the examiner. However, secrecy accorded to answer scripts evaluated in the context of public examinations can not be justified. Perhaps the fear is that disclosure in such cases may lead to flood of demands for re-evaluation, thereby derailing the whole examination process. Many Information Commissions have already given various judgments for showing the answer sheets by Staff Selection Commissions and other bodies. Some universities like IGNOU, New Delhi are not only showing but also giving zerox copies of answer sheets to the students. Government has to come out with clear guidelines on this matter keeping in mind the spirit of the RTI Act.

Q. 65. Some unscrupulous elements may tamper and misuse the copies of documents they get under the RTI Act. How does one prevent such misuse of information released under the RTI Act?

Ans. The Government has to devise means of authenticating documents released under the RTI Act to ensure that they are not misused. One suggestion is to mark every page of such documents with a rubber stamp impression stating – "Document released under the

RTI Act contains xx pages." If electronic files are requested the same may be provided in PDF or tiff format on floppies or CDs. This will also obviate the need for certifying the documents separately if the requestor wishes to use the same in some litigation.

8 Apprehensions and Operational Shortcomings of the Act

The enactment of the RTI Act, 2005 is one of the most progressive legislations enacted in our country. The Act covers not only the public sector but also the NGOs and the private sector to some extent. It is also one of the toughest legislations in the world, as it is the only RTI Act imposing penalty for any contravention of the provisions of the Act. After the completion of the four years of its implementation, the response to the Act has been very positive and it has received very wide and warm welcome from the people. People are learning the importance of the power of information. However, mere conferment of the right is not enough. There are various apprehensions in the minds of the stakeholders and also many operational impediments in the effective implementation of the Act.

Some of the major apprehensions and operational shortcomings in relation to the implementation of the RTI Act that have been expressed by various stakeholders are discussed below:

(i) Misuse of Information

There is an apprehension that some unscrupulous elements may misuse the copies of documents they access under the RTI Act. To prevent the misuse of document released under the RTI Act, the Government may have to devise a means of authenticating documents released under the RTI Act to ensure that they are not misused. One suggestion is to mark every page of a document accessed under the RTI Act with a rubber stamp impression saying, " Document released under the RTI Act containing xx pages." If electronic files are requested, the same may be provided in PDF or TIF format on floppies or CDs. This will also obviate the need for certifying the documents separately if the requester wishes to use the same in some litigation.

(ii) Officers may be Backmailed

There has also been the apprehension that the information requisioned under the RTI Act would be misused or used to blackmail officials or organizations. The situation of blackmailing the officials or organizations will only emerge when the official is placed in a privileged position to maintain secrecy of sensitive information. It is the situation of secrecy coupled with discretion of authority, which create a situation of blackmailing in favour of official position and not the other way round. Instead, the fact is that the Act requires making as much information as possible available with the public authorities in the public domain and it may actually prevent blackmail of honest and sincere officers. Thus , the question of blackmail or threatening may not arise. As far as possible, information, must be made public so as to reduce any possibility of blackmail. An honest and sincere officer need not fear blackmail at all. Strict adherence to the law would facilitate smooth functioning of such officers as they will be protected by law.

(iii) Disclosure of file notings

One of the most important concerns that has been raised in respect of RTI Act is the disclosure of file notings, as it will adversely affect the free and frank opinion by the public officials in decision-making process and would thereby undermine the spirit of bureaucratic openness and accountability, which the law embodies. The entire purpose of the Act is to open government's decision-making process to public scrutiny. The disclosure of notings will certainly ensure application of mind by the decision maker to the issues involved and thereby enhance the quality of the decisions. It may also be mentioned that compulsion of disclosure of file notings is likely to reduce, to a great extent, the administrative culture of putting something as part of record on dictation or in a mechanical manner. It may also be considered from the point of view of promoting the overall culture of good administrative practice. It would be appropriate to mention that the Central and State Information Commissions have held that the "file notings" were an integral part of a file.

(iv) Cost of Implementation

Another major concern has been the cost of implementing RTI Act. Such concerns are based on actual facts. The savings to the government through reduction in the level of corruption and maladministration by implementation of the Act would be more than the cost on its implementation. Additionally, the total cost on administration of the nation comes from the taxes, which the citizens pay to the government and the cost on implementation of RTI would be negligible as compared to the total cost on administration. And, the taxpayers have the right to know how their government is spending their money. Thus, the concern relating to cost on implementation of RTI Act is ill founded and has been blown out of proportion.

(v) Choice of Information Commissioners

Another major concern has been that the majority of Information Commissioners appointed at both the centre and the state levels are retired high-ranking members of the bureaucracy. They had been part of the secrecy regime for a long period during their careers. Their mindset may not be in favour of promoting transparency. The Act requires that the Commissioners may be appointed from the category of persons having "eminence in public life with wide knowledge and experience in law, science and technology, social science, management, journalism, mass media or administration and governance". Hence, the appointment of retired bureaucrats may not be justified. It rather goes against the express provision of the Act. In addition, this may also give an impression that all those who are responsible for administrative culture of secrecy are now trying to ensure transparency. Haryana has however, set the good trend by appointing majority of Information Commissioners from other categories.

Besides the apprehension discussed above, there are a **number of operational shortcomings in the Act. The following may be mentioned by way of illustrations.**

1. Appointment of Public Information Officers by Public Authorities

Though, Public Information Officers have been appointed by most of the Public Authorities, there are still many public authorities viz. NGOs and government aided institutions that are yet to designate/notify PIOs. This is despite the direction of the Information Commissions. Even where they have been designated, particulars of all such functionaries are still not available at one place. Most public authorities, particularly at the district level, do not display names and details of the PIOs on their notice boards making it difficult for the public to know where the application is to be submitted. Often, too junior officers are appointed as PIOs. There is also a lack of uniformity in the States in identifying the competent levels of officials for designation as PIOs.

2. Poor Infrastructural Facilities with the PIOs

PIO is the weakest link under the RTI Act. Although the PIO she/he can be penalised under the Act, is not provided the adequate infrastructure like photocopier, fax and accommodation etc. Moreover, PIO is not paid anything extra for performing the additional duties.

3. Enlisting Public Authorities

Given the huge number of public authorities, even enumeration of public authorities is a herculean task. There are doubts in the minds of the people as regards to various clarifications e.g. definitions of public authority or individual or substantially financed self-governing institutions etc. The CIC and SICs are also not very active in clearly defining the existing grey areas. Public Authorities have not given shape to any time-bound action plan for the implementation of RTI Act, with outcome budget and clear-cut physical targets. Consequently, public authorities have not been held accountable for not fulfilling the obligations under Section 4 and 5 during the last 3 years. No mechanism has been established for regular review of the Public Authorities for RTI implementation. Therefore, the status of proactive disclosure by the Public authorities is not available any where.

4. Suo Moto Disclosure

Publication of the 16 theme Manuals, as given in section 4 (1) (b), and dissemination widely in a suo moto mode is the most important obligation of all Public Authorities and the same has been found to have been done in an unsatisfactory manner in many public authorities. It is evasive, incomplete and mostly not adequate for the purpose for which it is required. In many cases the Acts Rules, Manuals, Codes, Regulations, Government. Resolutions/Government Orders, as section 4 (1) (b) have not been updated or printed in an updated manner. Incomplete/insufficient disclosures have no penal consequences for public authorities. There has also been no compliance of Section 4(2), which requires public authorities to explore what information is needed by the citizens and suo-moto disclose it.

5. Poor Experience of seeking information from Public Authorities

Experience regarding seeking information is also not very encouraging. Fees charged and the manner of payment is not uniform. Some states like Haryana, charge very high fees which is against the spirit of the Act. There is confusion about the head of accounts to which the application fee and other fee are to be credited. Bank drafts prescribed in some States cost bank commission Rs.35 for an application fee of Rs. 10. Payment by way of Postal Orders and non-judicial stamps is applicable only in few states. At the same time, applicants have to resort to sending their applications by Registered post since officials avoid accepting their applications in person. Most of the PIOs at state level and district level are not cooperative and they sometimes force the applicants to withdraw applications.

6. Appellate Authority at the State Capital Alone

People in rural areas find the appeal process expensive as they have to come to the capital for the hearings. In the School Education Department in Haryana, there is only one Appellate Authority at Chandigarh, even for information of a school in a block. This system of the location of first appeal discourages the poor from filing appeals.The location of the Information Commissioners in the States is at the State's capital cities and similar is the situation at the Centre, adding to the woes of the appellants. There is no provision of video conferencing in most of the states for hearing the cases.

7. Inadequate Strength and Lack of Autonomy of the Commission

Though in the recent times, the strength of the ICs has been increased at the centre and state levels, The Commissions have to rely on the government for all the support e.g. its infrastructure physical, financial and manpower, etc. The Commissions' autonomy is, therefore, compromised and they are unable to function autonomously without being subjected to directions by any other authority under this Act [S.12(4) and S.16(4)]. The restrictions on recruitment imply that the Commissions are understated. Their budgets are also subject to approval by the administrative departments to the extent that the CIC and some SICs have no powers of re-appropriation.

8. Misuse of BPL Exemption

The exemption of BPL category from fee under the Act is being misused by unscrupulous elements. Some of them even sell the information to a poor and unaware person at very high price. Due to this, the Police are flooded with requests from lawyers and the media. This, at times, hampers investigation and affects security.

9. Problems Regarding the Details on First Appeal Authority

Identification of First Appeal Authority is difficult particularly in cases, where applicants do not receive information within the stipulated time frame and have to file the first appeal. Under section 7(8) of the Act, PIOs are duty bound to provide details on the Appellate Authority to the applicant in case of refusal of information and the third party in case of disclosure of the information of the third party. But some of them do not provide it or provide incomplete information. As a result only very few are able to approach the First Appellate Authority and finally to the Information Commission.

10. Poor Compliance due to Reluctant use of Penalty Clause

The reluctance of the Information Commissioners to use the

penalty clause against officials providing wrong or no information has been an issue of discontent. The Commissioners feel that indiscriminate use of the clause may lead to collapse of the administrative machinery. Thus, an impression has been created that the government departments need not take this Act very seriously. Moreover, the government departments also don't always comply with the orders of the Information Commission. The powers under the Act for enforcing the Commission's orders are limited. Hence, there are instances of recalcitrance by public authorities. The ICs have also not been following up to check compliance. Further more, it has been observed that the ICs dismiss a case if the complainant does not turn on the hearing dates.

Few State Information Commissions like Haryana are not treating officials (Superintendent, Assistants and Clerks) as PIOs as per the mandate of Sections 5(4) & 5(5). These SICs are of the view that they are not officers as given in the above sections, therefore don't invite penalty. There is also a misunderstanding that the penalty is fixed and automatic, but the Act requires the Commission to follow principles of natural justice. The disposal of cases by the ICs is also low.

11. Lack of Awareness

The ground reality is that awareness is lacking not only among the information seekers but also among the information providers. Guidelines for information providers and seekers have not been widely disseminated. It has come to be known and used to some extent in the urban areas but the impact is much less in rural areas. So there is a need to create awareness about the RTI at the grassroots level.

Though some steps have been taken by the Government/ ICs in this regard but these are not sufficient. Administrative Training Institutes in the states have initiated the process of training RTI functionaries' viz. first appellate authorities, PIOs and APIOs. But these Institutes do not have adequate funds at their disposal. Unlike highlighting the achievement of other poverty alleviation and employment generation programmes, government has not undertaken any campaign, either in electronic or print media for making RTI popular among citizens. Though the NGOs and the media are playing an important role in spreading awareness about RTI yet all this is still not adequate.

12. Suffering from Railway Coach Syndrome

Spreading awareness of RTI Act is suffering from " Railway Coach Syndrome" wherein the passengers of an overcrowded Railway Coach are reluctant to let new passe-ngers get in and once a new passengers gets in, he also shows same behaviour. Similarly, a person who has undergone training and has knowledge of the RTI Act, he is not willing to disseminate it to others. Sincere efforts are required to bring about attitudinal change.

13. Problems on the part of judiciary

Judiciary has held in many cases that it does not fall in the ambit of the RTI Act. The Supreme Court has suggested an amendment to the act so that the second appeal in their cases may not lie before the Central Information Commission but with the Registrar General of the Supreme Court. The judiciary is expected to frame its own rules for dissemination of information under the Act. Though various high courts have framed RTI rules, some of these are in contravention of the RTI Act.

14. Lack of Uniformity of RTI Rules

There is no uniformity of RTI rules amongst different states of the country. This is also creating confusion in mind of the people. Some states have made the rules which are in contravention of the RTI Act viz Haryana has prescribed time limit for depositing additional fee.

Concluding Remarks

It is reiterated that mere conferment of the right is not enough. There have been various apprehensions like misuse of the Act, blackmailing of the officers and burden on government exchequer and also many operational impediments in the effective implementation of the Act. There are still many public authorities where RTI functionaries have not been designated. Many of them, particularly at the district level, do not display names and details of PIOs on their notice boards which continues making it difficult for the public to know where the application is to be submitted. Too junior officers are often appointed as PIOs. They are unable to collect information from the department employees. Moreover, while only PIOs can be penalised under the Act, they are not provided adequate infrastructure for performing their duties and responsibilities.

Public Authorities are yet to give shape to any time-bound action plan for the implementation of the RTI Act especially suo moto disclosure. This is due to the fact that, incomplete/insufficient disclosures have no penal consequences for Public Authorities.

Experience regarding seeking information is also not very encouraging. Fees charged and the manner of payment is not uniform. Some States like Haryana, charge very high fees which is against the spirit of the Act. There is confusion about the head of accounts to which the amount received as application fees and other fee are to be credited. Most of the PIOs at state and district levels are not cooperative and they sometimes force the applicants to withdraw applications.

People in rural areas find the appeal process expensive. Many times, there is just one First Appellate Authority for the whole department and that too, located at the capital cities. The location of Information Commissioners in the States and Centre at the capital cities has further added to their woes. BPL exemptions are also being misused by unscrupulous elements.

The Information Commissioners are not frequently using, the penalty clause against officials providing wrong or no information. As a result, an impression has been created that the government departments need not take this Act very seriously. The government departments also don't always comply with the orders of the Information Commission. The Commissions have not been provided with adequate infrastructure. They have to rely on the government for its entire infrastructure. The Commissions' autonomy is therefore compromised. The awareness is lacking not only among the information seekers but also among the information providers both in urban and rural areas. Finally, it can be said that making the legislation alone will not be able to ensure justice to the information seekers until it is implemented with strong conviction by removing the apprehensions from the minds of the people and removing hurdles in its effective implementation.

9 Right to Information Act : Roadmap for the Future

Despite the deficiencies, apprehensions and operational shortcomings given in the previous chapters, the RTI Act is a major step towards ensuring a participatory and transparent developmental process in the country. For the law to be truly effective, the active participation of the community at large is needed. Therefore, the Government, NGOs and the media, should strive to simplify the process and procedures and disseminate awareness about the same to the citizens. The RTI Act is, indeed, what Amartya Sen describes as "a momentous engagement with the possibilities of freedom". There are a number of steps, required for its effective implementation and operationalisation. Some of them are discussed below:

1. Activating Public Authorities

To remove ambiguity regarding the definition and status of Public Authorities ,the Competent Authority should notify all public authorities under Section 2(h) of the Act. The CIC and SICs should act in a pro-active manner as only such a role will help in identifying the grey areas. Each Public Authority needs to frame time-bound action plan for the implementa-tion of RTI Act, with outcome budget and clear-cut physical targets. They should also be made accountable for not fulfilling the obligations under Section 4 and 5. They should take a pro-active role in disclosing information as mandated under Section 4 and should facilitate access to information for the citizens. The details about the APIO/ PIO and First Appellate Authority should be there on the notice Board. Moreover, the responsibility about RTI implementation should not be left on the PIO alone. The Public Authority and the first Appellate Authority should also be equally responsive and accountable.

2. Computerisation of Records

Section 4(1) (a) of the Act requires records management policies and procedures made compatible with the RTI Act. In the spirit of this Act and for its effective implementation, the disclosure of the decisions should be the norm. The Public Authorities should initiate measures so that, as far as practical, all its decisions are mandatorily disclosed on its website. Extensive computerisation and networking is essential. Each Public Authority must provide a certain percentage of their budget for this purpose. At the same time, The Central and State Governments must necessarily make adequate fiscal allocations for computerization and connectivity from Information Commission level to District and Block level Public Authorities so as to effectively operationalise the provisions of the RTI Act.

3. Effective Suo Moto Disclosures by the Public Authorities

Disclosures under Section 4 and their adequacy should be made enforceable either through the Head of the Public Authority or through the PIO who needs to be of a sufficiently senior rank. Disclosures under this Section should be printed and periodically updated. It should be obligatory for the Public Authorities to publish the disclosures in their Annual Reports. The scope of "suo moto" disclosure of information by public authorities needs to be expanded to minimise citizen's resort to RTI to get the information needed by them. Citizen's Charter should therefore form an integral part of S. 4(1)(b) disclosures.

All Public Authorities must immediately update, multiply and develop hard and soft copies of all Acts, Rules, Manuals, Codes, Regulations, Govt. documentation. The Public Authorities (Ministries/Departments), who are administratively responsible to undertake it, must be made accountable for this task. They must report it to the CIC or the SIC, as the case may be. All Public Authorities must also re-visit their processes (viz. their decision-making systems/ processes) as section 4 (1) (b) (iii) provides for the disclosures as have been found wanting in most of these put on the web so far. It must be completed on a top-priority basis. Extensive use of IT may be resorted to for satisfactorily addressing the Obligations related to suo-moto disclosures.

It is suggested that strict directions be issued by the Central Government that all the State Governments/Public authorities should fulfill their obligations laid down under Section 4 of the RTI Act, 2005, failing which, may lead to penal provisions being invoked against such Public Authority. Secretary of the department may be held responsible in this regard and be clearly held culpable in case of non-compliance of Section 4(1) (b).

It is also essential to review the way the Public Authorities conduct their business. Without it, it would not be possible to undertake a satisfactory compliance of suo moto disclosures. For this, there should be monitoring of the record management and information disclosed in the suo-moto manner by the Public Authorities.The Central Information Commission and the State Information Commissions must use the Monitoring and Reporting powers given to them under Section 25 of the RTI Act to ensure their satisfactory compliance. This has also been recommended by the Second Administrative Reforms Commission in its report. Moreover, a mechanism should be devised for regularly reviewing the Public Authority for the efforts made to effectively implement the RTI Act.

4. Effective Record Management

The present status of record maintenance is in a state of utter neglect both in the Centre and the States. The public authorities have been facing enormous difficulties in cataloguing and indexing of records of all administrative units. The State Information Commission should be made powerful enough to ensure that public authorities take initiative in this regard. The weeding Rules which should have been drafted, and kept updated, are either in a state of utter neglect or non-existent in most of the Public Authorities. All Public Authorities, therefore, must review quickly the existing weeds Rules framed under the Destruction of Records Act, 1917. These must provide the period of retention of each type of records. Records in the Government offices need to be digitized and indexed for easy retrieval. Wherever any record/document is not traceable its absence must be explained in context of the Weeding Rules in place in a particular Public Authority. Clear cut accountability must be fixed for delays or non-traceable list of any document with reference to the Weeding Rules.

5. Appointment of APIOs/PIOs by Public Authorities

Effective steps should be taken by the ICs and concerned governments so that all the Public Authorities designate PIO/APIOs not only at the headquarter level but also at the district and block levels. Furthermore, to coordinate with other PIOs of the department and especially to ensure effective implementation of web based RTI system, one officer in each line department could be designated as Nodal PIO. Details of all RTI Act functionaries should be available at one place and these should be displayed on their notice boards, etc. so that the applicants don't face any problem while submitting the RTI application. As far as the competent level of officials for discharge of this function is concerned, there should be uniformity in the States.

The PIO is the only functionary under the Act who is at the receiving end. She/he can only be penalised under the Act. PIOs need to be of a senior rank. The organisation must provide adequate infrastructure such as photocopier, fax and accommodation for enabling him/her to handle the responsibility placed upon her/him under the Act. For this, there is a need to create a budget line to strengthen infrastructure. The mechanism for filing RTI applications also needs to be simplified and a centralized system of monitoring the applications, with a facility to the citizens to check the status of their applications through internet, should be made available.

6. Proper Training to the PIOs

Adequate training is needed to sensitize the PIOs to the needs of the people and about their functions. They should be suitably compensated for this additional work. Each Public Authority must review its decision relating to nomination of the PIO to ensure that they are not over-loaded with the RTI work and they share it equally within the organization. The Chief Executive of the Public Authorities must judiciously divide the PIO work. To avoid the problem of their frequent transfers and for their better sensitization on RTI Act, a separate cadre in civil services like IPS, IAS may be formed and named Indian Public Information service.

7. Incentives or Separate Cadre of PIO

PIOs should be relieved of the extra burden due to increase in volume of work. This should be addressed by way of incentives for this additional work. Each Public Authority must review its decision relating to nomination of the PIO to ensure that they are not over-loaded with the RTI work and they share it equally within the organization. The Chief Executive of the Public Authorities must judiciously divide the PIO work. To avoid the problem of their frequent transfers and for their better sensitization on RTI Act, a separate cadre in civil services like IPS, IAS may be formed and named Indian Public Information service.

8. Penalties for Ensuring Compliance from Public Authorities

Due to lack of number of cases of penalty, an impression is being created that the government departments needn't take this Act very seriously. Therefore, the Commissions should impose penalties in a larger number of cases. The rules must provide that the appeals/complaints under the Act shall not be dismissed due to non-appearance of appellants/complainants but shall be decided on merits in all cases based on available material. Moreover, unlike few State Information Commissions particularly SIC Haryana should treat the officials also as PIOs. CIC and RTI activists are not agreeing to this interpretation of Section 5(4) & 5(5) by the SICs.

9. Effective Working of ICs

Disposal of the cases in the ICs should be very fast. The CIC and SIC should form benches of more than one Commissioner to take up review of the decisions made by Single Commissioner. Video Conferencing too should be used extensively for hearing the appeals. Though till October, 2008 , CIC used video conferencing in about 1200 cases, other ICs have not used this facility. A time-limit should be put by the Commissions for suo moto taking up of the cases requiring disclosure of important information through their websites.

10. Autonomy of the Commissions

The ICs both at the centre and in the states should have financial autonomy so that they need not go to the Finance Department or to the concerned Administrative Department for funds. The Commission should also have autonomy in matters of creation of posts and recruitment of the personnel. There is a need to augment the power of the Commission so as to enable the Commission to enforce its decisions. The

Commission already has powers of a Civil Court for limited purposes. This power should be widened so as to enable the Commission to appropriately deal with contempt matters. Independence of Commissions and effective discharge of their duties cannot be guaranteed without granting them full financial and administrative autonomy. The Commission has to rely on the government for all its infrastructure including physical, financial and manpower, etc. Till date, Commissions, in most of the states, have not been provided with adequate infrastructure e.g. office, computers, staff, funds etc. Governments should keep up with their obligations under Section 13(6) of the Act to provide adequate staff. Each Public Authority should fulfill its obligations u/s 26 of dissemination of knowledge amongst citizens. Adequate budget for this purpose must be provided. The expenditure of the Commissions should therefore be 'charged' upon the Consolidated Fund of the State and Centre for respective Commissions.

11. Monitoring of Performance under the Act

There is a dire need for effective monitoring, review and auditing of the implementation of the Act. Annual Reports by the CIC/ SICs under Section 25 is based on information furnished by the Government departments without the benefit of any independent cross-check. The Commissions need to be given a separate set up with adequate staff for effective monitoring of its orders and for conducting cross-checks wherever necessary. They may engage the services of retired officers and renowned members of the Civil Society for this purpose. The Commissions should put in place mechanisms for Monitoring/review/auditing of information/orders with sustained follow-up to overcome deficiencies in implementation. The Commission should be empowered to enforce their decisions including penalising the Head of the Public Authority for continued contempt of its orders.

12. Moderate Fee and Simple Modes of Fee

Fee charged should be moderate and uniform throughout the country. To avoid confusion of depositing fee, there should be a receipt head in every public authority to which the application fee is to be credited. Instead of bank drafts prescribed in some States which cause undue extra burden, payment by way of postal Orders, cheques and non judicial stamps, banks debit and credit cards should be adopted as modes of fee payment.

13. Uniformity of Rules and Procedures

The RTI Act gives power of framing rules to competent authority which include the Central Government, State Governments and the High Courts and the Supreme Court. It is necessary that uniformity is maintained in formulating the rules and devising procedures.

14. Pro-Active Role of Judiciary

The judiciary needs to initiate measures for effective implementation of the RTI for which it should frame rules as required under the Act. The judiciary could also consider giving priority to disposal of cases where Public Authorities have withheld Information on the judicial stay of Commissioners' orders.

15. Pressure on Public Authorities

The civil society must continue building pressure on Public Authorities to ensure the implementation of the Act in letter and spirit. There is need for formal involvement of intermediary civil society organisations to train the PIOs and the APIOs in collaboration with other government nodal agencies. Social audit of certain public authorities by NGOs, Citizens Forum and Civic Bodies of repute would help in fighting corruption and effective Act implementation of the RTI.

16. Awareness Generation and Capacity-Building

Effective implementation would require capacity-building of the information providers and seekers. Capacity-building of the cutting edge level functionaries forms the key element as this level facilitates the first interface with the citizens. Creating a RTI regime in tune with the spirit and philosophy of the Act would require institutional mechanism for improving government-citizen interface. Capacity-building of officials is needed to meet citizen's information requirements besides awareness and empowerment of citizens to enable them to exercise right to information in the right earnest. A massive round of training of PIOs/APIOs must be undertaken to achieve the Objective of Maximum Disclosure and Promotion of Open Governance. The following steps may be taken in this regard:

(i) The RTI Act should be included in the syllabus at the High school and College level education.
(ii) RTI guidelines should be circulated widely and there should be training programmes for both the information seekers and the information providers.
(iii) Multimedia, especially TV Channels, should be used for the information dissemination.
(iv) Best practices in RTI should be show-cased.
(v) A week should be declared as RTI week, to spread awareness about the Act.
(vi) Nukkad Nataks, Talk Shows, etc should be organized regularly on various forms of media.

In this regard, particular attention of the CPIOs and SPIOs be drawn towards the provision contained in section 25 (5) wherein they are expected to exercise their functions conforming to "the provisions or spirit of" the RTI act. They must not be over-technical in meeting the demands made on them but also look at the spirit and intent behind asking of the question. This alone would promote an open-governance regime, one of the intended objectives of the RTI Act. At the same time, government should take steps to propagate this Act in the illiterate population living in the village and train Village Sarpanches, official and elected representatives of the PRIs.

17. Introduction of Call Centres and Common Service Contres as APIOs

For facilitating the access to information, the concept of RTI call centres can be introduced which, to some extent, is being practiced in Bihar. In this system, the government hires a call centre and gives two phone numbers to the public. One of the numbers would be, RTI Help Number (RHN) and the other would be RTI Application Number (RAN). RAN will be an ordinary number with normal call charges. If any citizen wants to get any help about how to use RTI, he can use this number. RAN will be a premium number. Anyone who wishes to file an RTI application will call up this number. Any call to this number will be charged the application fee, in addition to the normal call charges for the duration of the call. So, when a person calls up RAN, he will be asked to tell his name, address, what information he wants. This conversation will be voice recorded and also typed on computer simultaneously by the call centre executive receiving the call. The applicant will be given a unique ID no. for every RTI application filed on phone. The call centre will act as an APIO to be able to accept the applications and will transfer them to the concerned PIO. Haryana has established a call centre with six seats which would work on seven days basis i.e. without holiday and one shift basis.

Haryana has established 1159 rural Common Sevices coutres (CSC) (approximately ICSC for 6 Villages) all over Haryana. Besides, 104 urban CSCS are also in the Various stages of roll out all over Haryana. RTI applications for seeking information from various departments can be submitted at these CSCs. The applicatons thus received shall be e-mailed to the concerned APIO/PIO through a web based postal to be develped by NIC, State Unit.

18. Use of Post Offices

The State Governments in consultation with the Post Master General of the State can have a similar arrangement as already adopted by the Central Government, which has designated certain specified post offices in the country as APIOs to collect application on behalf of the Public Authorities of the Central Government and forward them to the concerned PIOs. Since, in most of the states, fee can be paid by way of postal order, this will be an easy method of sending applications especially for the people living in rural areas instead of visiting district headquarter or sub-divisional headquarter to get the draft prepared or payment by way of cash/treasury challan.

19. Confederation or Regular Meet of ICs

A Confederation/Conference of Information Commissions may be formed for regular meetings for having better coordination among the Commissions and cohesion in their decisions. So that there could be uniformity as regards the information relating to Annual Confidential Reports (ACRs), Answer Sheets, Annual Property Returns (APRs) and Income Tax Returns etc.

20. Public Interest First

Information Commissions should prioritize second-appeals /complaints , which are of public interest , over the once which are self-centric and self-serving.

Summing Up

The enactment of the RTI Act, 2005 is a laudable step. After completion of four years of its implementation, the response of this Act has been very positive and it has received very wide and warm welcome from the people. People are learning the importance of the power of information in their hands. That is why, the people of every section have been seeking information from the different authorities. Public Authorities and Public Information Officers are becoming increasingly aware of their full responsibilities. It has been a learning experience for each entity involved in the working of the law.

However, mere conferment of the right is not enough. Its successful implementation in the true spirit is needed. The revision and review of legislations contrary of this right is required. Suitable amendments in the conduct rules for public servants , attitudinal change in the behaviour of the bureaucracy , creation of efficient information management system , more frequent use of this right by press and will of the citizens are also required.

The RTI Act, 2005 is a major step towards ensuring participatory developmental process in the country. However, the success of the Act can only be achieved if the public authorities take the Act in right spirit and implement the Act effectively. And people began to use it as an instrument for pressing transparency and accountability on part of the public bodies.

To overcome the problems in its effective use, the governments should take steps to propagate this Act in the illiterate population living in the village. The states should increasingly use IT/e-governance. Records in the Government offices need to be digitized and indexed for easy retrieval. Video Conferencing should be used extensively for hearing the appeals. Proactive disclosure of public authorities should be audited by a team of Government officials and NGOs. Penal provisions, as stipulated under the Act for malicious and unreasonable refusal of information, by the Information Commission should be strictly implemented. Compulsory training of officers of Central and State Governments on RTI should be organized. What is most important at present juncture is to give honest chance to the Act to operate without creating negative stumbling blocks and bottlenecks. There is a special duty cast upon the organizations of the civil society and public authorities to be vigilant so that the objectives of the Act do not get frustrated by the bureaucratic manipulations. Attitudinal change for positive response in bureaucracy is a must for the successful implementation of the RTI Act, 2005.

Further, effective operationalisation of the RTI requires capacity-building of the information providers and seekers. Capacity-building of the cutting edge level functionaries forms the key element as it facilitates the first interface with the citizens. Creating the RTI regime in tune with the spirit and philosophy of the Act would require institutional mechanism for improved government citizen interface, capacity-building of officials to meet citizen's information requirements and awareness and empowerment of citizens to enable them to exercise RTI in the right earnest.

Realising the need to create awareness and build the capacity of various stakeholders, particularly the government employees about the RTI, Act, 2005 and its various implications, HIPA in association with the State Government and the State Information Commission has been organising capacity-building programmes for various categories of officers/officials of the state with an objective to create awareness about the need and importance of the RTI Act. Haryana has taken a lead over other states as far as coverage is concerned. RTI awareness programmes have been organized in all the districts of the state. About 4000 trainees from various categories of the employees of the state government have attended these programmes. Under the GOI – UNDP sponsored project on 'Capacity Building for Access to Information' HIPA, Gurgaon is working as the State Implementing agency and is the State Nodal Agency to implement the project in the State. Two districts Gurgaon and Jhajjar have been selected for implementing the project at the district level.

Above all, it can be said that strong will power is required to reap the fruit of this Act. Legislation alone will not ensure justice to the information seekers unless it is implemented with strong conviction. Laws by themselves are not adequate. What is needed is that these must be backed by people's movement. The RTI Act (2005) can be made effective only through people's active involvement. Much would depend on the seriousness of Central and State Governments and Public Authorities in fulfilling their obligations under the Act and in ensuring removal of difficulties in the operationalisation of the Act . Finally, it can be said that the enactment of RTI Act is indeed, a bold step and will go a long way in creating enabling environment for maturisation of our constitutional mandate by empowering the citizenry.

Annexure-I

THE RIGHT TO INFORMATION ACT, 2005
No. 22 of 2005

[15th June, 2005.]

An Act to provide for setting out the practical regime of right to information for citizens to secure access to information under the control of public authorities, in order to promote transparency and accountability in the working of every public authority, the constitution of a Central Information Commission and State Information Commissions and for matters connected therewith or incidental thereto.

WHEREAS the Constitution of India has established democratic Republic;

AND WHEREAS democracy requires an informed citizenry and transparency of information which are vital to its functioning and also to contain corruption and to hold Governments and their instrumentalities accountable to the governed;

AND WHEREAS revelation of information in actual practice is likely to conflict with other public interests including efficient operations of the Governments, optimum use of limited fiscal resources and the preservation of confidentiality of sensitive information;

AND WHEREAS it is necessary to harmonise these conflicting interests while preserving the paramountcy of the democratic ideal;

NOW, THEREFORE, it is expedient to provide for furnishing certain information to citizens who desire to have it.

BE it enacted by Parliament in the Fifty-sixth Year of the Republic of India as follows:—

CHAPTER I
Preliminary

1. (1) This Act may be called the Right to Information Act, 2005.
(2) It extends to the whole of India except the State of Jammu and Kashmir.
(3) The provisions of sub-section (*1*) of section 4, sub-sections (*1*) and (*2*) of section 5, sections 12, 13, 15,16, 24, 27 and 28 shall come into force at once, and the remaining provisions of this Act shall come into force on the one hundred and twentieth day of its enactment.

2. In this Act, unless the context otherwise requires,—
(*a*) "Appropriate Government" means in relation to a public authority which is established, constituted, owned, controlled or substantially financed by funds provided directly or indirectly—

(*i*) by the Central Government or the Union territory administration, the Central Government;
(*ii*) by the State Government, the State Government;

(*b*) "Central Information Commission" means the Central Information Commission constituted under sub-section (*1*) of section 12;
(*c*) "Central Public Information Officer" means the Central Public Information Officer designated under sub-section (*1*) and includes a Central Assistant Public Information Officer designated as such under sub-section (*2*) of section 5;
(*d*) "Chief Information Commissioner" and "Information Commissioner" mean the Chief Information Commissioner and Information Commissioner appointed under sub-section (*3*) of section 12;
(*e*) "competent authority" means—

(*i*) the Speaker in the case of the House of the People or the Legislative Assembly of a State or a Union territory having such Assembly and the Chairman in the case of the Council of States or Legislative Council of a State;

(*ii*) the Chief Justice of India in the case of the Supreme Court;

(*iii*) the Chief Justice of the High Court in the case of a High Court;

(*iv*) the President or the Governor, as the case may be, in the case of other authorities established or constituted by or under the Constitution; and

(*v*) the administrator appointed under article 239 of the Constitution;

(*f*) "information" means any material in any form, including records, documents, memos, e-mails, opinions, advices, press releases, circulars, orders, logbooks, and information relating to any private body which can be accessed by a public authority under any other law for the time being in force;

(*g*) "prescribed" means prescribed by rules made under this Act by the appropriate Government or the competent authority, as the case may be;

(*h*) "public authority" means any authority or body or institution of self- government established or constituted—

(*a*) by or under the Constitution;

(*b*) by any other law made by Parliament;

(*c*) by any other law made by State Legislature;

(*d*) by notification issued or order made by the appropriate Government, and includes any—

(*i*) body owned, controlled or substantially financed;

(*ii*) non-Government organisation substantially financed, directly or indirectly by funds provided by the Appropriate Government;

(*i*) "record" includes—

(*a*) any document, manuscript and file;
(*b*) any microfilm, microfiche and facsimile copy of a document;
(*c*) any reproduction of image or images embodied in such microfilm (whether enlarged or not); and
(*d*) any other material produced by a computer or any other device;

(*j*) "right to information" means the right to information accessible under this Act which is held by or under the control of any public authority and includes the right to—

(*i*) inspection of work, documents, records;
(*ii*) taking notes, extracts or certified copies of documents or records;
(*iii*) taking certified samples of material;
(*iv*) obtaining information in the form of diskettes, floppies, tapes, video cassettes or in any other electronic mode or through printouts where such information is stored in a computer or in any other device;

(*k*) "State Information Commission" means the State Information Commission constituted under sub-section (*1*) of section 15;

(*l*) "State Chief Information Commissioner" and "State Information Commissioner" mean the State Chief Information Commissioner and the State Information Commissioner appointed under sub-section (*3*) of section 15;

(*m*) "State Public Information Officer" means the State Public Information Officer designated under sub-section (*1*) and includes a State Assistant Public Information Officer designated as such under sub-section (2) of section 5;

(*n*) "third party" means a person other than the citizen making a request for information and includes a public authority.

CHAPTER II

Right to Information and Obligations of Public Authorities

3. Subject to the provisions of this Act, all citizens shall have the right to information.

4. (*1*) Every public authority shall—

(*a*) maintain all its records duly catalogued and indexed in a manner and the form which facilitates the right to information under this Act and ensure that all records that are appropriate to be computerised are, within a reasonable time and subject to availability of resources, computerised and connected through a network all over the country on different systems so that access to such records is facilitated;

(*b*) publish within one hundred and twenty days from the enactment of this Act,—

(*i*) the particulars of its organisation, functions and duties;

(*ii*) the powers and duties of its officers and employees;

(*iii*) the procedure followed in the decision making process, including channels of supervision and accountability;

(*iv*) the norms set by it for the discharge of its functions;

(*v*) the rules, regulations, instructions, manuals and records, held by it or under its control or used by its employees for discharging its functions;

(*vi*) a statement of the categories of documents that are held by it or under its control;

(*vii*) the particulars of any arrangement that exists for consultation with, or representation by, the members of the public in relation to the formulation of its policy or implementation thereof;

(viii) a statement of the boards, councils, committees and other bodies consisting of two or more persons constituted as its part or for the purpose of its advice, and as to whether meetings of those boards, councils, committees and other bodies are open to the public, or the minutes of such meetings are accessible for public;

(ix) a directory of its officers and employees;

(x) the monthly remuneration received by each of its officers and employees, including the system of compensation as provided in its regulations;

(xi) the budget allocated to each of its agency, indicating the particulars of all plans, proposed expenditures and reports on disbursements made;

(xii) the manner of execution of subsidy programmes, including the amounts allocated and the details of beneficiaries of such programmes;

(xiii) particulars of recipients of concessions, permits or authorisations granted by it;

(xiv) details in respect of the information, available to or held by it, reduced in an electronic form;

(xv) the particulars of facilities available to citizens for obtaining information, including the working hours of a library or reading room, if maintained for public use;

(xvi) the names, designations and other particulars of the Public Information Officers;

(*xvii*) such other information as may be prescribed; and thereafter update these publications every year;

(*c*) publish all relevant facts while formulating important policies or announcing the decisions which affect public;

(*d*) provide reasons for its administrative or quasi-judicial decisions to affected persons.

(2) It shall be a constant endeavour of every public authority to take steps in accordance with the requirements of clause (*b*) of sub-section (*1*) to provide as much information *suo motu* to the public at regular intervals through various means of communications, including internet, so that the public have minimum resort to the use of this Act to obtain information.

(3) For the purposes of sub-section (*1*), every information shall be disseminated widely and in such form and manner which is easily accessible to the public.

(4) All materials shall be disseminated taking into consideration the cost effectiveness, local language and the most effective method of communication in that local area and the information should be easily accessible, to the extent possible in electronic format with the Central Public Information Officer or State Public Information Officer, as the case may be, available free or at such cost of the medium or the print cost price as may be prescribed.

Explanation—For the purposes of sub-sections (*3*) and (*4*), "disseminated" means making known or communicated the information to the public through notice boards, newspapers, public announcements, media broadcasts, the internet or any other means, including inspection of offices of any public authority.

5. (*1*) Every public authority shall, within one hundred days of the enactment of this Act, designate as many officers as the Central Public Information Officers or State Public Information Officers, as the case may be, in all administrative units or offices under it as may be necessary to provide information to persons requesting for the information under this Act.

(*2*) Without prejudice to the provisions of sub-section (*1*), every public authority shall designate an officer, within one hundred days of the enactment of this Act, at each sub-divisional level or other sub-district level as a Central Assistant Public Information Officer or a State Assistant Public Information Officer, as the case may be, to receive the applications for information or appeals under this Act for forwarding the same forthwith to the Central Public Information Officer or the State Public Information Officer or senior officer specified under sub-section (*1*) of section 19 or the Central Information Commission or the State Information Commission, as the case may be:

Provided that where an application for information or appeal is given to a Central Assistant Public Information Officer or a State Assistant Public Information Officer, as the case may be, a period of five days shall be added in computing the period for response specified under sub-section (*1*) of section 7.

(*3*) Every Central Public Information Officer or State Public Information Officer, as the case may be, shall deal with requests from persons seeking information and render reasonable assistance to the persons seeking such information.

(*4*) The Central Public Information Officer or State Public Information Officer, as the case may be, may seek the assistance of any other officer as he or she considers it necessary for the proper discharge of his or her duties.

(*5*) Any officer, whose assistance has been sought under sub-section (*4*), shall render all assistance to the Central Public Information Officer or State Public Information Officer, as the case may be, seeking his or her assistance and for the purposes of any contravention of the provisions of this Act, such other officer shall be treated as a Central Public Information Officer or State Public Information Officer, as the case may be.

6. (*1*) A person, who desires to obtain any information under this Act, shall make a request in writing or through electronic means in English or Hindi or in the official language of the area in which the application is being made, accompanying such fee as may be prescribed, to—

(*a*) the Central Public Information Officer or State Public Information Officer, as the case may be, of the concerned public authority;

(*b*) the Central Assistant Public Information Officer or State Assistant Public Information Officer, as the case may be,

specifying the particulars of the information sought by him or her:

Provided that where such request cannot be made in writing, the Central Public Information Officer or State Public Information Officer, as the case may be, shall render all reasonable assistance to the person making the request orally to reduce the same in writing.

(2) An applicant making request for information shall not be required to give any reason for requesting the information or any other personal details except those that may be necessary for contacting him.

(3) Where an application is made to a public authority requesting for an information,—

(*i*) which is held by another public authority; or

(*ii*) the subject matter of which is more closely connected with the functions of another public authority,

the public authority, to which such application is made, shall transfer the application or such part of it as may be appropriate to that other public authority and inform the applicant immediately about such transfer:

Provided that the transfer of an application pursuant to this sub-section shall be made as soon as practicable but in no case later than five days from the date of receipt of the application.

7. (*1*) Subject to the proviso to sub-section (2) of section 5 or the proviso to sub-section (*3*) of section 6, the Central Public Information Officer or State Public Information Officer, as the case may be, on receipt of a request under section 6 shall, as expeditiously as possible, and in any case within thirty days of the receipt of the request, either provide the information on payment of such fee as may be prescribed or reject the request for any of the reasons specified in sections 8 and 9:

Provided that where the information sought for concerns the life or liberty of a person, the same shall be provided within forty-eight hours of the receipt of the request.

(2) If the Central Public Information Officer or State Public Information Officer, as the case may be, fails to give decision on the request for information within the period specified under sub-section (*1*), the Central Public Information Officer or State

Public Information Officer, as the case may be, shall be deemed to have refused the request.

(3) Where a decision is taken to provide the information on payment of any further fee representing the cost of providing the information, the Central Public Information Officer or State Public Information Officer, as the case may be, shall send an intimation to the person making the request, giving—

(a) the details of further fees representing the cost of providing the information as determined by him, together with the calculations made to arrive at the amount in accordance with fee prescribed under sub-section (*1*), requesting him to deposit that fees, and the period intervening between the despatch of the said intimation and payment of fees shall be excluded for the purpose of calculating the period of thirty days referred to in that sub-section;

(b) information concerning his or her right with respect to review the decision as to the amount of fees charged or the form of access provided, including the particulars of the appellate authority, time limit, process and any other forms.

(*4*) Where access to the record or a part thereof is required to be provided under this Act and the person to whom access is to be provided is sensorily disabled, the Central Public Information Officer or State Public Information Officer, as the case may be, shall provide assistance to enable access to the information, including providing such assistance as may be appropriate for the inspection.

(*5*) Where access to information is to be provided in the printed or in any electronic format, the applicant shall, subject to the provisions of sub-section (*6*), pay such fee as may be prescribed: Provided that the fee prescribed under sub-section (*1*) of section 6 and sub-sections (*1*) and (*5*) of section 7 shall be reasonable and no such fee shall be charged from the persons who are of below poverty line as may be determined by the appropriate Government.

(*6*) Notwithstanding anything contained in sub-section (*5*), the person making request for the information shall be provided the information free of charge where a public authority fails to comply with the time limits specified in sub-section (*1*).

(*7*) Before taking any decision under sub-section (*1*), the Central Public Information Officer or State Public Information Officer, as the case may be, shall take into consideration the representation made by a third party under section *11*.

(*8*) Where a request has been rejected under sub-section (*1*), the Central Public Information Officer or State Public Information Officer, as the case may be, shall communicate to the person making the request,—

(*i*) the reasons for such rejection;
(*ii*) the period within which an appeal against such rejection may be preferred; and
(*iii*) the particulars of the appellate authority.

(*9*) An information shall ordinarily be provided in the form in which it is sought unless it would disproportionately divert the resources of the public authority or would be detrimental to the safety or preservation of the record in question.

8. (*1*) Notwithstanding anything contained in this Act, there shall be no obligation to give any citizen,—

(*a*) information, disclosure of which would prejudicially affect the sovereignty and integrity of India, the security, strategic, scientific or economic interests of the State, relation with foreign State or lead to incitement of an offence;

(*b*) information which has been expressly forbidden to be published by any court of law or tribunal or the disclosure of which may constitute contempt of court;

(*c*) information, the disclosure of which would cause a breach of privilege of Parliament or the State Legislature;

(*d*) information including commercial confidence, trade secrets or intellectual property, the disclosure of which would harm the competitive position of a third party, unless the competent authority is satisfied that larger public interest warrants the disclosure of such information;

(*e*) information available to a person in his fiduciary relationship, unless the competent authority is satisfied that the larger public interest warrants the disclosure of such information;

(*f*) information received in confidence from foreign Government;

(*g*) information, the disclosure of which would endanger the life or physical safety of any person or identify the source of information or assistance given in confidence for law enforcement or security purposes;

(*h*) information which would impede the process of investigation or apprehension or prosecution of offenders;

(*i*) cabinet papers including records of

deliberations of the Council of Ministers, Secretaries and other officers:

Provided that the decisions of Council of Ministers, the reasons thereof, and the material on the basis of which the decisions were taken shall be made public after the decision has been taken, and the matter is complete, or over:

Provided further that those matters which come under the exemptions specified in this section shall not be disclosed;

(*j*) information which relates to personal information the disclosure of which has no relationship to any public activity or interest, or which would cause unwarranted invasion of the privacy of the individual unless the Central Public Information Officer or the State Public Information Officer or the appellate authority, as the case may be, is satisfied that the larger public interest justifies the disclosure of such information:

Provided that the information which cannot be denied to the Parliament or a State Legislature shall not be denied to any person.

(2) Notwithstanding anything in the Official Secrets Act, 1923 nor any of the exemptions permissible in accordance with sub-section (*1*), a public authority may allow access to information, if public interest in disclosure outweighs the harm to the protected interests.

(3) Subject to the provisions of clauses (*a*), (*c*) and (*i*) of sub-section (*1*), any information relating to any occurrence, event or matter which has taken place, occurred or happened twenty years before the date on which any request is made under Secton 6 shall be provided to any person making a request under that section:

Provided that where any question arises as to the date from which the said period of twenty years has to be computed, the decision of the Central Government shall be final, subject to the usual appeals provided for in this Act.

9. Without prejudice to the provisions of section 8, a Central Public Information Officer or a State Public Information Officer, as the case may be, may reject a request for information where such a request for providing access would involve an infringement of copyright subsisting in a person other than the State.

10. (*1*) Where a request for access to information is rejected on the ground that it is in relation to information which is exempt from disclosure, then, notwithstanding anything contained in this Act, access may be provided to that part of the record which does not contain any information which is exempt from disclosure under this Act and which can reasonably be severed from any part that contains exempt information.

(2) Where access is granted to a part of the record under sub-section (*1*), the Central Public Information Officer or State Public Information Officer, as the case may be, shall give a notice to the applicant, informing—

(*a*) that only part of the record requested, after severance of the record containing information which is exempt from disclosure, is being provided;

(*b*) the reasons for the decision, including any findings on any material question of fact, referring to the material on which those findings were based;

(*c*) the name and designation of the person giving the decision;

(*d*) the details of the fees calculated by him or her and the amount of fee which the applicant is required to deposit; and

(*e*) his or her rights with respect to review of the decision regarding non-disclosure of part of the information, the amount of fee charged or the form of access provided, including the particulars of the senior officer specified under sub-section (*1*) of section 19 or the Central Information Commission or the State Information Commission, as the case may be, time limit, process and any other form of access.

11. (*1*) Where a Central Public Information Officer or a State Public Information Officer, as the case may be, intends to disclose any information or record, or part thereof on a request made under this Act, which relates to or has been supplied by a third party and has been treated as confidential by that third party, the Central Public Information Officer or State Public Information Officer, as the case may be, shall, within five days from the receipt of the request, give a written notice to such third party of the request and of the fact that the Central Public Information Officer or State Public Information Officer, as the case may be, intends to disclose the information or record, or part thereof, and invite the third party to make a submission in writing or orally, regarding whether the information should be disclosed, and such submission of the third party shall be kept in view while taking a decision about disclosure of information:

Provided that except in the case of trade or commercial secrets protected by law, disclosure may be allowed if the public interest in disclosure outweighs in importance any possible harm or injury to the interests of such third party.

(2) Where a notice is served by the Central Public Information Officer or State Public Information Officer, as the case may be, under sub-section (*1*) to a third party in respect of any information or record or part thereof, the third party shall, within ten days from the date of receipt of such notice, be given the opportunity to make representation against the proposed disclosure.

(3) Notwithstanding anything contained in section 7, the Central Public Information Officer or State Public Information Officer, as the case may be, shall, within forty days after receipt of the request under section 6, if the third party has been given an opportunity to make representation under sub-section (2), make a decision as to whether or not to disclose the information or record or part thereof and give in writing the notice of his decision to the third party.

(4) A notice given under sub-section (*3*) shall include a statement that the third party to whom the notice is given is entitled to prefer an appeal under Section 19 against the decision.

CHAPTER III

The Central Information Commission

12. (*1*) The Central Government shall, by notification in the Official Gazette, constitute a body to be known as the Central Information Commission to exercise the powers conferred on, and to perform the functions assigned to, it under this Act.

(2) The Central Information Commission shall consist of—

(*a*) the Chief Information Commissioner; and

(*b*) such number of Central Information Commissioners, not exceeding ten, as may be deemed necessary.

(3) The Chief Information Commissioner and Information Commissioners shall be appointed by the President on the recommendation of a committee consisting of—

(i) the Prime Minister, who shall be the Chairperson of the committee;
(ii) the Leader of Opposition in the Lok Sabha; and
(iii) a Union Cabinet Minister to be nominated by the Prime Minister.

Explanation—For the purposes of removal of doubts, it is hereby declared that where the Leader of Opposition in the House of the People has not been recognised as such, the Leader of the single largest group in opposition of the Government in the House of the People shall be deemed to be the Leader of Opposition.

(4) The general superintendence, direction and management of the affairs of the Central Information Commission shall vest in the Chief Information Commissioner who shall be assisted by the Information Commissioners and may exercise all such powers and do all such acts and things which may be exercised or done by the Central Information Commission autonomously without being subjected to directions by any other authority under this Act.
(5) The Chief Information Commissioner and Information Commissioners shall be persons of eminence in public life with wide knowledge and experience in law, science and technology, social service, management, journalism, mass media or administration and governance.
(6) The Chief Information Commissioner or an

Information Commissioner shall not be a Member of Parliament or Member of the Legislature of any State or Union territory, as the case may be, or hold any other office of profit or connected with any political party or carrying on any business or pursuing any profession.

(7) The headquarters of the Central Information Commission shall be at Delhi and the Central Information Commission may, with the previous approval of the Central Government, establish offices at other places in India.

13. (1) The Chief Information Commissioner shall hold office for a term of five years from the date on which he enters upon his office and shall not be eligible for reappointment:

Provided that no Chief Information Commissioner shall hold office as such after he has attained the age of sixty-five years.

(2) Every Information Commissioner shall hold office for a term of five years from the date on which he enters upon his office or till he attains the age of sixty-five years, whichever is earlier, and shall not be eligible for reappointment as such Information Commissioner:

Provided that every Information Commissioner shall, on vacating his office under this sub-section be eligible for appointment as the Chief Information Commissioner in the manner specified in sub-section (3) of section 12:

Provided further that where the Information Commissioner is appointed as the Chief Information Commissioner, his term of office shall not be more than five years in aggregate as the Information Commissioner and the Chief Information Commissioner.

(3) The Chief Information Commissioner or an Information Commissioner shall before he enters upon his office make and subscribe before the

President or some other person appointed by him in that behalf, an oath or affirmation according to the form set out for the purpose in the First Schedule.

(4) The Chief Information Commissioner or an Information Commissioner may, at any time, by writing under his hand addressed to the President, resign from his office:

Provided that the Chief Information Commissioner or an Information Commissioner may be removed in the manner specified under section 14.

(5) The salaries and allowances payable to and other terms and conditions of service of—

(a) the Chief Information Commissioner shall be the same as that of the Chief Election Commissioner;

(b) an Information Commissioner shall be the same as that of an Election Commissioner:

Provided that if the Chief Information Commissioner or an Information Commissioner, at the time of his appointment is, in receipt of a pension, other than a disability or wound pension, in respect of any previous service under the Government of India or under the Government of a State, his salary in respect of the service as the Chief Information Commissioner or an Information Commissioner shall be reduced by the amount of that pension including any portion of pension which was commuted and pension equivalent of other forms of retirement benefits excluding pension equivalent of retirement gratuity:

Provided further that if the Chief Information Commissioner or an Information Commissioner if, at the time of his appointment is, in receipt of retirement benefits in respect of any previous service rendered in a Corporation established by or under any Central Act or State Act or a Government company owned or controlled by the Central Government or the State Government, his salary in respect of the service as the Chief Information Commissioner or an Information Commissioner shall be reduced by the amount of pension equivalent to the retirement benefits:

Provided also that the salaries, allowances and other conditions of service of the Chief Information Commissioner and the Information Commissioners shall not be varied to their disadvantage after their appointment.

(*6*) The Central Government shall provide the Chief Information Commissioner and the Information Commissioners with such officers and employees as may be necessary for the efficient performance of their functions under this Act, and the salaries and allowances payable to and the terms and conditions of service of the officers and other employees appointed for the purpose of this Act shall be such as may be prescribed.

14. (*1*) Subject to the provisions of sub-section (3), the Chief Information Commissioner or any Information Commissioner shall be removed from his office only by order of the President on the ground of proved misbehaviour or incapacity after the Supreme Court, on a reference made to it by the President, has, on inquiry, reported that the Chief Information Commissioner or any Information Commissioner, as the case may be, ought on such ground be removed.

(2) The President may suspend from office, and if deem necessary prohibit also from attending the

office during inquiry, the Chief Information Commissioner or Information Commissioner in respect of whom a reference has been made to the Supreme Court under sub-section (*1*) until the President has passed orders on receipt of the report of the Supreme Court on such reference.

(3) Notwithstanding anything contained in sub-section (*1*), the President may by order remove from office the Chief Information Commissioner or any Information Commissioner if the Chief Information Commissioner or a Information Commissioner, as the case may be,—

(*a*) is adjudged an insolvent; or

(*b*) has been convicted of an offence which, in the opinion of the President, involves moral turpitude; or

(*c*) engages during his term of office in any paid employment outside the duties of his office; or

(*d*) is, in the opinion of the President, unfit to continue in office by reason of infirmity of mind or body; or

(*e*) has acquired such financial or other interest as is likely to affect prejudicially his functions as the Chief Information Commissioner or a Information Commissioner.

(4) If the Chief Information Commissioner or a Information Commissioner in any way, concerned or interested in any contract or agreement made by or on behalf of the Government of India or participates in any way in the profit thereof or in any benefit or emolument arising therefrom otherwise than as a member and in common with the other members of an incorporated company,

he shall, for the purposes of sub-section (*1*), be deemed to be guilty of misbehaviour.

CHAPTER IV
The State Information Commission

15.(*1*) Every State Government shall, by notification in the Official Gazette, constitute a body to be known as the .... (name of the State) Information Commission to exercise the powers conferred on, and to perform the functions assigned to, it under this Act.

(2) The State Information Commission shall consist of—

(a) the State Chief Information Commissioner, and

(b) such number of State Information Commissioners, not exceeding ten, as may be deemed necessary.

(3) The State Chief Information Commissioner and the State Information Commissioners shall be appointed by the Governor on the recommendation of a committee consisting of—

(i) the Chief Minister, who shall be the Chairperson of the committee;

(ii) the Leader of Opposition in the Legislative Assembly; and

(iii) a Cabinet Minister to be nominated by the Chief Minister

Explanation—For the purposes of removal of doubts, it is hereby declared that where the Leader of Opposition in the Legislative Assembly has not been recognised as such, the Leader of the single largest group in opposition of the Government in the Legislative Assembly shall be deemed to be the Leader of Opposition.

(*4*) The general superintendence, direction and management of the affairs of the State Information Commission shall vest in the State Chief Information Commissioner who shall be assisted by the State Information Commissioners and may exercise all such powers and do all such acts and things which may be exercised or done by the State Information Commission autonomously without being subjected to directions by any other authority under this Act.

(*5*) The State Chief Information Commissioner and the State Information Commissioners shall be persons of eminence in public life with wide knowledge and experience in law, science and technology, social service, management, journalism, mass media or administration and governance.

(*6*) The State Chief Information Commissioner or a State Information Commissioner shall not be a Member of Parliament or Member of the Legislature of any State or Union territory, as the case may be, or hold any other office of profit or connected with any political party or carrying on any business or pursuing any profession.

(*7*) The headquarters of the State Information Commission shall be at such place in the State as the State Government may, by notification in the Official Gazette, specify and the State Information Commission may, with the previous approval of the State Government, establish offices at other places in the State.

16.(*1*) The State Chief Information Commissioner shall hold office for a term of five years from the date on which he enters upon his office and shall not be eligible for reappointment:

Provided that no State Chief Information Commissioner shall hold office as such after he has attained the age of sixty-five years.

(2) Every State Information Commissioner shall hold office for a term of five years from the date on which he enters upon his office or till he attains the age of sixty-five years, whichever is earlier, and shall not be eligible for reappointment as such State Information Commissioner:

Provided that every State Information Commissioner shall, on vacating his office under this sub-section, be eligible for appointment as the State Chief Information Commissioner in the manner specified in sub-section (3) of section 15:

Provided further that where the State Information Commissioner is appointed as the State Chief Information Commissioner, his term of office shall not be more than five years in aggregate as the State Information Commissioner and the State Chief Information Commissioner.

(3) The State Chief Information Commissioner or a State Information Commissioner, shall before he enters upon his office make and subscribe before the Governor or some other person appointed by him in that behalf, an oath or affirmation according to the form set out for the purpose in the First Schedule.

(4) The State Chief Information Commissioner or a State Information Commissioner may, at any time, by writing under his hand addressed to the Governor, resign from his office.

Provided that the State Chief Information Commissioner or a State Information Commissioner may be removed in the manner specified under Section 17.

(5) The salaries and allowances payable to and other terms and conditions of service of—

(a) the State Chief Information Commissioner

shall be the same as that of an Election Commissioner;

(b) the State Information Commissioner shall be the same as that of the Chief Secretary to the State Government:

Provided that if the State Chief Information Commissioner or a State Information Commissioner, at the time of his appointment is, in receipt of a pension, other than a disability or wound pension, in respect of any previous service under the Government of India or under the Government of a State, his salary in respect of the service as the State Chief Information Commissioner or a State Information Commissioner shall be reduced by the amount of that pension including any portion of pension which was commuted and pension equivalent of other forms of retirement benefits excluding pension equivalent of retirement gratuity:

Provided further that where the State Chief Information Commissioner or a State Information Commissioner if, at the time of his appointment is, in receipt of retirement benefits in respect of any previous service rendered in a Corporation established by or under any Central Act or State Act or a Government company owned or controlled by the Central Government or the State Government, his salary in respect of the service as the State Chief Information Commissioner or the State Information Commissioner shall be reduced by the amount of pension equivalent to the retirement benefits:

Provided also that the salaries, allowances and other conditions of service of the State Chief Information Commissioner and the State Information Commissioners shall not be varied to their disadvantage after their appointment.

(*6*) The State Government shall provide the State Chief Information Commissioner and the State Information Commissioners with such officers and employees as may be necessary for the efficient performance of their functions under this Act, and the salaries and allowances payable to and the terms and conditions of service of the officers and other employees appointed for the purpose of this Act shall be such as may be prescribed.

17.(*1*) Subject to the provisions of sub-section (*3*), the State Chief Information Commissioner or a State Information Commissioner shall be removed from his office only by order of the Governor on the ground of proved misbehaviour or incapacity after the Supreme Court, on a reference made to it by the Governor, has on inquiry, reported that the State Chief Information Commissioner or a State Information Commissioner, as the case may be, ought on such ground be removed.

(2) The Governor may suspend from office, and if deem necessary prohibit also from attending the office during inquiry, the State Chief Information Commissioner or a State Information Commissioner in respect of whom a reference has been made to the Supreme Court under sub-section (*1*) until the Governor has passed orders on receipt of the report of the Supreme Court on such reference.

(3) Notwithstanding anything contained in sub-section (*1*), the Governor may by order remove from office the State Chief Information Commissioner or a State Information Commissioner if a State Chief Information Commissioner or a State Information Commissioner, as the case may be,—

(*a*) is adjudged an insolvent; or

(*b*) has been convicted of an offence which, in the opinion of the Governor, involves moral turpitude; or

(c) engages during his term of office in any paid employment outside the duties of his office; or

(d) is, in the opinion of the Governor, unfit to continue in office by reason of infirmity of mind or body; or (e) has acquired such financial or other interest as is likely to affect prejudicially his functions as the State Chief Information Commissioner or a State Information Commissioner.

(4) If the State Chief Information Commissioner or a State Information Commissioner in any way, concerned or interested in any contract or agreement made by or on behalf of the Government of the State or participates in any way in the profit thereof or in any benefit or emoluments arising therefrom otherwise than as a member and in common with the other members of an incorporated company, he shall, for the purposes of sub-section (1), be deemed to be guilty of misbehaviour.

CHAPTER V
Powers and Functions of the Information Commissions, Appeal and Penalties

18.(1) Subject to the provisions of this Act, it shall be the duty of the Central Information Commission or State Information Commission, as the case may be, to receive and inquire into a complaint from any person,—

(a) who has been unable to submit a request to a Central Public Information Officer or State Public Information Officer, as the case may be, either by reason that no such officer has been appointed under this Act, or because the Central Assistant Public Information Officer or State Assistant Public Information Officer, as the case may be, has refused to accept his or her application for information or appeal under this Act for forwarding the same to the Central Public Information Officer or State Public Information Officer or senior officer specified in sub-section (*1*) of section 19 or the Central Information Commission or the State Information Commission, as the case may be;

(b) who has been refused access to any information requested under this Act;

(c) who has not been given a response to a request for information or access to information within the time limit specified under this Act;

(d) who has been required to pay an amount of fee which he or she considers unreasonable;

(e) who believes that he or she has been given incomplete, misleading or false information under this Act; and

(f) in respect of any other matter relating to requesting or obtaining access to records under this Act.

(2) Where the Central Information Commission or State Information Commission, as the case may be, is satisfied that there are reasonable grounds to inquire into the matter, it may initiate an inquiry in respect thereof.

(3) The Central Information Commission or State Information Commission, as the case may be, shall, while inquiring into any matter under this section, have the same powers as are vested in a civil court while trying a suit under the Code of Civil Procedure, 1908, in respect of the following matters, namely:—

(a) summoning and enforcing the attendance of persons and compel them to give oral or written evidence on oath and to produce the documents or things;

(b) requiring the discovery and inspection of documents;

(c) receiving evidence on affidavit;

(d) requisitioning any public record or copies thereof from any court or office;

(e) issuing summons for examination of witnesses or documents; and

(f) any other matter which may be prescribed.

(*4*) Notwithstanding anything inconsistent contained in any other Act of Parliament or State Legislature, as the case may be, the Central Information Commission or the State Information Commission, as the case may be, may, during the inquiry of any complaint under this Act, examine any record to which this Act applies which is under the control of the public authority, and no such record may be withheld from it on any grounds.

19. (*1*) Any person who, does not receive a decision within the time specified in sub-section (*1*) or clause (*a*) of sub-section (*3*) of section 7, or is aggrieved by a decision of the Central Public Information Officer or State Public Information Officer, as the case may be, may within thirty days from the expiry of such period or from the receipt of such a decision prefer an appeal to such officer who is senior in rank to the Central Public Information Officer or State Public Information Officer as the case may be, in each public authority:

Provided that such officer may admit the appeal after the expiry of the period of thirty days if he or she is satisfied that the appellant was prevented by sufficient cause from filing the appeal in time.

(2) Where an appeal is preferred against an order made by a Central Public Information Officer or a State Public Information Officer, as the case may be, under Section 11 to disclose third party information, the appeal by the concerned third party shall be made within thirty days from the date of the order.

(3) A second appeal against the decision under sub-section (*1*) shall lie within ninety days from the date on which the decision should have been made or was actually received, with the Central Information Commission or the State Information Commission:

Provided that the Central Information Commission or the State Information Commission, as the case may be, may admit the appeal after the expiry of the period of ninety days if it is satisfied that the appellant was prevented by sufficient cause from filing the appeal in time.

(4) If the decision of the Central Public Information Officer or State Public Information Officer, as the case may be, against which an appeal is preferred relates to information of a third party, the Central Information Commission or State Information Commission, as the case may be, shall give a reasonable opportunity of being heard to that third party.

(5) In any appeal proceedings, the onus to prove that a denial of a request was justified shall be on the Central Public Information Officer or State Public Information Officer, as the case may be, who denied the request.

(6) An appeal under sub-section (*1*) or sub-section (*2*) shall be disposed of within thirty days of the receipt of the appeal or within such extended period not exceeding a total of forty-five days from

the date of filing thereof, as the case may be, for reasons to be recorded in writing.

(*7*) The decision of the Central Information Commission or State Information Commission, as the case may be, shall be binding.

(*8*) In its decision, the Central Information Commission or State Information Commission, as the case may be, has the power to—

(*a*) require the public authority to take any such steps as may be necessary to secure compliance with the provisions of this Act, including—

(i) by providing access to information, if so requested, in a particular form;

(ii) by appointing a Central Public Information Officer or State Public Information Officer, as the case may be;

(iii) by publishing certain information or categories of information;

(iv) by making necessary changes to its practices in relation to the maintenance, management and destruction of records;

(v) by enhancing the provision of training on the right to information for its officials; and

(vi) by providing it with an annual report in compliance with clause (*b*) of sub-section (*1*) of section 4;

(*b*) require the public authority to compensate the complainant for any loss or other detriment suffered;

(*c*) impose any of the penalties provided under this Act;

(*d*) reject the application.

(*9*) The Central Information Commission or State Information Commission, as the case may be, shall give notice of its decision, including any right of appeal, to the complainant and the public authority.

(*10*) The Central Information Commission or State Information Commission, as the case may be, shall decide the appeal in accordance with such procedure as may be prescribed.

20. (*1*) Where the Central Information Commission or the State Information Commission, as the case may be, at the time of deciding any complaint or appeal is of the opinion that the Central Public Information Officer or the State Public Information Officer, as the case may be, has, without any reasonable cause, refused to receive an application for information or has not furnished information within the time specified under sub-section (*1*) of section 7 or malafidely denied the request for information or knowingly given incorrect, incomplete or misleading information or destroyed information which was the subject of the request or obstructed in any manner in furnishing the information, it shall impose a penalty of two hundred and fifty rupees each day till application is received or information is furnished, so however, the total amount of such penalty shall not exceed twenty-five thousand rupees:

Provided that the Central Public Information Officer or the State Public Information Officer, as the case may be, shall be given a reasonable opportunity of being heard before any penalty is imposed on him:

Provided further that the burden of proving that he acted reasonably and diligently shall be on the Central Public Information Officer or the State Public Information Officer, as the case may be.

(2) Where the Central Information Commission or the

State Information Commission, as the case may be, at the time of deciding any complaint or appeal is of the opinion that the Central Public Information Officer or the State Public Information Officer, as the case may be, has, without any reasonable cause and persistently, failed to receive an application for information or has not furnished information within the time specified under sub-section (*1*) of section 7 or malafidely denied the request for information or knowingly given incorrect, incomplete or misleading information or destroyed information which was the subject of the request or obstructed in any manner in furnishing the information, it shall recommend for disciplinary action against the Central Public Information Officer or the State Public Information Officer, as the case may be, under the service rules applicable to him.

CHAPTER VI
Miscellaneous

21. No suit, prosecution or other legal proceeding shall lie against any person for anything which is in good faith done or intended to be done under this Act or any rule made thereunder.

22. The provisions of this Act shall have effect notwithstanding anything inconsistent therewith contained in the Official Secrets Act, 1923, and any other law for the time being in force or in any instrument having effect by virtue of any law other than this Act.

23. No court shall entertain any suit, application or other proceeding in respect of any order made under this Act and no such order shall be called in question otherwise than by way of an appeal under this Act.

24. (*1*) Nothing contained in this Act shall apply to the intelligence and security organisations specified in the Second Schedule, being organisations established by the Central Government or any information furnished by such organisations to that Government:

Provided that the information pertaining to the allegations of corruption and human rights violations shall not be excluded under this sub-section:

Provided further that in the case of information sought for is in respect of allegations of violation of human rights, the information shall only be provided after the approval of the Central Information Commission, and notwithstanding anything contained in section 7, such information shall be provided within forty-five days from the date of the receipt of request.

(2) The Central Government may, by notification in the Official Gazette, amend the Schedule by including therein any other intelligence or security organisation established by that Government or omitting therefrom any organisation already specified therein and on the publication of such notification, such organisation shall be deemed to be included in or, as the case may be, omitted from the Schedule.

(3) Every notification issued under sub-section (2) shall be laid before each House of Parliament.

(4) Nothing contained in this Act shall apply to such intelligence and security organisation being organisations established by the State Government, as that Government may, from time to time, by notification in the Official Gazette, specify:

Provided that the information pertaining to the allegations of corruption and human rights violations shall not be excluded under this sub-section:

Provided further that in the case of information sought for is in respect of allegations of violation of human rights, the information shall only be provided after the approval of the State Information Commission and, notwithstanding anything contained in section 7, such information shall be provided within forty-five days from the date of the receipt of request.

(5) Every notification issued under sub-section (*4*) shall be laid before the State Legislature.

25. (*1*) The Central Information Commission or State Information Commission, as the case may be, shall, as soon as practicable after the end of each year, prepare a report on the implementation of the provisions of this Act during that year and forward a copy thereof to the Appropriate Government.

(2) Each Ministry or Department shall, in relation to the public authorities within their jurisdiction, collect and provide such information to the Central Information Commission or State Information Commission, as the case may be, as is required to prepare the report under this section and comply with the requirements concerning the furnishing of that information and keeping of records for the purposes of this section.

(3) Each report shall state in respect of the year to which the report relates,—

(*a*) the number of requests made to each public authority;

(*b*) the number of decisions where applicants were not entitled to access to the documents pursuant to the requests, the provisions of this Act under which these decisions were made and the number of times such provisions were invoked;

(*c*) the number of appeals referred to the Central Information Commission or State Information Commission, as the case may be, for review, the nature of the appeals and the outcome of the appeals;

(*d*) particulars of any disciplinary action taken against any officer in respect of the administration of this Act;

(*e*) the amount of charges collected by each public authority under this Act;

(*f*) any facts which indicate an effort by the public authorities to administer and implement the spirit and intention of this Act;

(*g*) recommendations for reform, including recommendations in respect of the particular public authorities, for the development, improvement, modernisation, reform or amendment to this Act or other legislation or common law or any other matter relevant for operationalising the right to access information.

(4) The Central Government or the State Government, as the case may be, may, as soon as practicable after the end of each year, cause a copy of the report of the Central Information Commission or the State Information Commission, as the case may be, referred to in sub-section (*1*) to be laid before each House of Parliament or, as the case may be, before each House of the State Legislature, where there are two Houses, and where there is one House of the State Legislature before that House.

(5) If it appears to the Central Information Commission or State Information Commission, as the case may be, that the practice of a public authority in relation to the exercise of its functions under this Act does not conform with the provisions or spirit

of this Act, it may give to the authority a recommendation specifying the steps which ought in its opinion to be taken for promoting such conformity.

26. (*1*) The Appropriate Government may, to the extent of availability of financial and other resources,—

(*a*) develop and organise educational programmes to advance the understanding of the public, in particular of disadvantaged communities as to how to exercise the rights contemplated under this Act;

(*b*) encourage public authorities to participate in the development and organisation of programmes referred to in clause (*a*) and to undertake such programmes themselves;

(*c*) promote timely and effective dissemination of accurate information by public authorities about their activities; and

(*d*) train Central Public Information Officers or State Public Information Officers, as the case may be, of public authorities and produce relevant training materials for use by the public authorities themselves.

(2) The Appropriate Government shall, within eighteen months from the commencement of this Act, compile in its official language a guide containing such information, in an easily comprehensible form and manner, as may reasonably be required by a person who wishes to exercise any right specified in this Act.

(3) The Appropriate Government shall, if necessary, update and publish the guidelines referred to in sub-section (2) at regular intervals which shall, in particular and without prejudice to the generality of sub-section (2), include—

(*a*) the objects of this Act;

(*b*) the postal and street address, the phone and fax number and, if available, electronic mail address of the Central Public Information Officer or State Public Information Officer, as the case may be, of every public authority appointed under sub-section (*1*) of section 5;

(*c*) the manner and the form in which request for access to an information shall be made to a Central Public Information Officer or State Public Information Officer, as the case may be;

(*d*) the assistance available from and the duties of the Central Public Information Officer or State Public Information Officer, as the case may be, of a public authority under this Act;

(*e*) the assistance available from the Central Information Commission or State Information Commission, as the case may be;

(*f*) all remedies in law available regarding an act or failure to act in respect of a right or duty conferred or imposed by this Act including the manner of filing an appeal to the Commission;

(*g*) the provisions providing for the voluntary disclosure of categories of records in accordance with section 4;

(*h*) the notices regarding fees to be paid in relation to requests for access to an information; and

(*i*) any additional regulations or circulars made or issued in relation to obtaining access to an information in accordance with this Act.

(*4*) The Appropriate Government must, if necessary, update and publish the guidelines at regular intervals.

27. (*1*) The Appropriate Government may, by notification in the Official Gazette, make rules to carry out the provisions of this Act.

(2) In particular, and without prejudice to the generality of the foregoing power, such rules may provide for all or any of the following matters, namely:—

(*a*) the cost of the medium or print cost price of the materials to be disseminated under sub-section (*4*) of section 4;

(*b*) the fee payable under sub-section (*1*) of section 6;

(*c*) the fee payable under sub-sections (*1*) and (*5*) of section 7;

(*d*) the salaries and allowances payable to and the terms and conditions of service of the officers and other employees under sub-section (*6*) of section 13 and sub-section (*6*) of section 16;

(*e*) the procedure to be adopted by the Central Information Commission or State Information Commission, as the case may be, in deciding the appeals under sub-section (*10*) of section 19; and

(*f*) any other matter which is required to be, or may be, prescribed.

28. (*1*) The competent authority may, by notification in the Official Gazette, make rules to carry out the provisions of this Act.

(2) In particular, and without prejudice to the generality of the foregoing power, such rules may provide for all or any of the following matters, namely:—

(*i*) the cost of the medium or print cost price of the materials to be disseminated under sub-section (*4*) of section 4;

(ii) the fee payable under sub-section (*1*) of section-6;

(iii) the fee payable under sub-section (*1*) of section 7; and

(iv) any other matter which is required to be, or may be, prescribed

29. (*1*) Every rule made by the Central Government under this Act shall be laid, as soon as may be after it is made, before each House of Parliament, while it is in session, for a total period of thirty days which may be comprised in one session or in two or more successive sessions, and if, before the expiry of the session immediately following the session or the successive sessions aforesaid, both Houses agree in making any modification in the rule or both Houses agree that the rule should not be made, the rule shall thereafter have effect only in such modified form or be of no effect, as the case may be; so, however, that any such modification or annulment shall be without prejudice to the validity of anything previously done under that rule.

(2) Every rule made under this Act by a State Government shall be laid, as soon as may be after it is notified, before the State Legislature.

30. (*1*) If any difficulty arises in giving effect to the provisions of this Act, the Central Government may, by order published in the Official Gazette, make such provisions not inconsistent with the provisions of this Act as appear to it to be necessary or expedient for removal of the difficulty:

Provided that no such order shall be made after the expiry of a period of two years from the date of the commencement of this Act.

(2) Every order made under this section shall, as soon as may be after it is made, be laid before each House of Parliament.

31. The Freedom of Information Act, 2002 is hereby repealed.

THE FIRST SCHEDULE
[*See* sections 13 (*3*) and 16(*3*)]
Form of Oath or Affirmation to be made by the Chief Information Commissioner/the Information Commissioner/the State Chief Information Commissioner/the State Information Commissioner

"I, ..., having been appointed Chief Information Commissioner/Information Commissioner/State Chief Information Commissioner/State Information Commissioner *swear in the name of God* ***Solemnly affirm*** that I will bear true faith and allegiance to the Constitution of India as by law established, that I will uphold the sovereignty and integrity of India, that I will duly and faithfully and to the best of my ability, knowledge and judgment perform the duties of my office without fear or favour, affection or ill-will and that I will uphold the Constitution and the laws."

THE SECOND SCHEDULE (*See* section 24)
Intelligence and Security Organisation established by the Central Government

1. Intelligence Bureau.
2. Research and Analysis Wing of the Cabinet Secretariat.
3. Directorate of Revenue Intelligence.
4. Central Economic Intelligence Bureau.
5. Directorate of Enforcement.
6. Narcotics Control Bureau.
7. Aviation Research Centre.
8. Special Prontier Force.
9. Border Security Force.

10. Central Reserve Police Force.
11. Indo-Tibetan Border Police.
12. Central Industrial Security Force.
13. National Security Guards.
14. Assam Rifles.
15. Special Service Bureau
16. Special Branch (CID), Andaman and Nicobar.
17. The Crime Branch-C.I.D.-CB, Dadra and Nagar Haveli.
18. Special Branch, Lakshadweep Police.

T. K. VISWANATHAN,
Secy. to the Govt. of India.

Annexure - II

Jammu and Kashmir Right to Information Act, 2004 (J & K Act, 1 of 2004)

[5th January, 2004)

An Act to make provision for securing right to *information in the State of Jammu and Kashmir.*

Be it enacted by Jammu and Kashmir State Legislature in the Fifty-fourth year of the Republic of India as follows:

1. Short title, extent and commencement :

    (1) This Act may be called the Jammu and Kashmir Right to Information Act, 2004.
    (2) It shall extend to the whole of the State of Jammu and Kashmir.
    (3) It shall come into force on such date as the, Government may, by notification in the Government Gazette, appoint.

2. *Definitions:* In this Act, unless—the context otherwise requires:—

    (a) *"Controlling Officer"* means the immediate superior officer above the incharge of office, who supervises and controls the work of incharge of office or such officer as may from time to time, be specified as such by the Government for the purposes of this Act;
    (b) *"Department"* means any department or office of the Government;
    (c) *"Government"* means the Government of Jammu and Kashmir;
    (d) *"In-charge of the Office"* means an Officer/ functionary of a department of the Government

or a public body, who is in actual control of any office of the Government or public body, as the case may be, or such officer/functionary as may, from time to time, be specified as such by the Government for the purposes of this Act;

(e) *"Information"* means any document or information relating to the affairs of the State or a public body;

(f) *"Public body"* shall include:—

(i) offices of all local bodies and other authorities constituted under any law for the time being in force; or

(ii) any other statutory authority constituted by the Government under any law for the time being in force; or

(iii) a Government Company/Corporation incorporated under the Companies Act, 1956 (Central Act No.1 of 1956) in which not less than fifty-one per cent of the paid up share capital, is held by the Government or a trust established by the Government under any law for the time being in force and controlled by it; or

(iv) a Society or a Co-operative Society or any other organization established under any law for the time being in force, by the Government and directly controlled or funded by it; or

(v) any other body, which may be receiving substantial financial assistance from the Government, as may be specified by notification, in the Government Gazette for the purposes of this Act;

(g) *"Right to information"* means right to obtain information relating to the affairs of the State or Public bodies by means of—

(i) obtaining certified copies of documents or records; or
(ii) inspection of accessible records and taking notes and extracts; or
(iii) inspection of public works; or
(iv) taking of samples of material from public works; or
(v) diskettes, floppies or in any other electronic mode or through print outs where such information is stored in a computer or in any other device.

3. Obligation of Departments and Public Bodies— Every Department and public body shall—

(a) maintain all its records, in such manner and form as is consistent with its operational requirements dilly catalogued and indexed;
(b) publish at such intervals as may be prescribed by the Government—

(i) the particulars of its organization, functions and duties;
(ii) the powers and duties of its officers and employees and the procedure followed by them in the decision-making process;
(iii) the norms set by the public authority for the discharge of its functions;
(iv) rules, regulations, instructions, manuals and other categories of records under its control used by its employees for discharging its functions;
(v) the name, designation and other particulars of the incharge of the office and of the Controlling Officer;

(c) publish all relevant facts concerning important.

decisions and policies that affect the public while announcing such decisions and policies;

(d) give reasons for its decisions, whether administrative or quasi-judicial to those affected by such decisions; and

(e) before initiating any project, publish or communicate to the public generally or to the persons affected or likely to be affected by the project in particular, the facts available to it or to which it has reasonable access which in its opinion should be known to them in the best interests of maintenance of democratic principles.

4. Right to information— Subject to the provisions of this Act, every citizen shall have right to obtain information from the incharge of office and such incharge shall be liable to provide information under and in accordance with the provisions of this Act.

5. Procedure for supply of information— Any person seeking information shall make an application to the incharge of the office giving particulars of the matter relating to which information is sought,

(a) if the incharge of the office is in possession of the information requested and the information does not fall in anyone or more categories mentioned in Section 6, the incharge of the office shall supply the. information to the applicant as far as may be practical within a period of thirty working days from the receipt of the application;

(b) Fifth incharge of the office is in possession of the information requested but, the information sought falls in anyone or more categories mentioned in Section 6, the incharge of the office shall reject the request and communicate the reasons for the rejection to the applicant as early as possible;

(c) if the incharge of the office is dealing with the

subject-matter but the information cannot be compiled without considerable financial expenditure or without considerable extra work, the incharge of the office may after recording the reasons in writing, send a regret reply to the applicant. The incharge of the office shall, however, supply any related information readily available.

(d) the incharge of the office may seek the assistance of any other officer as he may consider necessary for the proper discharge of his duties; and

(e) any officer whose assistance has been sought under clause *(d)* shall render all assistance to the incharge of the office seeking his assistance.

6. Restriction of right to information— (l) Notwithstanding anything hereinbefore contained, the following information shall be exempted from disclosure, namely:—

(a) information, the disclosure of which would prejudicially affect the sovereignty and integrity of India, security of the State, or conduct of international relations;

(b) information, the disclosure of which would prejudically affect public order and investigation of an offence, or

(c) information, the disclosure of which would prejudicially affect the conduct of Centre-State relations, including information exchanged in confidence between the Central and State Government or any of their authorities/ agencies;

(d) Cabinet papers including record of deliberations of the Council of Ministers;

(e) minutes of records of advice including legal advice, opinions of recommendations made by any officer of a public authority during the decision-

making process prior to the executive decision or policy formulation;

(f) information, the disclosure of which may result in the breach of privileges of Parliament or the Legislature of the State, or contravention of a lawful order of a court; and

(g) information held in consequence of having been supplied in confidence by a person who—

(i) gave the information under a guarantee that its confidentiality would be protected; or

(ii) was not under any legal obligation, whether actual or implied, to supply, and has not consented to its disclosure.

(2) The incharge of the office may, for reasons to be recorded in writing, withhold—

(a) information, the disclosure of which—

(i) would prejudicially affect the enforcement of any, law including detection, prevention, investigation or suppression of crime or contravention of any law or the apprehending of offenders and the operations of any intelligence organization;

(ii) would endanger the life or physical safety of any person, or identify the source offfiformation or assistance given in confidence for law enforcement or security purposes;

(iii) would prejudicially affect fair trial or adjudication of a pending case or the proceedings of any tribunal, public inquiry;

(iv) would reveal the existence or identity of a confidential record, or would prejudice future supply of information relating to violation or contravention of any law; and

(iv) may help or facilitate escape of any person from legal custody to affect his present security;

(b) information, the disclosure of which would prejudicially affect the Government's ability to manage the economy or the legitifi.1.ate economic and commercial interests of a public authority; or would use if; unfair gain or loss to any individual or organization; these would include trade and commercial secrets protected by law;

(c) personal information, the disclosure of which has no relationship to any public activity or which would cause unwanted invasion of the privacy of an individual;

(d) the record and information referred to in Sections 123 and 124 of the Evidence Act,. *Samvat* 1977 and, claimed privileges; and

(e) information on the following grounds also—

(i) that the request is too general or is of such nature that, having regard to the volume of information required to be retrieved or processes for fulfiling, it, it would involve disproportionate diversion of the resource of a public authority or would adversely interfere with the functioning of such authority:
Provided that, where access is being refused on the ground that the request is too general, it would be duty of the incharge, of office concerned to render help, as far as possible, to the persons seeking information to reframe his request in such a manner as may facilitate supply of information;

(ii) that the request relates to information that is required by law or convention to be published at a particular time;

(iii) that the request relates to information that is contained in published material for sale.

7. Third party information— Where an incharge of office intends to disclose information on a request made by a party which relates to or has been supplied by a third party and has been treated as confidential by that party, the incharge of office shall by notice to that third party invite representation against such proposed disclosure.

8. Act not to apply to certain organizations.—Nothing contained in this Act shall apply to intelligence and security organizations by whatever name called, discharging their functions as such under the Government.

9. Appeals.—

(1) Any person aggrieved by the order of the incharge of the office or any person who has not received required information within the time stipulated under Section 5, may appeal to the controlling officer, within thirty days of the decision rejecting, his request for information or the expiry of period stipulated under Section 5 for furnishing such information:

Provided that the controlling officer may entertain appeal after the expiry of the said period of thirty days, if it is satisfied that the appellant was prevented by sufficient cause from filing the appeal.

(2) A second appeal against the decision under sub-section (1) shall lie within 30-days such decision (the Government).

Provided that the Government may entertain appeal after the expiry of the said period of thirty days if it is satisfied that the appellant was prevented by sufficient cause from filing the appeal.

(3) The appeals preferred under sub-sections (1) and (2) shall be heard and decided expeditiously and by all means be disposed of within thirty days of presentation of appeal:

Provided that no order adversely affecting the person making the appeal shall be passed unless an opportunity of being heard is afforded to him.

(4) The appeal shall be accompanied with the proof of fee deposited or tendered in the manner provided in accordance with Section 10.

10. Fee—

(1) The request for seeking information under this Act shall be accompanied by a proof of payment of such fee as may be prescribed for furnishing of information.

(2) If requisite fee as prescribed under sub-section (1) is not paid for the required information, the information sought under Section 5 may not be made available.

(3) The appeal shall be accompanied with such fee, and be deposited and tendered in such manner, as may be prescribed.

11. Obligation of the Incharge of Office —

(1) Every incharge of the office shall have a duty to maintain all records in accordance with the procedure laid down under relevant law or Departmental manuals.

(2) While maintaining the record proper indexing, listing, numbering and paging of records shall be done and the same may be kept ready for access to information, subject to the provisions of this Act, to any citizen requesting for such access.

(3) Any person responsible for providing any information under this Act shall be personally liable for furnishing information within the period specified under this Act.

12. *Penalties*—Where any person responsible for making available information under this Act, fails without any r-easonable cause to furnish information sought by any citizen under the provisions of this Act within the time specified or furnishes any information which is false with regard to any material particulars and which he knows and has reasonable cause to believe it to be false or does not believe it to be true, he shall be liable, after such inquiry as may be required under rules pertaining to disciplinary action applicable to him, for imposition of such penalty as may be determined by the disciplinary authority under such rules.
13. Protection of action taken in good faith—No suit, prosecution or legal proceedings shall lie against any person for anything done or intended to be done in good faith in pursuance to the provisions of this Act or rules made thereunder.
14. Bar to the legal proceedings—No court shall entertain any suit, application or other proceedings in respect of any order made under this Act and no such order shall be called in question otherwise, than by way of appeal under this Act.
15. Power to make Rules—

    (1) The Government may make rules for carrying out the purposes of this Act.
    (2) All rules under this Act shall be laid, as soon as may be after they are made, before the two Houses of the State Legislature. If the State Legislature makes any modification in such rules, or resolves that any such rule should not be made, such rules thereafter have effect only in such modified form or be of no effect, as the case may be:
    Provided that any such modification or annulment shall be without prejudice to the validity of anything previously done thereunder.

Annexure - III

The Delhi Right to information Act, 2001
(Delhi Act No.7 of 2001)

14 May, 2001

An Act to make provision for securing right to information in the National Capital Territory of Delhi and for matters relating thereto.

Be it enacted by the Legislative Assembly of the National Capital Territory of Delhi in the Fifty-second Year of the Republic of India as follows:

1. Short title and commencement—

(1) This Act may be called the Delhi Right to Information Act, 2001.

(2) It shall come into force on such date as the Government may, by notification in the official Gazette, appoint.

2. Definitions—In this Act, unless there is anything repugnant in the subject or contexts—

(a) *"competent authority"* means any authority or officer notified by the Government from time to time in official Gazette for the purpose of this Act;

(b) *"electronic form"* with reference to information means any information generated, sent, received or stored in media, magnetic, optical, computer memory, microfilm, computer generated micro fiche or similar device;

(c) *"Government"* means the Lt. Governor referred in Article 239-AA of the Consti-tution";

(d) *"information"* means any material or information relating to the affairs of the National Capital Territory of Delhi except matters with respect to Entries I, 2 and 18 of the State List and Entries 64, 65 and 66 of that list in so far as they relate to the said Entries 1,2 and 18 embodied in the Seventh Schedule of the Constitution;

(e) *"Lt. Governor"* means the Lt. Governor of the National Capital Territory of Delhi appointed by the President under Article 239 of the Constitution;

(f) *"prescribed"* means as prescribed in rules;

(g) *Public authority"* means any authority or body established or constituted—

(i) by or under the Constitution;

(ii) by any law made by the Government and includes any other body owned, controlled or substantially financed by funds provided directly or indirectly by the Government;

(h) *"Public Grievances Commission"* means the Public Grievances Commission set up by the Government *vide,* their. Resolution No. 4/14/94-AR dated the 25th September, 1997 as amended from time to time;

(i) *"right to information"* means the right of the access to information and includes the inspection of works, documents, records, taking notes and extracts and obtaining certified copies of documents or records, or taking samples of material.

3. Right to information—Subject to the provisions of this

Act, every citizen shall have right to obtain information from a competent authority.

4. Obligations on public authorities.-Every public authority shall—

(*a*) maintain all its records, in such a manner and form as is consistent with its operational requirements duly catalogued and indexed;

(*b*) publish at such intervals as may be prescribed by the Government—

(*i*) the particulars of its organisation, functions and duties;

(*ii*) the powers and duties of its officers and employees and the procedure followed by them in the decision-making process;

(*iii*) the norms set by the public authority for the discharge of its functions;

(iv) laws, bye-laws, rules, regulation, instructions, manuals and other categories of records under its control used by its employees for discharging its functions;

(*v*) the details of facilities available to citizens for obtaining information; and

(*vi*) the name, designation and other particulars of the competent authority;

(*c*) publish all relevant facts concerning important decisions and policies that affect the public while announcing such decisions and policies;

(*d*) give reasons for its decisions, whether administrative or quasi- judicial to those affected by such decisions; and

(*e*) before initiating any project, publish or communicate to the public generally or to the 5.
Procedure for supply of information—

(1) A person desiring information shall make a request in writing or through electronic form, to the competent authority giving the particulars of the matter relating to which he seeks information:
Provided that where a person *cannot* for valid reasons make a request in writing the competent authority may either accept an oral request which *may* subsequently be reduced in writing or render reasonable assistance to such person in making a written request.

(2) Upon receipt of an application requesting for an information the competent authority shall consider it and furnish the information required by the applicant or pass orders thereon refusing the request as soon as practicable but normally within fifteen days and in any case within thirty days from the date of receipt of application.

(3) The information shall be supplied in writing either in English or in the official language.

(4) Where a request is rejected under sub-section *(2)1* the competent authority shall communicate to the person making the request—

(i) the reasons for such rejection;
(ii) the period within which the appeal against such rejection may be preferred;
(iii) the particulars of the appellate authority.

6. Restrictions on right to information.—The competent authority *may* for reasons to be recorded in writing withhold—

(a) the information disclosure or contents of which will prejudicially affect the sovereignty and

integrity of India or security of the National Capital Territory of Delhi or international relations or which leads to incitement to an offence;

(b) the information relating to an individual or other information, the disclosure of which would constitute a dear and unwarranted invasion of personal privacy and has no relationship to any activity of the Government or which will not subserve any public interest;

(c) papers containing advice, opinion recommendations or minutes submitted to the Lt. Governor for discharge of his constitutional functions and any information, disclosure of which would prejudicially affect the conduct of the Centre/State/Union Territory relations, including information exchanged in confidence between the Centre and the Government or any of their authorities or agencies;

(d) trade and commercial secrets or any other information protected by law;

(e) information whose release would constitute a breach of privilege of Parliament or Legislative Assembly of the National Capital Territory of Delhi:

Provided that the competent authority shall before withholding information under this clause, refer the matter to the Legislative Assembly Secretariat for determination of the issue and according to the advice tendered by that Secretariat:

Provided further that no appeal shall be under Section 7 against an order withholding supply of information under this clause;

(f) information whose disclosure would endanger the life or physical safety of any person OT identify the source of information or assistance given in confidence for law enforcement or security purposes orin public interest:

Provided that the information which cannot ·be

denied to the Legislative Assembly of the National Capital Territory of Delhi, shall not be denied to any person;

(g) minutes or records of advice including legal advice, opinions or recommendations made by an officer of a public authority during the making process prior to the executive decision or policy formulation;

(h) Cabinet papers including records of the deliberations of the Council of Ministers, Secretaries and other officers.

7. Appeal—

(1) Any person aggrieved by an order of the competent authority or any person who has not received any order from the competent authority within thirty working days, may appeal to the Public Grievances Commission.

(2) The decision of the Public Grievances Commission shall be final.

(3) No order adversely affecting any person shall be passed, except after giving that person a reasonable opportunity of being heard.

(4) Every appeal shall be disposed of as expeditiously as possible and endeavour shall be made to dispose of the appeal within thirty days from the date on which it is presented.

8. Obligation on competent authority—Every competent authority shall be under a duty to maintain all its records, as per its operational requirements, duly catalogued and indexed, and grant access to information, subject to the provisions of this Act, to any citizen requesting for such access.

9. Penalties—

(1) Any person responsible for providing any information under this Act shall be personally

liable for furnishing the information within the period specified.

(2) Where a person responsible to supply information fails to furnish the information asked for under this Act within the time specified or furnishes any information which is false in any material particulars, and which he knows or has reasonable cause to believe to be false or does not believe it to be true, he shall be liable, after such inquiry as may be required under the service rules pertaining to disciplinary addition applicable to him, for imposition of such penalty as may be determined by the disciplinary authority under such rules or as prescribed in the Rules.

10. State Council for Right to Information—

(1) The Government shall by notification in the Official Gazette, establish with effect from such date as specified in the notification, a Council to be known as State Council for Right to Information.

(2) The State Council shall consist of the following members, namely:—

(a) the Chief Minister, Government of National Capital Territory of Delhi shall be its Chairman;

(b) the Minister-in-charge of the Department of Administrative Reforms in the Government shall be its member:
Provided if the Chief Minister is the Minister In-charge of Administrative Reforms Department, then the Finance Minister shall be the Member;

(c) such number of other officials not exceeding ten of which three member shall be elected representatives of the Legislative Assembly of the NCT of Delhi and of which 'one shall be woman to be nominated by the Speaker of Assembly of NCT of Delhi and non-official members not exceeding ten representing such interests as may be prescribed by the Government.

(3) The time and place of the meeting of the Council shall be as the Chairman may decide and it shall observe such procedures as may be laid down by the Council to transact its business.

(4) The object of the State Council shall be to promote the right to information in the National Capital Territory of Delhi and it shall deal with all matters related to Right to Information, such as—

(*a*) review of the operation of this Act and the rules made there under;

(*b*) review of the administrative arrangements and procedures to secure for citizens the fullest possible access to information;

(c) research and documentation as regards management of information with a view to improve the extent and accuracy of information being made available under this Act; and

(*d*) to advise the Government on all matters related to the right to information, including training, development and orientation of employees to bring in a culture of openness and transparency.

11. Act to have overriding effect—The provisions of this Act shall have effect notwithstanding anything inconsistent therewith contained in any other enactment of the Legislative Assembly of Delhi for the time being in force.

12. Protection of action taken in good faith—No suit, prosecution or other legal proceedings shall lie against,

any person for anything done in good faith or intended to be done in pursuance of this Act.

13. Charging of fees—The competent authority shall charge such for supply of information as may be prescribed by rules, but which shall not exceed the cost of processing and making available of the information.

14. Laying of Annual Report of State Council—The Chairperson shall cause to be laid on the Table of the House Annual Report of the State Council.

15. Power to make rules.—

(1) The Government may, by notification in the Official Gazette, make rules to carry out the purposes of this Act.

(2) In particular, and without prejudice to the generality of the foregoing power, such rules may provide for all or any of the following matters, namely:

(*a*) the interval at which particulars and other material and information shall be published by the public authorities;

(*b*) the composition of the State Council with reference to the interest to be represented therein;

(*c*) prescription of fee to be charged for supply of information; and

(*d*) any matter which is to be, or may be prescribed under this Act.

(3) Every rule made under this Act shall be laid, as soon as may be after it is made, before the House of the Legislative Assembly of the Capital Territory of Delhi while it is in session, for a total period of thirty days which may be comprised in one session or in two or more successive sessions, and if, before the expiry of the session immediately following the session or the successive sessions aforesaid,

the House agrees in making any modification in the rule or the House agrees that the rule should not be made; the rule shall thereafter have effect only in such modified form or be of no effect, as the case may be; so, however, that any such modification or annulment shall be without prejudice to the validity of anything previously done under that rule.

16. Removal of difficulties.—

(1) If any difficulty arises in giving effect to the provisions of this Act, the Government may, by general or special order published in the Official Gazette, make such provision not inconsistent with the provisions of this Act as appear to it to be necessary or expedient for the purpose of removing difficulty:

Provided that not such order shall be made after the expiration of two years from the commencement of this Act.

(2) Every order made under this section shall, as soon as may be after it is made, be laid before the Legislative Assembly of the National Capital Territory of Delhi.

* The Delhi RTI Act, 2001is mainly for redressal of grievances, therefore, an appeal against its contravention goes to Public Grievances Commission. After the RTI Act, 2005, Delhi Government has neither framed RTI Rules, 2005, nor it has constituted Delhi Information Commission instead the Central Government. RTI Rules, 2005 are applicable to it and Central Information Commission handles the Delhi State RTI cases.

Annexure - IV

Right to Information Rules : Central and States

**The Central Government RIT
(Regulation of Fee and Cost) Rules, 2005
Dated: 16th September, 2005
F.No.34012/8 (S)/2005-Estt.b**

In exercise of the powers conferred by clauses (b) and (c) of sub-section (2) of section 27 of the Right to Information Act, 2005 (22 of 2005), the Central Government makes the following rules, namely:—

1. Short title and commencement:—

   (1) These rules may be called the Right to Information (Regulation of Fee and Cost) Rules, 2005.
   (2) They shall come into force on the date of their publication in the official gazette.

2. Definitions:—
   In the rules, unless the context otherwise requires—

   (a) "Act" means the Right to Information Act, 2005.
   (b) "section" means section of the Act.
   (c) all other words and expressions used herein but not defined an defined in the Act shall have the meanings assigned to them in the Act.

3. A request for obtaining information under sub-section (1) of section 6 shall be accompanied by an application fee of rupees ten by way of cash against proper receipt or by demand draft or bankers cheque payable to the Accounts Officer of the public authority .

4. For providing the information under sub-section (1) of section 7, the fee shall be charged by way of cash against proper receipt or by demand draft or bankers cheque payable to the Account Officer of the public authority at the following rates:—

   (a) rupees two for each page (in A4 and A3 size paper) created or copied.
   (b) actual charge or cost price of a copy in large size paper;
   (c) actual cost or price for samples or models; and
   (d) for inspection of records, no fee for the first hour and a fee of rupees five for each subsequent hour (or fraction thereof).

5. For providing the information under sub-section (5) of section 7, the fee shall be charged by way of cash against proper receipt or by demand draft or bankers cheque payable to the Accounts Officer of the public authority at the following rates:—

   (a) for information provided in diskette floppy rupees fifty per diskette or floppy; and
   (b) for information provided in the printed form at the price fixed for publication or rupees two per page of photocopy for extracts from the publication.

Note : These rules are also followed by Delhi Government.

The Central Information Commission (Appeal Procedure) Rules, 2005

Notification
Dated: 28th October, 2005
No. F.No. 1/4/2005-AR

In exercise of the powers conferred by clauses (e) and (f) of sub-section (2) of section 27 of the Right to Information Act 2005 Central Act No. 22 of 2005, the Central Government hereby makes the following rules, namely:—

1. Short title and commencement: —

   (1) These rules may be called the Central Information Commission (Appeal Procedure) Rules 2005.
   (2) They shall come into force on the date of their publication in the official gazette.

2. Definitions:
   In the rules, unless the context otherwise requires.

   (a) "Act" means the Right to Information Act, 2005.
   (b) "Section" means section of the Act.
   (c) "Commission" means the Central Information Commission
   (d) Words and expressions used herein and not defined but defined in the Act, shall have the meaning respectively assigned to them in that Act.

3. Contents of Appeal:—
   An appeal to the Commission shall contain the following information namely:—

   (i) name and address of the appellant;

(ii) name and address of the Central Public Information Officer against the decision of whom the appeal is preferred;
(iii) particulars of the order including number, if any, against which the appeal is preferred;
(iv) brief facts leading to the appeal;
(v) if the appeal is preferred against deemed refusal, the particulars of the application, including number and date and name and address of the Central Public Information Officer to whom the application was made;
(vi) prayer or relief sought;
(vii) grounds for the prayer or relief;
(viii) verification by the appellant; and
(ix) any other information which the Commission may deem necessary for deciding the appeal.

4. Documents to accompany the appeal: —
Every appeal made to the Commission shall be accompanied by the following documents namely: —

(i) self attested copies of the orders or documents against which the appeal is being preferred;
(ii) copies of documents relied upon by the appellant and referred to in the appeal; and
(iii) an index of the documents referred to in the appeal.

5. Procedure in deciding appeal: —
In deciding the appeal Commission may: —

(i) hear oral or written evidence on oath or on affidavit from concerned or interested person;
(ii) Peruse or inspect documents, public records or copies thereof;
(iii) inquire through authorized officer further details or facts;

(iv) hear Central Public Information Officer, Central Assistant Central Public Information Officer or such Senior Officer who decide the first appeal, or such person against whom the complaint is made, as the case may be;

(v) hear third party; and

(vi) receive evidence on affidavit from Central Public Information Officer, Central Assistant Public Information Officer, such Senior Officer who decided the first appeal, such person against whom the complaint lies or the third party.

6. Mode of Servicing of notice by Commission.
Notice to be issued by the Commission may be served in any of the following modes: —

(i) service by the party itself;
(ii) by hand delivery (*dasti*) through process server;
(iii) by registered post with acknowledgement due; or
(iv) through Head of the office or Department.

7. Personal presence of the appellant or complainant:—

(1) The appellant or the complainant, as the case may be, shall in every case be informed of the date of hearing at least seven clear days before that date.

(2) The appellant or the complainant, as the case may be, may at his discretion at the time of hearing of the appeal or complaint by the Commission be present in person or through his duly authorized representative or may opt, not to be present.

(3) Where the Commission is satisfied that the circumstances exist due to which the appellant or the complainant, as the case may be, is being prevented from attending the hearing of the Commission, then, the Commission may afford the appellant or the complainant, as ,the case may be, another opportunity of being heard before a final

decision is taken or take any other appropriate action as it may deem fit.

(4) The appellant or the complainant, as the case may be, may seek the assistance of any person in the process of the appeal while presenting his points and the person representing him may not be a legal practitioner.

8. Order of the Commission:

Order of the Commission shall be pronounced in open proceedings and be in writing duly authenticated by the Registrar or any other officer authorized by the Commission for this purpose.

Note : Central Information Commission also acts as Information Commission for Delhi Government.

Andhra Pradesh RTI Rules, 2005

Notification
Dated: 13.10.2005
G.O.Ms. 454

In exercise of the powers conferred by clauses (b) and (c) of sub-section (2) of section 27 of the Right to Information Act, 2005 (Central Act 22 of 2005). Government of Andhra Pradesh hereby makes the following rules, namely: —

RULES

1. Short title and commencement

   (i) These Rules may be called the Andhra Pradesh Right to Information (Regulation of fee and cost) Rules, 2005.
   (ii) They shall come into force from the date of publication in the Official Gazette.

2. Definitions
   In these rules, unless the context otherwise requires: -

   (a) 'State' means, the State of Andhra Pradesh;
   (b) 'Act' means the Right to Information Act, 2005;
   (c) 'Section' means section of the Act;
   (d) 'Commission' means, the State Information Commission, constituted under Section 15(I) of the Act;
   (e) All other words and expressions used here in but not defined and defined in the Act shall have the meanings assigned to them in the Act.

3. Applications fee to accompany request for obtaining Information. A request for obtaining information under sub-section (I) of section 6 shall be accompanied by an application fee by way cf cash or by demand draft or by bankers Cheque payable to the Accounts Officer or any other duly authorized officer of the Public Authority, against proper receipt, at the following rates: —

(a) In respect of public authorities at the Village Level – no fee;
(b) In respect of public authorities at Mandal Level- Rs. 5 per application.
(c) In respect of public authorities other than those covered above Rs. 10 per application.

4. Fee to be charged for providing information.
Fee for providing information under sub-section (1) of sub-section (5) of Section 7, a fee shall be charged by the way of cash or demand draft or bankers cheque payable to the Accounts Officer of any other duly authorized officer of the Public Authority against proper receipt at the following rates:—

(A) Priced Material:—
Publications , printed matter, text, maps, plans, floppies, CDs, samples, models or material in any of the form, which are prices, the sale price thereof;
(B) Other than priced material:

(i) Material re-printed or text form (in A 4 or A 3 size paper) Rs. 2 per page per copy.
(ii) Material re-printed or text form in larger than A 4 and A 3 size paper— actual cost thereof;

(iii) Maps and plans actual cost thereof;

(iv) Information in Electronics format viz. Floppy, CD or DVD

  (a) Rupees fifty for Floppy of 1.44 MB;

  (b) Rupees one hundred for CD of 700 MB; and

  (c) Rupees two hundred for CD (DVD)

(v) Samples and Models— actual cost thereof;

(vi) Inspection of records— no fee for the first hour; and a fee of rupees five for each fifteen minutes (or fraction thereof) thereafter;

(vii) Material to be sent by post— the actual postal charges in addition to the charges payable as per these rules.

The Arunachal Pradesh Right to Information Rules, 2005

Notification

Dated: 15th September, 2005

No. Om-43/2003

In exercise of the powers conferred by sub-section (1) of section 28 of the Right to Information Act, 2005 (Act No. 22 of 2005), the Governor of Arunachal Pradesh hereby makes the following rules, namely:

1. Short title and commencement: —

(1) These rules may be called the Arunachal Pradesh Right to Information Rules, 2005.

(2) They shall come into force from the date of their publication in the official Gazette.

2. Definition:

(1) In these rules, unless the context otherwise requires:—

(a) 'Act' means the Right to Information Act, 2005 (Act No. 22 of 2005);

(b) 'Competent Authority' means the Competent Authority to accept fee prescribed under these rules;

(c) 'Form' means the 'Form' appended to these rules;

(d) 'Section' means a section of the Act.

(2) Words and expression used but not defied in these rules shall have the meaning as assigned to them in the Act.

3. Application for seeking information: — Any person seeking information under the Act shall make an application in Form 'A' to the competent authority and deposit application fees as per rule 8 with the authorized person. The competent authority shall duly acknowledge the application as provided in Form 'A'. Provided that a person who makes a request through electronic form shall ensure that the requisite fee is deposited in Treasury Challan under the Head of Account .0070 – other administrative service within seven days of his request sent through electronic form, failing which his application shall be treated as withdrawn by the applicant.

4. Disposal of application by the competent authority:—

(1) If the requested information does not fall within the jurisdiction of the competent authority, it shall order return of the application to the applicant in Form 'B' as soon as practicable, normally within fifteen days and in any case within thirty days of the receipt of the application.

(2) If the requested information falls within the competent authority's jurisdiction and also in one or more of the categories of restrictions listed in section 8 of the Act, the competent authority, on being satisfied, will issue the rejection order in Form 'C' as practicable, normally within fifteen days and any case, within thirty days from the date of the receipt of the application.

(3) If the requested information falls within the competent authority's jurisdiction but not in one or more of the categories listed in section 8 of the Act, the competent authority, on being so satisfied, shall supply the information to the applicant in Form 'D', falling within his jurisdiction. In case,

the information sought is party outside the jurisdiction of the competent authority or partly falls in the categories listed in section 8 of the Act, the competent authority shall supply only such information as is permissible under the Act and is within its own jurisdiction and reject the remaining part giving reasons thereof.

(4) The information shall be supplied as soon as practicable, normally within fifteen days and in any case within thirty days from the date of the receipt of the application on deposit of the balance amount, if any, in Treasury Challan and original copy of the Challan is submitted to the authorized person, before collection of information. A proper acknowledgement shall be obtained from the applicant in token of receipt of information.

5. Appeal:

(1) Any person —

(a) who fails to get a response in Form 'B' or Form 'C' from the competent authority within thirty days of submission of Form 'A' or

(b) who is aggrieved by the response received within the prescribed period, may appeal in Form 'E' to the State Information Commission and deposit fee for appeal as per rule 8 in Treasury Challan and original copy of the Challan is submitted with the authorized person.

(2) On receipt of the appeal, the State Information Commission shall acknowledge the receipt of appeal and after giving the applicant an opportunity of being heard, shall endeavor to dispose it of within thirty days from the date on which it is presented and send a copy of the

decision to the competent authority concerned.

(3) Where the appeal is filed on the ground specified in clause (a) of sub-rule (1) of this rule, no appeal shall be admissible after sixty days of the submission of the application in Form 'A'

(4) In case the appeal is allowed, the information shall be supplied to the applicant by the competent authority within such period as ordered by the appellate authority. This period shall not exceed thirty days from the date of the receipt of the order.

6. Penalties :

(1) Whoever being bound to supply information under sub-section (1) of section 20 of the Act fails to furnish the information asked for under the Act within the time specified or fails to communicate the rejection order under section 9 of the Act, shall be liable to pay a penalty of fifty rupees per day for the delayed period beyond thirty days subject to a maximum of five hundred rupees per application filed under rule 3.

(2) Where the information supplied is found to be false in any material particular and which the person bound to supply it knows or has supplying the information shall liable to pay a penalty of one thousand rupees per application, filed under rule 3.

7. Suo moto Publication of Information by public authorities:

(1) The public authority shall suo-moto publish information as per sub-section (3) of section 26 of the Act by publishing booklets, folders and pamphlets at the following intervals: —

1. Particular of its organization, functions and duties — Once in five years.
2. Powers and duties of its officers and employees and the procedure followed by them in the decision-making process — Once in two years.
3. Norms set by the public authority for the discharge of its functions — Once in two years.
4. Laws, bye-laws, rules, regulations, instruction, manuals and other categories of records under its control used by its employees for discharging its functions — Once in five years.
5. (1) Details of facilities available to citizens for obtaining information — Annually.
   (2) Such information shall also be made available to the public through information counters, medium of internet and display on notice board at conspicuous places in the office of the competent authority and the State Public Information Commission

8. Charging of Fees :

(1) The competent authority shall charge the fee at the following rates, namely: —

(A) Application Fees

(i) Information relating to tender documents/ bids/quotation/Business contracts — Five hundred rupees per application.

(ii) Information other than (i) above — Fifty rupees per application

(B) Other Fees: —

1. Where the information is available in the

form of a priced publication price so fixed.

2. For other than priced publication — Five rupees per page.
3. The appellate authority shall charge a fee of fifty rupees per appeal through Treasury Challan.
4. The fees charged shall be depsited through Treasury Challan in the Head of Account "0070-Other administrative charge" by the applicant.

9. State Information Commission: —

(1) The State Information Commission shall be constituted by the State Government by a separate notification.

10. Maintenance of Records: —

(1) The competent authority shall maintain records of all applicants received for supply of information and fee charges and deposited in the Government account.

(2) The State Information Commission shall maintain records of all appeals filed before it and fee charged and deposited in the Government account.

The Assam Right to Information Rules , 2005

NOTIFICATION
Dated: 2nd January, 2006
No. AR.78/2005/142

In exercise of powers conferred by clause (b) and (c) of sub-section (2) of section 27 of the "Right to Information Act, 2005 (22 of 2005)" enacted by Parliament, the State Government hereby makes the following rules, namely: —

1. Short title and commencement:

(1) These rules may be called the "Assam Right to Information (Regulation of Fee and Cost) Rules, 2005".
(2) They shall come into force on the date of their publication in the Official Gazette.

2. Definitions:
In these rules, unless the context otherwise requires:—

(a) "Act" means the "Right to Information Act, 2005" enacted by Parliament:
(b) 'Authorized person' means a person nominated by the "State Public Information Officer and Assistant State Public Information Officer as defined under Section 2 (m) of the Act" or "Appellate Authority under Section 19 (1) of the Act", as the case may be, to accept fee prescribed under these rules;
(c) "Section" means section of the Act; and
(d) all other words and expressions used herein but not defined and defined in the Act shall have he meaning assigned to them in the Act.

3. A request for obtaining information under sub-section (1) of section 6 shall be accompanied by an application fee of rupees ten by way of cash against proper receipt or by demand draft or banker's cheque payable to the Authorized Officer of the public authority.
4. For providing the Information under sub-section (1) of section 7, the fee shall be charged by way of cash against proper receipt or by demand draft or banker's cheque payable to the Authorized Officer of the public authority at the following rates: —

   (a) rupees two for each page (in A-4 or A-3 size paper) created or copied;
   (b) actual charge or cost price of a copy in larger size paper;
   (c) actual cost or price for samples or model; and
   (d) for inspection of records, no fee for the first hour; and a fee of rupees five for each fifteen minutes (or fraction thereof) thereafter.

5. For providing the Information under sub-section (5) of section 7 the fee shall be charged by way of cash against receipt or by demand draft or banker's cheque payable to the Authorized Officer of the public authority at the following rates:

   (a) for information provided in diskete or floppy Rupees fifty per diskette or floppy; and
   (b) for information provided in printed form at the price fixed for such publication or Rupees two per page of photocopy for extracts from the publication.

Assam State Information Commission
RTI Rules, 2005
NOTIFICATION
No. AR. 87/2005/89

In exercise of powers conferred by clauses (e) of sub-section (2) of section 27 of the "Right to Information Act, 2005 (Central Act No.22 of 2005)" the State Government hereby makes the following rules, namely :

1. Short title and commencement: —

   (i) These rules may be called the Assam State Information Commission (Appeal Procedure) Rules, 2005,

   (ii) They shall come into force on the date of their publication in the official Gazette

2. Definitions:
   In these rules, unless the context otherwise requires:—

   (a) 'Act' means the Right to Information Act, 2005;

   (b) 'Commission' means the Assam State Information Commission:

   (c) "Section" means section of the Act.

   (d) Words and expressions used herein and not defined but defined in the Act shall have the meanings respectively assigned to them in that Act.

3. Contents of Appeal: An appeal to the Commission shall contain the following information, namely :—

(i) name and address of the appellant;
(ii) name and address of the Public Information Officer;
(iii) particulars of the order against which he appeal is made including number, date and the State Public Information Officer who passed the order;
(iv) Brief facts leading to the appeal;
(v) Prayer or relief sought;
(vi) Grounds for the prayer or relief;
(vii) Provisions of the Act or the rules;
(viii) verification by the appellant; and
(ix) any other information which the Commission may deem necessary for deciding the appeal.

4. Documents to accompany appeal: - Every appeal made to the Commission shall be accompanied by the following documents, namely: —

(i) Attested true copy of the Order against which the appeal is being preferred;
(ii) copies of documents relied upon by the appellant and referred to in the appeal; and
(iii) an index of the documents referred to in the appeal.

5. Procedure in deciding appeal:
In deciding the appeal the Commission shall—

(i) hear oral or written evidence on oath or on affidavit from concerned or interest person;
(ii) peruse or inspect documents, public records or copies thereof;
(iii) inquire through authorized officer, Assistant State Public Information Officer or such Senior Officer who decide the first appeal, as the case may be;
(iv) hear third party; and
(vi) receive evidence on affidavits from State Public Information Officer, Assistant State Public Information Officer, such Senior Officer who decided the first appeal or third party.

6. Service of notice by Commission:
Notice to be issued by the Commission may be served in any of the following modes, namely:—

(i) service by the party itself;
(ii) by hand delivery through Process Server;
(iii) by registered post with acknowledgement due; and
(iv) through Head of officer or Department.

7. Signing of Order—Order of the Commission pronounced in open proceedings shall be in writing and authenticated by the Registrar or any other officer authorized by the Commission for the purpose.

The Bihar Right to Information Rules, 2005

NOTIFICATION

Dated: 15 dated 28.06.06.

No. 8/Su.A. 15.02/2006 – Ka- 6161

In exercise of the powers conferred by section 27 of the Right to Information Act, 2005 (22 of 2005), the Government of Bihar hereby makes the following rules, for implementation of the provisions of the said act, namely:

1. Short title, extent and commencement:

   1. These rules may be called the Bihar Right to Information Rules 2006
   2. hese rules extend to the whole State of Bihar
   3. It shall come into force with immediate effect.

2. Definition (1) In these rules, unless, the context otherwise required—

   (a) Act means the Right to Information Act, 2005
   (b) Commission means from State Information Commission constituted under Section 15 of the act.
   (c) From means from appended to these rules.
   (d) Fee means rates determined under schedule 1 of these rules which may be redetermined by the State Government by a separate notification from time to time.
   (e) Public Information Officer means State Public Information Officer as designated under sub-section 1 of section 5 of the act and includes State Assistant Public Information .
   (f) State Government means the Government of Bihar.

3.Application for obtaining information:

(1) A person who desired to obtain information shall make an application in form a accompanied with the prescribed fees, or through the e medium to public Information officer. The receipt of the application shall be given to the applicant in form B. The fees may be paid in cash wherever facility for cash receipt is available otherwise by Demand Draft or by pay order or in the form of non-judicial stamp.

(2) The applicant applying through the e-medium shall have to pay the fees within seven days from the date of application, failing which the application shall be deemed to be withdrawn.

(3) The Public Information Officer shall inform the applicant in form C regarding other fees and charges to be paid as determined by the Government.

(4) Provided that no fees and charges shall be payable by a person belonging to the below poverty line familied provided that such person enclosed with the application, certified copy of the below poverty line card or a certificate issued in that behalf by the district magistrate of the concerned district or sub-divisional officer of the concerned sub division.

(5) The amount received as charges and fees shall be deposited in the receipt head prescribed by the finance department.

4. Disposal of the application

(1) Ihe Public Information Officer shall be required to provide the information sought for, to the applicant within thirty days of the receipt of the request inform D or inform the application about

rejection of application in Form F taking into consideration the provisions of the Section 8 and 9 of the Act.

Provided that the applicant shall be given reasons for not giving the information which is exempted from disclosure under section 8 or under section 9 of the act.

Provided further that where the information sought for concerns the life or liberty of a person the Public Information Officer shall be required to provide such information within forty-eight hours of the receipt of the application and inform the application and inform the applicant immediately about such transfer.

5. Rate of Fees: The rates of fees and other charges for obtain required information and documents shall be such as determined under schedule 1. The State Government may from time to time predetermines the fees and charges by amendment in schedule 1 through a notification published in the official gazette.

6. Appeal: Any person aggrieved by a decision of the Public Information officer in Form D or does not received any decision as the case may be he may prefer an appeal in From G within thirty days from the date of receipt or non-receipt or non-receipt of such decision, to the appellate authority appointment by the State Government in this behalf.

(2) The application aggrieved by an order of the appellate authority under sub-rule 1 may prefer the second appeal to the State Information Commission within ninety days from thedate of the receipt of the appellate authority giving following details.

(i) Name and address of the applicant.

(ii) Name and office address of the Public Information Officer.
(iii) Number date and details of the order aginst which the second appeal is filed.
(iv) Brief facts leading to second appeal.
(v) Ground for appeal.
(vi) Verification by the appellant.
(vii) Any information which Commission may deem necessary for deciding the appeal.

(3) Every appeal made to the Commission shall be accompanied by the certified copy of the order against which second appeal is preferred.

(4) While deciding appeal the commission may:

(i) take a oral or written evidence on oath or on affidavit,
(ii) evaluate the record;
(iii) inquire through the authorized officer further detail or truthfulness;
(iv) summon the public information officer or the appellate authority who has heard the first appeal;
(v) hear the third party and

(5) The Commission shall serve the notice in any one of the following modes—

(i) service by the party itself.
(ii) by hand delivery after taking receipt;
(iii) by registered post with acknowledgement due or;
(iv) through the Head of Department or its subordinate office;

(6) The commission shall after hearing the parties to

the appeal, pronounce in open proceedings its decision and issue a written order which shall be authenticated by the Registrar or such officer as may be authorized by the Commission in this behalf.

7. Maintenance of records— The Public Information Officer shall maintain the records in respect of the application received for information and fees collected for giving the information.
8. The department appellate authority will maintain the records in respect of all appeals received and disposed off.
9. Miscellaneous — The forms as prescribed under these rules need not be in authorized reprinted stationery, but in any formal neatly typed, handwritten or in electronic form containing essential details prescribed in the form.

The Chhattisgarh RTI Rules, 2005

NOTIFICATION

Dated: 09 March, 2006

No. F2-10/2006/1/6

In exercise of the powers conferred by sub-section (1) of read with sub-section (9) of section 7 of the Right to Information Act, 2005 (No. 22 of 2005) the State Government hereby makes the following Rules namely :

Rules

1. Short title and commencement :

   (1) Short title and commencement:— these rules may be called the Chhattisgarh Right to Information (fees and charged) Rules, 2006

   (2) It shall come into force from the date of its Publication of the Official Gazette.

2. Definitions:— In the rules, unless the context otherwise requires: —

   (a) "Act" means the Right to Information Act, 2005 (No. 22 of 2005)

   (b) "Section" means section of the Act.

   (c) The words and expressions used but not defined in these rules carry of the provisions of the Act.

3. Information sought under the Act, shall be provided as described hereunder:

   (A) For information sought by persons below poverty line :—

(i) If the information sought relates to his/her life then the information will be provided in the form in which it is demanded.

(ii) If the information sought is not pertaining to self but If the information can be given in 50 photocopied pages (of A4 size) or the cost of production of information is within Rs. 100 (Rupees one hundred only) then the sought information will be provided in the form it is sought.

(iii) If the information, sought involves photocopying of more than 50 pages or the cost of production exceeds Rs. 100 (Rupees one hundred only) then by recording reasons under Section 7(9) of the Act the applicant will be requested to inspect the records/files in the office.

(B) For the information sought in question-answer form (for non-BPL people)

(i) If the information pertains to individual life of the applicant then the information will be provided in the form demanded. But the cost of such information produced will be Rs. 100 (Rupees one hundred only) per page.and

(ii) The cost of producing information by considering cost of human resources computer time and other resources or the cost of photocopying the records from which such information will be prepared shall be calculated. The applicant shall be communicated to deposit the cost of his/her choice. The information will be provided in the form as per the choice of fee deposit exercised by the applicant. Otherwise inspection of file/records will be allowed.

4. The fee for inspection of file for first hour which was free till date shall be now Rs. 50 (Rupees fifty only). Details of Fee and Costs—
Application — Rs. 10; Mode of Payment — cash against receipt/treasury challan. Appeal fees–Cash or non-judicial stamp paper; (A-4/ A-3) paper created or photo copies - Rs. 2 per page; Publication and printed form- Actual cost fixed; Large size paper -Actual cost price; Floppy/ CD/ Diskette or any other electronic mode - Rs. 50 per item; First Appeal Fee - Rs. 50 (Rs. 75 where appeal is made by post); Second Appeal- Rs. 100 (Rs. 125 where it made by post)

The Goa State Information Commission
Right to Information Rules, 2005
NOTIFICATION
February 16, 2006
No: D1/INF/RTI/BILL/2005/6475

In exercise of the powers conferred by Section 27 of the Right to Information Act, 2005 (Central Act 22 of 2005), the Government of Goa hereby makes the following rules, namely:—

1. Short title and commencement —

   (1) These rules may be called the Goa State Information Commission (Appeal Procedure) Rules, 2006.
   (2) They shall come into force from the date of their publication in the Official Gazette.

2. Definitions – In these rules, unless the context other wise requires—

   (a) "Act" means the Right to Information Act, 2005 (Central Act No. 22 of 2005);
   (b) "Section" means a section of the Act;
   (c) "Commission" means the State Information Commission;
   (d) words and expressions used herein and not defined but defined in the Act, shall have the same meaning respectively assigned to them in the Act.

3. Contents of appeal — An appeal to the Commission shall contain the following information, namely :—

(i) name and address of the appellant;
(ii) name an address of the State Public Information Officer against whose decision the appeal is preferred;
(iii) particulars of the order including number, if any, against which the appeal is preferred;
(iv) brief facts leading to the appeal.
(v) If the appeal is preferred against deemed refusal, the particulars of the application, including number and date as also the name and address of the State Public Information Officer to whom the application was made;
(vi) prayer or relief sought;
(vii) grounds for the prayer or relief;
(viii) verification by the appellant; and
(ix) any other information which the Commission may deem necessary for deciding the appeal.

4. Documents to accompany appeal — Every appeal made to the Commission shall be accompanied by the following documents, namely :—

(i) self-attested copies of the Orders or documents against which the appeal is being preferred, unless the appeal is preferred against deemed refusal;
(ii) copies of documents relied upon by the appellant and referred to in the appeal; and
(iii) an index of the documents referred to in the appeal.

5. Procedure in deciding appeal — In deciding an appeal, the Commission may—

(i) take oral or written evidence on oath or on affidavit from the concerned or interested person;
(ii) peruse or inspect documents, public records or copies thereof;
(iii) inquire, through authorised officer, about further details or facts;
(iv) hear State Public Information Officer, State Assistant Public Information Officer or such Senior

Officer who had decided the first appeal, or such person against whom the complaint is made, as the case may be ;

(v) hear a third party ; and

(vi) receive evidence on affidavits from State Public Information Officer, State Assistant Public Information Officer, such Senior Officer who decided the first appeal, such person against whom the complaint lies or the third party.

6. Service of notice by Commission – Notice to be issued by the Commission may be served in any of the following modes, namely :—

(i) service by the party itself;
(ii) by hand delivery (dasti) through Process Server;
(iii) by registered post with acknowledgement due; or
(iv) through the Head of Office or Department.

7. Personal presence of the appellant or complainant –

(1) The appellant or the complainant, as the case may be, shall in every case be informed of the date of hearing at least seven clear days before that date.

(2) The appellant or the complainant, as the case may be, may, at his discretion, at the time of hearing of the appeal or complaint by the Commission, be present in person or through his duly authorised representative or may opt not to be present.

(3) Where the Commission is satisfied that circumstances exist due to which the appellant or the complainant, as the case may be, is being prevented from attending the hearing of the Commission, then the Commission may afford the

appellant or the complainant, as the case may be, another opportunity of being heard before a final decision is taken or take any other appropriate action as it may deem fit.

(4) The appellant or the complainant, as the case may be, may seek the assistance of any person in the process of the appeal while presenting his points and the person representing him need not be a legal practitioner.

8. Order of the Commission – Order of the Commission shall be pronounced in proceeding and shall be in writing duly authenticated by the Registrar or any other officer authorised by the Commission for this purpose.

Goa Right to Information Rules, 2005

NOTIFICATION

February 15, 2006

No: D1/INF/RTI/BILL/2005/6474

In exercise of the powers conferred by Section 27 of the Right to Information Act, 2005 (Central Act 22 of 2005), the Government of Goa hereby makes the following rules, namely:—

1. Short title and commencement –

   (1) These rules may be called the Goa Right to Information (Regulation of fee and cost) .

   (2) They shall come into force on the date of their publication in the Official Gazette.

2. Definitions – In these rules, unless the context otherwise requires—

   (a) "Act" means the Right to Information Act, 2005 (Central Act No. 22 of 2005)

   (b) "Section" means a section of the Act;

   (c) words and expressions used herein but not defined and defined in the Act, shall have the same meaning respective assigned to them in the Act.

3. Fee for information—

   (1) A request for obtaining information under sub section of Section 6 of the Act, shall be accompanied by an application fee of Rs. ten by way of cash against proper receipt or by demand draft or by bankers cheque payable to the concerned Public Information Officer.

(2) For providing the information under sub-section (1) of section 7 of the Act, the fee shall be charged by way of cash against proper receipt or by demand draft or bankers cheque payable to the concerned Public Information Officer at the following rates :—

(a) rupees two for each page (in A-4 or A-3 size paper) created or copied ;

(b) actual charge or cost price of a copy in larger size paper;

(c) actual cost or price for samples or models; and

(d) for inspection fo records, no fee for the first hour; and a fee of rupees five for each subsequent hour (or fraction thereof) thereafter.

(3) For providing the information under sub-section (5) of section 7 of the Act, the fee shall be charged by way of cash against proper receipt or by demand draft or bankers cheque payable to the concerned Public Information Officer at the following rates :—

(a) for information provided in diskette or on a floppy, rupees fifty per diskette or per floppy; and

(b) for information provided in printed form at the price fixed for such publication or rupees two per page of photocopy for extracts from the publication.

The Gujarat Right to information Rules, 2005

In exercise of the powers conferred by Section 27 of Right to Information Act 2005(Central Act No. 22 of 2005), the Government of Gujarat hereby makes the following rules, namely:—

1. Short title and commencement: —

    (1) These rules may be called by the Gujarat Right to Information Rules, 2005.
    (2) They shall come into force on the 12th October, 2005.

2. Definitions:

    (1) In these rules, unless the context otherwise requires: —

        (a) "Act" means the Right to Information Act, 2005.
        (b) "Commission" means the State Information Commission constituted under Section 15 of the Act.
        (c) 'Form' means form appended to these rules;
        (d) 'Fee' means fee prescribed under rule 5.

    (2) The words and expressions used in these rules but not defined shall have the meaning assigned to them in the Act.

3. Application for obtaining information: —

(1) A person who desires to obtain information shall make an application in Form A accompanying with the fees prescribed in rule 5 or through the e-media to the Public Information Officer and the receipt of the application shall be given to the applicant in Form B. The fee may be paid in cash wherever facility for cash receipt is available, or by Demand Draft or by pay order or in the form of non-judicial stamp.

(2) (i) The applicant shall be required to pay the application fee as provided under clausc (a) of sub-rule (1) of rule 5:

Provided that a person applying through e-media shall have to pay the fees within seven days from the date of application, failing which the application shall be treated as withdrawn.

(ii) The Public Information Officer shall inform the applicant in Form C regarding other fees and charges to be paid as provided under clause (b) of sub- rule (1) of rule 5;

Provided that no fees and charges shall be payable by a person belonging to the Below Poverty Line families.

Provided that such person encloses with the application, a certified copy of the Below Poverty Line Card or a Certificate issued in that behalf by the concerned authority.

(3) The charges payable under clause (b) of sub-rule (l) of rule 5 may be paid in cash wherever facility for cash receipt is available, or by demand draft or by pay order.

4. Disposal of the application—

(1) The Public Information Officer shall be required

to provide information sought for to the applicant within thirty days of the receipt of the request in Form 'D' or inform the applicant about rejection of application in Form-F taking into consideration the provisions of section 8 and 9 of the Act .

(2) In case where the information sought for does not fall within the jurisdiction of the Public Information Officer to whom the application has made, he shall transfer such application in Form E to concerned Public Authority/Public Information Officer within five days of the receipt of the application and inform the applicant immediately about such transfer.

Provided that where the information sought for concerns the life or liberty of a person, the Public Information Officer shall be required to provide such information within forty-eight hours of the receipt of such request or application.

5. Rates of fees:—

(1) The rates of fees and other charges for obtaining required information and documents shall be as under:—

(a) Application fee: Rs 20 per application.

(b) Other fees and charges

(i) Any information available in the publication form — Actual price of publication

(A) Information Provided in.—

(i) A4,A3 size paper — Rs. 2 per page

(ii) Larger size paper — Actual cost

(B) For Sample, Model Photographs — Actual cost

Note: Procedure stipulated by the department for the sample or the model shall have to be followed.

(C) Inspection of records— No fees for the first half an-hour and thereafter Rs. 20 for each half an-hour.

(D) For information to be furnished in a of floppy disc- Rs. 50 per floppy or disk.

Note: 'the existing rates' wherever possible fees for inspection of records shall continue wherever such system or procedure exist an the a fore said fees shall not be applicabie.

6. Appeal: —

(1) Any person aggrieved by a decision of the Public Information Officer in Form D and in Form F, or does not receive any decision, as the case may be, he may prefer an appeal in Form G within thirty days from the date of receipt or non-receipt of such decision, to appellate authority appointed by the Government in this behalf.

(2) The applicant aggrieved by an order of the appellate authority under sub - rule (1) may prefer the second appeal fo the State Information Commission within ninety days from the date of receipt of the order of the appellate authority giving following details:

(i) name and address of the appellant;

(ii) name and address of the State Public Information Officer;

(iii) Number, date and details of the order against which the second appeal is filed;

(iv) brief facts leading to the appeal;
(v) grounds for the prayer or relief;
(vi) verification by the appellant; and
(vii) any other information which the commission may deem necessary for deciding the appeal.

(3) Every appeal shall be accompanied by the following documents namely.

(i) certified copy of the order against which second appeal is preferred.
(ii) copies of documents referred or relied upon by the appellant with a list thereof.

(4) While deciding appeal the Commission may.—

(i) take oral and written evidence on oath or an affidavits. (ii) evaluate the record.
(ii) inquire through the authorized officer details or truthfulness.
(iv) summon the Public Information Officer or the appellate authority which has heard the first appeal.
(v) hear the third party; and
(vi) obtain necessary evidence from the Public Information Officer or the appellate authority who has heard the first appellate.

(5) The Commission shall serve the notice in anyone of the following modes:—

(i) service by the party itself;
(ii) by hand delivery;
(iii) by registered post with acknowledgement due; and
(iv) through the Head of the Department or its subordinate office.

(6) The Commission shall, after hearing the parties to the appeal, pronounce in open proceedings its decision and issue a written order which shall be authenticated by the registrar or such officers as may be authorized by the Commission on this behalf.

7. Maintenance of Records :

(1) The Public Information Officer shall maintain records in respect of the applications received for information and fee collected for giving the information.

(2) The State Information Commission shall maintain records of all appeals received and disposed off.

8. Miscellaneous :

For the purpose of removing any doubt it is herby clarified that the forms as prescribed under these rules need not be in authorized pre-printed stationery, but any format neatly typed, handwritten or in electronic form which covers essential details prescribed in the form shall be valid.

Haryana Right to Information Rules, 2005

Notification

The 28th October, 2005 No.5/4/200-IAR.

In exercise of the powers conferred by sub-section (I) read with sub section (2) of section 27 of the right to Information Act, 2005 (Central Act 22 of 2005), the Governor of Haryana hereby makes the following rules providing for information under the said Act, namely:—

1. Short title and commencement—

   (1) These rules may be called the Haryana Right to Information Rules, 2005.

   (2) They shall come into force on the date of their publication in the Official Gazette.

2. Definitions –

   (1) In these rules, unless the context otherwise requires—

      (a) "Act" means the Right to Information Act, 2005 (Central Act 22 of 2005).

      (b) "Commission" means the Haryana Information Commission.

      (c) "Form" means a form, appended to these rules.

      (d) "Section" means the section of the Act.

   (2) The words and expressions used in these rules, but not defined, shall have the same meanings as assigned to them in the Act.

3. Application for obtaining information:

(1) A person, who desires to obtain any information admissible under the Act, shall make an application in Form A to the State Public Information Officer/State Assistant Public Information Officer alongwith a fee as specified in rule 5 of these rules. Sections 2(m), 6 and 27.

(2) On the receipt of an application, made under sub-rule(1), the State Public Information Officer/State Assistant Public Information Officer shall give a receipt in token there of to the applicant.

4. Deposit of fee:

(1) the fee shall be deposited with the State Public Information Officer/State Assistant Public Information Officer either in cash against proper receipt by treasury challan/IPO/Bank Draft.

(2) The amount of fee shall be credited to the receipt head/account number of the concerned public authority.

(3) On receipt of an application, submitted under sub-rule(1) of the 3, the State Public Information Officer/State Assistant Public Information Officer shall scrutinize the application and shall assess how much see is required to be paid by the applicant for obtaining the information.

(4) The fee assessed under sub-rule (3), shall be informed to the applicant by the State Public Information Officer/State Assistant Public Information Officer in Form B within a period of seven days from the receipt of application.

(5) In case the applicant fails to deposit the issuance of the intimation given to him under sub-rule (4), it shall be construed that the applicant is no longer

interested in obtaining the information, sought for, and his application shall be deemed to have been filed.

5. Quantum of fee.

(1) An application for obtaining any information under sub-section (1) of section 6 shall be accompanied with a fee of Rs. 50
Section 6 and 7:

(2) For providing an information under sub-section (1) of section 7, the fee shall be charged from the applicant at the following rate, namely:—

(a) Rs. 10 for each page in A-4 or A-4 size paper, created or copied; and

(b) If information is to be provided on a large size of paper than that of specified in clause (a), the actual cost price of such a paper shall be charged.

(3) For providing an information under sub-section (5) of section 7, the fee shall be charged from the applicant at the following rates, namely:—

(a) Rs. 50 for providing information in a floppy;

(b) Rs. 100 for providing information on a diskette; and

(c) If information sought is of such a nature, which is contained in a printed document of which a price has been fixed, then that information shall be provided after charging the price, fixed for that printed document. However, if only an extract or page of such a printed document is asked for, then a fee of Rs.10 per page shall be charged.

(4) No fee for inspection of record shall be charged, if such an inspection is made for one hour only. However, if inspection is made for a period of more than one hour, then a fee of rupees ten shall be charged for every fifteen minutes in excess of first hour. Every fraction of the period above fifteen minutes, shall be construed as a complete period of fifteen minutes and it shall be charged as full period of fifteen minutes.

6. Procedure to be followed in deciding appeal:
Before deciding an appeal, the Commission shall,—
Section 19(10)

(a) serve notice to the concerned persons;
(b) entertain any evidence in support of appeal, which may be oral or in writing form the concerned persons;
(c) examine on oath or by having affidavits from the persons concerned;
(d) persue or inspect the documents or any records or copies thereof;
(e) inquire through the authorized officer the facts of an appeal or may require facts in details, if it so deems appropriate, hear the State Public Information Officer or any other senior officer who had decided the first appeal, as the case may be; and
(f) receive evidence on affidavits from the State Public Information Officer or any officer who had decided the first appeal or from any other person from whom the evidence may be deemed necessary.

7. Mode of serving notice—

The Commission may serve notice to the persons concerned in any of the following modes, namely:—
Section 19(10)

(a) by hand delivery(dasti) through process server; or
(b) by registered post with acknowledgement due; and
(c) by publication in the newspaper.

8. Order by the Commission:

(1) The Commission shall make order in writing and pronounce the same in the presence of the concerned parties.
Section 19(10)
(2) The party concerned may, obtain the copy of the order from the Commission.

Form A

To

The State Public Information Officer/
State Assistant Public Information Officer,
(Name of the office with address)

1. Full name of the applicant
2. Address:
3. Particulars of information required:—

(i) Subject matter of Information*
(ii) The period to which the information relates**
(iii) Description of the information by post or in person
(iv) Whether information is required by post or in person (the actual postal shall be included in addition to the fees.***
(v) In case by post (Ordinary, Registered or Speed)

Place: Signature of the Applicant.
Date:

* Broad category of the subject to be indicated (such as Grant/Government land/Service matters/ Licenses etc.)

** Relevant period for which information is required to be indicated.

*** Specific details of the information are required to be indicated.

ACKNOWLEDGEMENTS

Received your application dated_____________, vide Dairy No._______________ dated_______________.

The State Public Information Officer/
State Assistant Public Information Officer
Name of the Department /Office

Form B

From

The State Public Information Officer/
State Assistant Public Information Officer,
(Name of the office with address)

To

Name and address of the applicant.

Sir,

Please refer to your application dated_______________ addressed to the undersigned requesting information regarding __________. The additional fee for the supplying this information to you is Rs. _______________.

2. You are hereby informed to pay the fee at this office either in cash/Government treasury challan/IPO/ Bank Draft and send a copy of the challan to this office

within a period of fifteen days and collect the information on ___________.

3. The amount of fee shall be deposited in the receipt head/account No................(to be intimated to the applicant by the concerned department.)

State Public Information Officer/
State Assistant Public Information Officer.

Annexure – C

Appeal under Section 19 (3) of the Right to Information Act, 2005

From

Applicant's Name and Address.

To

Name/Designation/Address of the appellate authority.

1. Full Address of the appellant
2. Address
3. Particulars of the Public Information Officer
4. Date of receipt of the order appealed against
5. Last date for filing the appeal
6. Particulars of Information: —
   - (i) Nature and subject matter of the information required.
   - (ii) Name of the officer or department to which the information relates.
   - (iii) The ground for appeal

Place Signature of the Appellant
Date

Haryana Government Administrative Reforms Department

Notification

The 29th December, 2005

No.5/4/2005-1AR

In exercise of the powers conferred by sub-section (4) of section 24 of the Right to Information Act, 2005 (Central Act 22 of 2005) the Governor of Haryana hereby specifies the intelligence and security organizations as mentioned in the schedule given below for the purpose of the said sub-section :—

SCHEDULE

(i) State Criminal Investigation Department (C.I.D.); including the Crime Branch
(ii) Haryana Armed Police;
(iii) Security Organizations of Police;
(iv) Haryana Police Telecommunication Organization;
(v) India Reserve Battalion;
(vi) Commando.

S.C.Choudhary
Financial Commissioner & Principal
Secretary to Government. Haryana,
Administrative Reforms Department

The Himachal Pradesh RTI Rules, 2005

In exercise of the powers conferred by clauses to sub-section (2) section 27 of "The Right to Information act 2005"(Central Act No. 22 of 2005), the Governor of Himachal Pardesh is pleased to make the following rules, namely:-

1. Short title and commencement: —

(1) These rules may be called by the Himachal Pardesh Right to Information Rules, 2006.
(2) They shall come into force on the date of their publication in the official Gazette.

2 Definitions:—

(1) In these rules, unless the context otherwise requires:—

(a) 'Act' means the Right to Information Act, 2005 (Central Act No. 22 of 2005).
(b) 'Form' means a form appended to these rules;
(c) 'Section' means section of the Act ;
(d) 'Appendix' means the appendix appended to these rules.

(2) The words and expressions used but not defined, shall have the meaning assigned to them in that Act.

3. Application for seeking information—

(1) Any person seeking information under the Act

shall make an application in Form "A" to the Public Information Officer/Assistant Public Information Officer accompanied by fee prescribed in Rule 5 and the Public Information Officer/Assistant Public Information Officer shall duly acknowledge the receipt thereof and shall enter the particulars in Part I of the application Register maintained for the purpose in Appendix I.

(2) Except in the case of an applicant who is determined by the state Government as being below poverty line the application shall be accepted only if it is accompanied by a challan in support of payment of the requisite application fees as specified in Rule 5. A separate application shall be made in respect of each subject and in respect of each year to which the information relates.

(3) When the information sought for is ready and requires payment of additional fee, if any, the Public Information Officer/Assistant Public Information Officer shall communicate to the applicant the fact in Form "B" specifying the additional fee to be paid on his address given in application. The particulars of information being supplied shall be entered in Part II of the application register.

(4) When the information is ready the Public Information Officer / Assistant Public Information Officer will inform the applicant in form.

(5) Any information supplied under sub-rule (4) shall be in the language available in the office record.

4. Inspection of record :—

(1) Any person who seeks to inspect the record before making an application under Section 4 shall make application in Form D for the purpose indicating the record to be inspected.

(2) An Inspection Register shall be maintained with the Public Information Officer / Assistant Public Information Officer in form given in Appendix II and details of the application and inspection shall be recorded therein.

(3) During inspection the applicant shall not take photographs etc., of the record/ document.

(4) Except if inspection of the record is disallowed under Section 8 and 9 of the Act, Public Information Officer/Assistant Public Information Officer shall allow the inspection on payment of the requisite fee prescribed in Rule 5.

5. Charges of Fee :—

(1) Except in the case of persons who are below poverty line as determined by the State Government, the Public Information Officer/ Assistant Public Information Officer shall charge the fee for supply of information at the following rates, namely: —

Description of information Prices/Fees in Rupees

1. Fee alongwith application : Rs. 10 per application
2. Where the information is : On printed price available in the form of priced publication.
3. For other than priced : Rs. 10 per page of A-4 size or publication smaller and actual cost subject to minimum of Rs. 20 per page in case of larger.
4. Where information is available in electronic form : Rupees 50 per floppy and Rs. 100 per CD. and is to be supplied in electronics form, e.g Floopy, CD etc.
5. Fee for inspection of record : Rs. 10 per 15

minutes or document fraction thereof.

(2) Every page of information to be supplied shall be duly authenticated giving the name of the applicant (including below poverty line status if that is the case), and shall bear the dates signatures and seal of the concerned Public Information Officer supplying the information.

(3) Fee Charged shall be deposited in a Government Treasury under the head of 'account "0070-0AS, 60-05, 8000R, 11 — Receipt Head under Right to Information Act, 2005" Accruals into this head of account may be placed in a separate fund by way of grant -in - aid for furthering the purposes of the Accruals, including purchase of equipment and consumables, providing training to staff etc.

(4) When the Appellate Authority / Commission may calls for the records, it shall in any case shall return the original record within 10 days after retaining an authenticated copy if required.

(5) On the date of hearing or on any other day to which hearing may be adjourned, the parties shall put their appearance before the Appellate Authority / Commission. If the appellant fails to appear on the such date, the Appellate Authority / Commission may in its discretion either dismiss the appeal or decide the matter ex-parte on merits.

(6) The appellant shall not, except by leave of the Appellate Authority/ Commission, urge or be heard in support of any ground of objection which has not been set forth in the memorandum, but the Appellate Authority / Commission, in deciding the appeal, need not confine itself to the grounds of objection set forth in the memorandum:

Provided that the Appellate Authority/ Commission shall not rest its decision on any ground than those specified in memorandum, unless the party likely to be affected thereby, has been given, an opportunity of being heard by the Appellate Authority/ Commission.

(7) The Commission may frame regulations in respect of its day-to-day proceedings.

6. Procedure in appeals before the Appellate Authorities:—

1. Contents of appeal:— The Memorandum of appeal to the Appellate Authority/Commission shall contain the following information, namely.—

(i) name and address of the appellant;
(ii) name and address of the State Public Information Officer
(iii) particulars of the orders against which the appeal is made including number and date;
(iv) brief facts leading to the appeal;
(v) if the appeal is preferred against refusal, the particulars of the application including number an date and name and address of the Public Information Officer to whom the application was made;
(vi) prayer or relief sought;
(vii) grounds or the prayer or relief;
(viii) verification by the appellant; and
(ix) any other information which the commission may deem necessary for deciding the appeal;

(2) The appellant shall submit four copies of the memorandum of appeal for official purpose.

(3) Every appeal made to the Appellate Authority/ Commission shall be accompanied by the following documents namely—

(i) self-attested copies of the orders or documents

against which the appeal is being preferred;

(ii) challan in proof of the payment of the prescribed fee;

(iii) copies of documents relied upon by the appellant and referred to in the appeal; and

(iv) an index of the documents referred to in the appeal.

(4) When the Appellate Authority / Commission calls for the record, it shall in any case shall return the original record within ten days after retaining and authenticated copy if required.

The Jammu and Kashmir Right to Information Rules, 2005

Notification

Srinagar, the 30th June, 2005

SRO 181

In exercise of the powers conferred by sub-section (1) of section 15 of the Jammu and Kashmir Right to Information Act, 2004 (Act No. 1 of 2004), the Government of Jammu and Kashmir hereby makes the following rules, namely:—

1. Short title and commencement—
   (i) These rules may be called the Jammu and Kashmir Right to Information Rules, 2005.
   (ii) These rules shall come into force from the date of their publication in the official Gazette.

2. Definitions:
   In these rules, unless the context otherwise requires—

   (a) 'Act' means the Jammu and Kashmir Right to Information Act, 2004
   (b) 'Authorized person' means a person nominated by the Incharge of the Office to accept fee prescribed under these rules.
   (c) 'Controlling Officer' means the Officer as specified in Schedule I specified as such in schedule annexed to these rules.
   (d) 'Form' means the form appended to these rules.
   (e) 'Incharge of the Office' means an Officer/functionary specified as such in schedule annexed to these rules.
   (f) 'Section' means a section of the Act.
   (j) Words and expressions used buy not defined in these rules shall have the same meaning as has been assigned in the Act.

3. Application for seeking information—

(i) Any person seeking information under the Act shall make an application in Form 'A' to the Incharge of the office and deposit application fee as per rule 8 with the authorized person. The Incharge of the Office shall duly acknowledge the application as provided in Form 'A.'

Provided that the person who makes a request shall ensure that the requisite fee is deposited in cash with the Authorized person with 7 days of his request, failing which his application shall be treated as withdrawn.

4. Disposal of application seeking information—

(i) If the information sought for falls in any of the restrictions mentioned in section 6 of the Act and/or pertains to the organizations mentioned in Section 8 of the said Act, the Incharge of the office shall order return of the application to the applicant in Form 'B' as soon as practicable, within 15 days of receipt of the application assigning the reason(s) for such return. The application fee deposing in such cases shall not be refunded.

(ii) If the information sought for does not fall within any of the restrictions mentioned in section 6 and do not pertain to the organizations mentioned in section 8 of the Act, the Incharge of the Office, on being satisfied, shall supply the information to the applicant in Form 'C.' In case the information sough is partially falling under the preview of section 6 and/or 8 of the Act and partly falls outside the restrictions, the Incharge of the office shall supple only such information as is permissible under the Act and reject the remaining part giving reasons thereof.

(iii) The information shall be supplied as soon as

practicable within a period of thirty (30) working days from the receipt of the application on deposit of fee. A proper acknowledgement shall be obtained from the applicant in token of receipt of the information.

5. Inspection of documents:—

(i) In case the applicant desires the inspection of documents, the applicant shall deposit fee with the Incharge of the Office in addition to the application fee as prescribed in Rule 8. Only those documents shall be allowed for inspection, copies of which can be given under the Act.

(ii) Inspection of public works:— In case the applicant desires the inspection of public works, the applicant shall deposit fee with the authorized person in addition to the application fee as prescribed in Rule 8. Inspection of only such public works shall be allowed which are provided by this Act and not prohibited by any other law.

(iii) Taking of samples or material from public works:—In case the applicant desires taking samples or material from public work, the Incharge of the Office shall decide the quantum of fee on case to case basis so as to cover the cost of the material and the labour in providing such sample. The applicant shall deposit the fee so calculated with the Authorized person in addition to application fee as prescribed in rule 8. Only such sample and material shall be made available which is permissible under the provision of this Act.

6. Appeal—

(1) Any person

(a) who fails to get a response in Form 'C' from

the Incharge of the Office within 30 working days of submission of Form 'A' or

(b) is aggrieved by the response received within the prescribed period, may appeal in Form 'D' to the controlling officer within 30 days of the decision of Incharge of the office.

(2) On receipt of the appeal, the controlling officer shall acknowledge the receipt of appeal and after giving the applicant the opportunity of being heard, shall endeavor to disposed it off within 30 days from the date on which it is presented and send a copy of the decision to the Incharge of the office concerned.

(3) The second appeal against the decision of the controlling officer shall lie within 30 days of such decision with the Government in Form 'E.'

(4) In case the appeal is allowed, the information shall be supplied to the applicant by the Incharge of the Office within such period as ordered by the appellate authority. This period shall not exceed thirty working days from the date of receipt of the order.

7. Publication of information

(i) Every department and public body shall publish the information as per the sub-section (b) of section 3 of the Act, in the form of booklets, folders and pamphlets within three months from the date these rules are notified in the official Gazette and then at the following intervals:

S. No. Particular of Information to be published — Interval

1. Particulars of its organizations, functions and duties — Once in five years
2. Powers and duties of its Officers and employees

and the procedure followed by them in the decision-making process — Once in two years

3. Norms set by the public authority for the discharge of its functions — Once in two years
4. Laws, bye-laws, rules, regulations, instructions, manuals and other categories of records under its control used by its employees for discharging its functions — Once in five years
5. Details of facilities available to citizens for obtaining information — Annually
6. Name, designation and other particulars of the Incharge of the Office and Controlling Officer — Annually

(ii) Such information shall also be made available to the public information counters, medium of Internet and display on notice board at conspicuous places in the office of the Incharge of the Office and in the office of the Controlling Officer.

8. Charging of fee —

(i) The Incharge of the Office shall charge the fee at the following rates

1. Application fee Five rupees per application

Other Fees :

S. No. *Description of Information Fees in Rupees*

1. Where the information is available in the form of a priced publication Price fixed for the publication
2. For other than priced publication as fixed or determined for the same

3. Inspection of documents Rupees 5 (Five)
4. Inspection of public works Rupees 500.
5. Taking of samples of material from public works Rupees 500.

(ii) The Appellate Authority shall charge a fee of Ten rupees per appeal.
Provided that the said prescribed fee shall be deposited in the Government Treasury under:— Major Head: 0070 — Other Administrative Services 60 — Other Services 800 — Other Receipts on account of Right to Information Act

9. Interpretation— In case there seems any ambiguity in these rules the interpretation of the Government in the General Administration Department in consultation with Law Department shall be the final.

10. Maintenance of Records:—

(i) The Incharge of the office shall maintain records of all applications received for supply of information and fee charged.

(ii) The controlling officer shall maintain records of all appeals filed before him and the fee charged.

The Jharkhand State Information Commission RTI Rules, 2005

Notification

Ranchi, Dated 27Feb. 2008

No. 7/vi.Vi.San.03-97/2005 (Part – 1) ka 1178

In exercise of powers conferred u/s 27 (2) (d), (e) of Right to Information Act, 2005, Government of Jharkhand makes the following Rules of procedure in deciding appeals by Jharkhand State Information Commission and also the Rules for condition of service of the officers and employee of the Commission:—

1. Short title and Commencement —

   (i) These rules may be called Jharkhand Right to Information Commission— (Procedure for deciding appeals and conditions of service of officers and employees rules, 2008.

   (ii) These Rules shall come into force from the date of Notification

2. Definitions

   (i) In these rules, unless the context otherwise requires—

   (a) 'Act', means the Right to Information Act, 2005 Central Act 22 of 2005

   (b) 'Commission' means the Jharkhand State Information Commission as constituted u/s of the Act

   (c) 'Section' means section of the Act.

   (d) 'State Government' means the Government of Jharkhand

(ii) Words and expressions used and not defined in these rules but defined in the act, shall have—

CHAPTER – 1

The procedure to be adopted in deciding appeals—

3. Memorandum of Appeal : Every appeal shall be preferred in the form of memorandum of appeal signed by the appellant and presented before the Commission or an officer appointed by the Commission in that behalf.

(iii) The Memorandum shall contain the following information namely:

(a) Name and Address of appellant;
(b) The name and address of PIO against the decision of whom the appeal u/s 191 of the Act has been preferred;
(c) The name and address of the appellate authority against whose order appeal is being preferred;
(d) Brief facts leading to the appeal;
(e) The concise and distinct heads of the grounds of objection to the appellate order, appealed against;
(f) The Memorandum shall be accompanied by a copy of order passed by appellate authority u/s 191 of the Act;
(g) Copies of document relied upon by the appellant and referred to in the appeal; and
(h) The Memorandum shall accompany verification by the appellant.

4. Institution and admission of appeal :
On receipt of the Memorandum of appeal, the officer

of the Commission appointed in this behalf, shall make scrutiny of the Memorandum and if on scrutiny it is found that the Memorandum is in order it shall be duly registered and a serial number of registration be given thereon.

Then before such imposition a reasonable opportunity of being heard be given to such public authority and the commission shall pass a reasoned order for imposing such penalty.

5. Recovery of Compensation amount: Where a compensation was ordered to be given to the appellant, the Commission on an application made before it by the appellant issue a certificate for the amount to the Collector and the Collector shall proceed to recover the same in the manner as an arrear of Land Revenue.
6. If any fine is imposed by the Commission, the same shall be deposited before an officer authorized in this behalf by the Commission and the said officer shall enter the same in a register and issue receipt thereof. The officer shall deposited the amount realized as fine on the next working day in the Treasury through Treasury Challan. Any dereliction on the part of such officer shall entail disciplinary action against him.

(ii) Where the Commission has imposed any fine against a public authority and such public authority has not deposited the said fine in the Commission as per sub-rule (i) the same shall be realized as per the procedure prescribed under Section 42 1 b of the Code of Criminal Procedure.

CHAPTER –2

Condition of Service of the Officers and Employees of the Commission.

7. Salary and Allowance: The officers and employees of the Commission provided by the State Government under sub-section 6 of section 16 of the Act shall get such salaries and allowances as prescribed in Notification No. 3120 date 17th June, 2006 and 245 dated 17 January, 2007 and will be in accordance with the posts to be created in future by the Department of Personnel Administrative Reforms and Rajbhasha, Government of Jharkhand.
8. Leave and other Service Condition: The officers and employees of the Commission provided by the State Government under sub-section 6 of section 16 of the Act shall avail such leave and their conditions of service will also be such as prescribed by the State Government from time to time.

CHAPTER – 3

1. Repeal and savings: The previous rules notified by the Government of Jharkhand, Department of Personnel Administrative Reforms and Rajbhasha on the subject *vide* notification No. 3889 dated 14.11.05 and its amendment notification No. 2780 dated 04.06.07 are hereby repealed.

   (ii) Notwithstanding the repeal of the above rules any judgment order issued under the repealed rules or nay other action taken under the repealed rules before the commencement of present rules, so far as it is not inconsistent with the provisions of the Act, be deemed to have been duly issued and made under the corresponding provisions of these rules.

The Karnataka RTI Rules, 2005

In exercise of the powers conferred by sub-section (1) and (2) of section 27 of the Right to Information Act, 2005 (Central Act 22 of 2005), the Government of Karnataka hereby made the following rules namely:—

1. Title and Commencement:—

    1. These rules may be called the Karnataka Right to Information Rules, 2005.
    2. They shall come into force with effect from the date of their publication in the Official Gazette.

2. Definition:—

    (i) 'Act' means the Right to Information Act, 2005 (Central Act 22 of 2005);

    (ii) 'Section' means section of the Act.

3. Publication of certain other information's etc., under Section 4

    1. The information under Section 4 (4) shall be easily accessible to the public. It shall be indicated on the notice board by the Public Information Officer where these particulars are available. Further the public authorities can adopt any of the methods provided under the Act for disseminating the information.
    2. The information so disseminated shall also contain the details of phone number, fax number

etc. of the State Public Information Officers and the Assistant State Public Information Officers of the office in question.

4. Fee: —

1. Any person desirous of obtaining information under sub-section (1) of section 6 of the Act shall make an application in Form-A or in any other format as far as possible containing the particulars specified under the format to the State Public Information Officer or State Assistant Public Information Officer as the case may be alongwith an initial fee of Rs. 10 with his application. Every officer receiving request under the Act shall give an acknowledgement.
2. (a) For providing information under sub-section (1) of section 7, the fees for supplying the information shall be charged at Rs. 2 for each page in the respect of matters in A4 size paper.
   (b) For providing information under sub-section (1) of section 7, in the case of Maps, Plans, Reports, a Partial record or any Technical data or Sample or Models, a reasonable fee shall be fixed by he State Public Information Officer in each case depending upon the cost of labour and material required to be employed.
   (c) As regards inspection of records and documents, no fee for the first hour. For every subsequent half an hour or fraction thereof, Rs. 20 shall be charged from persons making application with initial payment as prescribed under rule 4(1) above. For inspection of works a reasonable fee shall be fixed by the State Public Information Officer in each case depending upon the cost of labour and material required to be employed apart from initial fees as prescribed under rule 4(1).

(3) For providing information under sub-section (5) of section 7, the fees for supplying information in Diskette or Floppy or CD or in any other electronic mode shall be Rs. 50.

(4) The fee shall be collected in the form of Indian Postal Order or DD or Bankers Cheque or Pay order drawn in favour of the State Public Information Officer or in cash or by remitting it to the Treasury as per Karnataka Financial Code (KFC).

(5) A person claiming exemption under proviso to sub-section (5) of section 7 shall produce a valid certificate issued by the concerned authority that he/she belongs to the Below Poverty Line category.

(6) Salary and allowances and conditions of service of officers and employees of the State Information Commission: —

  (1) The salary and allowance payable to the officers and employees of State Information Commission shall be on par with other State Government employees of equivalent rank.

  (2) The rules governing conditions of service and disciplinary matter of the State Government employee shall mutates-mutandis apply to the employees of State Information Commission subject to modifications specified in schedule to these rules.

  (3) The method of recruitment shall be in accordance with the provisions under KCS (General Recruitment) Rule, 1977 by Deputation of Government Servants of equivalent rank from any of the State Civil Services or Public sector undertaking or by outsourcing:

  Provided that the outsourcing shall be restricted to post of Cleaning, Housekeeping, Home Orderlies and Security Guards.

6. Appeal under sub-section (1) of section 19: —

(1) The Public Authority shall by notification specify

the designation of the officer to whom the appeals under sub-section (1) of section 19, shall lie.

(2) Every such appeal shall be accompanied by a copy of the order, if any, appealed against, and it shall specify:—

(i) the name and address of the applicant and the particulars regarding the State Public Information Officer appealed against.

(ii) the date of receipt of order, if any, from the State Public Information Officer appealed against:

(iii) the grounds of appeal; and

(iv) the relief which the applicant claims.

(3) The Appellate Authority under sub-section (1) of section 19 shall fix a day for hearing of the appeal. On the date fixed for hearing the appeal or on further date to which, the appeal may be adjourned, the Appellate Authority shall after hearing the parties pass such orders of the appeal as it deems fit.

7. Procedure in Appeals under sub-section (3) of Section 19:—The provisions of rule 6 shall mutates-mutandis apply to an appeal preferred under-section 19(3).

The Kerala Right to information Rules, 2005

Notification
No. 11259/Cdn.5/2006/GAD
Dated,, 9th May, 2006
S.R.O. No. 385/2006

In exercise of the powers conferred by sub-section (1) and clauses (b) and (c) of sub-section 27 of the Right to Information Act, 2005 (Central Act 22 of 2005), the Government of Kerala hereby made the following rules namely:—

1. Short title and commencement:

   (1) These rules may be called the Kerala Right to Information (Regulation of Fee and Cost) Rules, 2006.
   (2) They shall come into force at once.

2. Definition :

   (1) in these rules, unless the context otherwise requires:—

      (a) 'Act' means the Right to Information Act, 2005 (Central Act 22 of 2005).
      (b) 'Commission' means the Kerala State Information Commission constituted under sub-section (1) of section 15 of the Act.
      (c) 'Section' means section of the Act.
      (d) All other words and expressions used in these rules but not defines and defined in the Act shall have meanings, respectively, assigned to them in the Act.

3. Procedure for seeking information: —

(1) A request for obtaining information under sub-section (1) of section 6 of the Act shall made to the concerned State Public Information Officer or through the State Assistant Public Information Officer, as the case may be, accompanied by an application fee of rupees ten.

(2) The application fee shall be paid in any of the following manners, namely:—

(a) by affixing Court fee stamp;

(b) by remitting the amount in the Government Treasury, under the head of account "0070 other administrative services-60 other services-800 other receipts-42 other items",

(c) by cash remittance against proper receipt in the office of the State Public Information Officer / State Assistant Public Information Officer, as the case may be;

(d) by demand draft/bankers cheque/pay order payable to the State Public Information Officer/State Assistant Public Information Officer.

(3) An application under sub-rule(1) may specify, as far as possible, the particulars mentioned in the Form appended to these rules.

4. Fee for providing information:—

(1) For providing information under sub-section (1) of section 7, the fee shall be charged at the following rates, namely: —

(a) rupees two for each page in 'A4' size paper;

(b) actual charge or cost price of the copy in larger size paper;

(c) Actual cost or price for samples or models, maps, plans etc; and

(d) For inspection of records, no fee for the first hour, and a fee of rupees ten for every subsequent thirty minutes or fraction thereof.

(2) For providing information under sub-section (5) of section 7, the fee shall be charged at the following rates, namely: —

(a) for information provided in diskette or floppy or CD or any other electronic mode, rupees fifty (for each); and

(b) for information provided in printed form, rupees two each page or the actual price fixed for such publication.

(3) The fee specified in sub-rules (1) and (2), shall be collected by way of cash against proper receipt or by remitting the amount in the Treasury under the head of account "0070 other administrative services-60 other service-800 other receipts-42 other items" or by demand draft or bankers cheque or pay order payable to the concerned State Public Information Officer.

(4) Notwithstanding anything contained in sub-rules (1) and (2), no fee shall be charged from the person who are below poverty line as may be determined by the Competent Authority. Such persons shall produce valid certificate along with the application providing that they belong to the category of below poverty line.

(5) Remittance of fee by way of demand draft etc.: — Every demand draft bankers cheque or pay order mentioned in rule 3 or rule 4 shall be taken in favour of the State Public Information Officer/

Assistant Public Information Officer in their official designation and every demand draft shall be drawn in such a way that the same shall be encashed at the branches of any Nationalized Bank / Scheduled Bank situated near the Office of the State Public Information Office / State Assistant Public Information Officer.

The Madhya Pradesh RTI Rules, 2005

Notification

NO. F- 11-37-05-I-9

In exercise of the powers conferred by section 27 of the Right to Information Act – 2005 (NO. 22 of 2005) the State Government, hereby makes the following rules namely:-

RULES

CHAPTER –1

1. Short title and commencement :

   (1) These rules may be called the Madhya Pradesh Right to Information (Fees and Appeal) Rules, 2005.

   (2) They shall come into force with effect from the date of publication in the Madhya Pradesh Gazettes.

2. Definitions:

   In these rules, unless the context otherwise requires,

   (a) Act means the Right to Information Act- 2005 (No. 22 of 2005)

   (b) 'Below Poverty Line' means such citizen of State of Madha Pradesh who is declared as below poverty line by the Government of Madhya Pradesh.

   (c) 'Cost means' the cost which is chargeable for providing information as defined in clause (1) of section 2 of the Act.

(d) 'Fees' means the fee payable under the provisions of the Act.
(e) 'Forms' means the forms attached to these rules
(f) 'Sections' means the sections of the Act.
(g) The words used in these rules but not defined shall have the same meaning as they are defined in section 2 of the Act.

CHAPTER – 2

FEES

3. (1) Any person who is not below the poverty line, desires any material under sub-section 4 of the section 4 of the Act shall submit the application himself to the State Public Information Officer/ Assistant Public Information Officer on judicial stamp Rs. 10 or with the receipt of Rs. 10 (Rupees ten) after making payment in cash. If the application is being sent by post, the applicant shall enclose the non judicial stamp of Rs. 10 (Rupees ten).

(2) After receiving the application by the State Public Information Officer or the State Assistant Public Information Officer as the case may be, the printing cost or medium cost price of the material of the information as determined by above officers shall be deposited by the applicant with the above said officers in cash or in the form of non judicial stamp. If the amount is deposited in cash by the applicant, the State Public Information Officers or the officers as directed by him shall give a receipt of such amount. The amount so deposited shall be deposited into the treasury by a challan.

4. Any person who is not below the poverty line, desired to seek an information under sub-section (1) of section

6 and sub-section (1) of section 7 of the Act shall produce the application before the public authority or State Public Information Officer or State Assistant Information Officer, as the case may be, with the non-judicial stamp of Rs. 10 or with the receipt of Rs. 10 by paying in cash.

5. (1) For the purpose of sub-section 5 of section 7 where access to information is to be provided in the printed or in any electronic format, the applicant, who is not below the poverty line, shall deposit the actual cost of the information as determined by the public authority or State Public Information Officer or State Assistant Public Information Officer in cash or in the form of non-judicial stamp within three days from the date of direction to such officers as directed by the public authority or State Public Information Officer.

(2) If the applicant wants to examine any document or record, the State Public Information Officer or State Public Information Officer shall depute any subordinate officer for such purpose and the applicant, who is not below the poverty line, shall pay Rs. 50 for first hour or fraction thereof and Rs. 25 for every additional fifteen minutes or fraction therefore in cash or in the form of non-judicial stamp.

(3) If the applicant wants the certified samples of any material, the cost determined by the State Public Information Officer or State Public Information Officer of such material, shall be deposited by the applicant to such officer who is directed by the State Public Information Officer in cash or in the form of non judicial stamp.

(4) Where the information is stored in the computer the actual cost of the diskettes or floppies or tape or video cassette as determined by the State Public

Information Office or the State Public Information Officer shall be deposited by the applicant in cash or in the form of non judicial stamp.

CHAPTER -3
Pay and other Service Conditions

6. The officer and servants deputed under sub-section (6) of the section 16 shall be paid the same pay and allowances as they were receiving before deputation and for these service conditions the same rules shall be applicable as were applicable before such deputation.

CHAPTER-4
Appeal

7. First Appeal :

(1) Any person who does not receives a decision within the time specified in sub-section (1) or clause (a) of Sub-section (3) of section 7, or is aggrieved by a decision of the State Public Information Officer, may within thirty days from the expiry of such period or from the receipt of such a decision prefer an appeal , with a memorandum of appeal and the fee of Rs.50 (Rupces. Fifty) either in cash or in the form of non-judicial stamp, to such officer who is senior in rank to the State Public Information Officer in each public authority:

Provided that such officer may admit the appeal after the expiry of the period of thirty days if he is satisfied that the appellant was prevented by sufficient cases from filing the appeal in time.

(2) In the memorandum of appeal the name and address of the appellant , the basis of the subject

matter of the information , with the name and the post of the competent officer, the orders of the competent authority and payment of fee shall be clearly specified.

(3) An appeal under sub-rule (1) shall be disposed of within thirty days of the receipt of the appeal or within such extended period not exceeding a total of forty-five days from the date filing thereof, as the case may be, for reasons to be recorded in writing.

(4) The copy of order passed in appeal shall be given free of cost.

8. Second Appeal—

(1) A second appeal against the decision under sub-rule (3) of rule 7 shall lie within ninety days from the date on which the decision should have been make or was actually received, with the State Information Commission:
Provided that the State Information Commission may admit the appeal after the expiry of the period of ninety days if it is satisfied that the appellant was prevented by sufficient cause from filing the appeal in time.

(2) With the memorandum of appeal filed before the State Information Commission the fee of Rs.100 (Rs. One hundred) in case or in the form of non-judicial stamp shall be deposited.

(3) The State Information Commission shall after giving reasonable opportunity being heard to public authority or State Public Information Officer or appellant as the case may be disposed of the appeal within thirty days from the date of the receipt of the appeal for reasons to be recorded in writing.

(4) The decision of the State Information Commission shall be final and binding.

(5) A copy of the decision of the State Information Commission shall be given free of cost if the appellant wants to receive the copy of the order by post then after receiving the fee of postal charges shall be sent within three days.

9. The fee chargeable under rule 7 and 8 shall not be charged from the person who are of below poverty line.

The Maharashtra Right to Information Rules, 2005

NOTIFICATION

No. RTI.2005/C.R.315/05/5

In exercise of the powers conferred by sub-section (2) of section 27 of the Right to Information Act 2005, the Government of Maharashtra hereby makes the following rules, namely:—

1. Short title and commencement: —

   (1) These rules may be called the Maharashtra Right to Information Rules, 2005.

   (2) They shall into force on the 12th October, 2005.

2. Definitions: —

   (1) In these rules, unless the context otherwise requires: —

      (a) "Act "means the Right to Information Act, 2005.

      (b) "Section "means section of the Act.

   (2) The words and expressions used in these rules but not defined shall have the meaning assigned to them in that Act.

3. Procedure for seeking information.—A request for obtaining information under sub-section (1) of section 6 shall be made to the concerned State Public Information Officer on plain paper or in the format given in Annexure 'A' and shall be accompanied by

an application fee of rupees ten by way of cash against proper receipt or by the demand draft or banker's cheque payable to the public authority or by affixing a court stamp of rupees ten.

4. Fee for information:—

(1) For providing the information under sub-section (1) of section 7, the fee shall be charged by way of cash against proper receipt or by demand draft or bankers cheque payable to the public authority at the following rates, namely:—

(A)(a) When the concerned department has already fixed the price of some documents, maps. etc, the price so fixed plus postal .

(b) When the information is readily available either by way of photocopying or by other way (copy)

(i) rupees two for each page (in A4 & A3 size paper) created or copied plus postal charges; or

(ii) Actual charge or cost price of a copy in large size paper plus postal charges.

(B) for inspection of records, no fee for the first hour and a fee of rupees five for each 15 minutes (or fraction thereof) thereafter:
Provided that no postal charges shall be charged if the applicant collects information personally.

(2) For Providing the information under sub-section (5) of section 7, the fee shall be charged by way of cash against proper receipt or by demand draft or bankers cheque payable to the public authority at the following rates: —

(a) for information provided in diskette or floppy rupees fifty per diskette or floppy; and

(b) for information provided in printed form at the price for such publication or rupees two per page of photocopy for extracts from the publication plus postal charges.

Provided that no postal charges shall be charged if the applicant collects information personally.

5 Appeal :—

(1) Any person who does not receive a decision within the time specified in sub-section (1) or clause (a) of sub-section (3) of section 7, or is aggrieved by an order of the State Public Information Officer, prefer an appeal to the concerned appellate authority on plain paper in the format given in Annexure" B" which shall be accompanied by an appeal fee of rupees twenty by way of cash against proper receipt or by demand draft or banker's cheque payable to the public authority or by affixing a court fee stamp of rupees twenty, with a copy of such order appealed against.

(2) Any person aggrieved by an order of the appellate authority under sub-section (1) of section 19 may, within ninety days from the date of receipt of the order of the appellate authority, prefer a second appeal to the State Information Commission on plain paper in the format given in Annexure "C" which shall be accompanied by an appeal fee of rupees twenty by way of cash against proper receipt or by demand draft or banker's cheque payable to the public authority or by affixing a court fee stamp of rupees twenty, with a copy of such order appealed against.

The Manipur RTI Rules, 2005

NOTIFICATION

The 14Th October, 2005

No. 11/4/2005-AR

In Exercise of the powers conferred by clause (b) and (c) of sub section 2 of section 27 of the Right to Information Act, 2005 (22 of 2005) the Government of Manipur hereby hereby makes the following rules namely.

1. Short title and commencement: These rules may be called the Manipur Right to Information Act, 2005 (Regulation of Fee and cost Rule, 2005)
2. They shall come into force on the dated of their publication in official gazette.
   Definitions: In the rules, unless the context otherwise requires:

   (a) 'Act' menas the Right to Information Act, 2005
   (b) 'section' means section of the Act
   (c) all other words and expression used herein but not defined and defined in the Act shall have the meanings assigned to them in the Act.

3. A request for obtaining information under sub-section (1) of section 6 shall be accompanied by an application fee of rupees ten by way of cash against proper receipt or by demand draft or bankers cheque payable to the Accounts officer of the Public Authority.
4. For providing information under sub-section 91) of section 7, the fee shall be charged by way of cash against proper receipt or by demand draft or bankers cheque payable to the Accounts officer of the public authority at the following rates:

(a) Rupees two for each page a-4 or a-3 size paper, created or copied;
(b) Actual charge or cost price of a copy in large size paper;
(c) Cost or price for samples or models; and
(d) For inspection or records, no fee for the first hour and a fee of rupees five for each fifteen minutes (or fraction thereof) thereafter.

5. For providing the information under sub-section (5) of section 7, the fee shall be charged by way of cash against proper receipt or by demand draft or bankers cheque payable to the Accounts Officer of the public authority at the following rates:—

(a) for information provide in diskette or floppy rupees fifty per diskette or floopy; and
(b) for information provided in printed form at the price fixed for such publication or rupees two per page of photocopy for extracts from the publication.

The Meghalaya RTI Rules, 2005.

NOTIFICATION

Dated: 8th October, 2005

No. IPR. 112/96/Pt. IV/2075.

In exercise of the powers conferred by clauses (b) and (c) of sub section (2) of section 27 of the Right to Information Act, 2005 (22 of 2005), the Government of Meghalaya hereby adapts the Right to Information (Regulation of Fee and Cost) Rules, 2005, made by the Central Government and published vide Notification No. GSR. 34012 / 8 (s) / 2005 –Estt. (B), dated 16th September, 2005 in Part-II, Section 3, Sub-Section (1) of the Gazette of India.

(H. Marwein)

Commissioner & Secretary to
the Government. of Meghalaya
Information and Public Relation
Department

The Mizoram Right to information Rules, 2006

In exercise of the power conferred by section 27 of the RTI Act, 2005, the Governor of Mizoram made the Mizoram Right to Information Rules, 2006, which was notified vide Government Notification No. F.13011/4/2005-IPR, dated 21st June,2006.

Defects in the Rules

It is pertinent to note that section 27 of the Act authorizes the Government to make rules to carry out the provisions of the Act. In this connection, certain provisions in the rules merit re-examination,

Identity

Identity has been defined under clause (e) of sub-rule (1) of rule 1 to mean "an evidence to show the citizenship like an electoral photo identity card, a passport or any other document which can satisfy the authority about citizenship of the person". Identity of the applicant is one of the essential particulars of the Application Form in FORM'A' prescribed under rule 4 of the Rules.

The provisions of RTI Act, 2005 nowhere require any authority to satisfy himself about the citizenship of an applicant person. On the other hand, sub-section (2) of section 6 of the Act prohibits (the authority) from requiring an applicant to give any reason for requesting the information or any other personal details except those that may be necessary for contacting him. Accordingly, the definition of "identity" in the rules is unnecessary and its use in FORM

'A' is contrary to the provisions of sub-section (2) of section 6 of the Act.

Recommendation

Amendment in accordance with the provisions of the Act is recommended.

Mizoram Legislative Assembly Right to Information Rules, 2006

Rule 3(1) of the Mizoram Legislative Assembly Right to Information Rules, 2006 prescribes that a person desirous to obtain information pertaining to Mizoram Legislative Assembly shall make an application in Form A. This rule requiring application to be in Form A has technical flaw of being not supported by any provision of the Act. The Act mandates that the request for information should be in writing. Prescription of Application Form is not intended.

Form A, which is Application Form, seems to be quite in accordance with the provisions of the Act in respect of making an application for information.

Recommendation

Deletion of the word "shall" appearing in between 'Legislative Assembly' and 'make an application' will render making an application in 'Form A' not mandatory and, would look more conforming with the provisions of sub-section (1) of section 6 of the Act.

Appreciation

Though the Commission have earnestly made every effort to include the implementation, progress and conduct on the Act by each and every Public Authority under the State Government, it is regretted that only a handful have complied to this effort, thus Enabling the Commission to produce, but a vivid picture of the State in the implementation of RTI, Act 2005. However, it is heartening to mention that 125 public authorities of the State Government have rendered some effort in the implementation of the Act. It is further worth mentioning that among the eight districts, Public Authorities within Serchhip District has duly submitted their reports which may be credited to the untiring efforts and motivation of the Serchhip Deputy Commissioner. The following directorates, Industries and Power & Electricity have also duly complied by furnishing reports of not only the directorate but also of every subordinate offices under it. The performances of these public authorities have set an example and will hopefully encourage other public authorities in the implementation and due submission of reports in future.

Conclusion

A reasonably good beginning had been made. Much has been done. Much more remains to be done. It is believed that we shall overcome.

BPL Card

The Provision to sub-section (5) of section 7 exempts persons of below poverty line as may be determined by the appropriate Government from payment of fees both application fee as well as fees representing cost of providing information. The first Proviso to sub-rule (1) of rule 4 prescribes that such person should produce BPL Card. The law and the rule are perfectly complementary and supplementary to each other. But, it is learnt that under the State Government of Mizoram, three Departments, viz. Rural Development Department, Food and Civil Supplies and Local Administration Department have issued their own list of persons belonging to BPL and that each of these Departments recognized only the list issued by them. This situation, it is learnt, creates confusion and problems under R.T.I. Act for getting information.

Recommendation

Government may look into the matter and settle the problem in accordance with the provisions of section 7(5) of the Act.

Intimation of Rejection in FORM 'C':

Sub-rule (1) of rule 5 prescribes that the SPIO should intimate the applicant in FORM 'C' if his application is rejected. FORM 'C' specifies the following as grounds of rejection of application, thus.—

(i) It comes under the exempted category covered under Sections 8 and 9 of the Act;
(ii) Your application was not complete in all respect.
(iii) Your identity is not satisfactory;
(iv) The information is contained in published material available to Public. You did not pay the required cost for providing information within the prescribed time;
(v) The information sought for is prohibited as per section 24(4) of the Act; and
(vi) The information would cause unwarranted invasion of the privacy of any person.

The foregoing six reasons of rejection of application for information prescribed in FORM 'C' are neither supported by any provision of the Act nor are in accordance with the letter and spirit of the Act. Section 7 of the Act requires the SPIO to make a decision, giving reasons, either to provide information or reject the application. Section 4(1)(d) also requires similar reasoning. It is not proper to prescribe reasons of rejection for SPIO in a FORM. Decision means written decision with reasons. FORM 'C' forecloses decision.

(i) "It comes under the exempted category covered under Sections 8 and 9 of the Act" is inaccurate. Section 8 contains 10 grounds on the basis of which the SPIO may not be obliged to give the information. SPIO should specify the ground of rejection. It cannot be all the ten of them in each case. Moreover, some of the so-called exempted information can be allowed in larger public interest. To foreclose the powers and functions of the SPIO in FORM 'C' is not 'to carry out the provisions of' the Act as authorized under section 27 of the Act.

(ii) "Your application was not complete in all respect" in FORM 'C' has the effect of making the Application form in FORM 'A" mandatory and is contrary to the provisions of the Act. Section 6 of the Act does not visualize any prescribed application form. FORM 'A' requires 'identity' of the applicant which is prohibited by sub-section (2) of section 6. FORM 'A' can be only model in nature and not mandatory. If so, FORM 'C' becomes redundant.

(iii) 'Your identity is not satisfactory' is contrary to the provisions of sub-section (2) of section 6 of the Act.

(iv) 'The information is contained in published material available to Public. You did not pay the required cost for providing information within the prescribed time.' These grounds of rejection contained in FORM 'C' are not supported by any provision of the Act. Non-payment of required cost will disentitle the applicant to get the information, i.e. until he pays, he would not get the information; but cannot be a ground for rejection of his application.

(v) 'The information sought for is prohibited as per section 24(4) of the Act' is an inaccurate ground. Section 24(4) does not prohibit any information; it keeps those notified organizations outside the purview of the Act.

(vi) 'The information would cause unwarranted invasion of the privacy of any person' is more like a pre-judged decision. Clause (j) of sub-section (1) of section 8 of the Act has a lot of room for discussion, for or against giving the information and, SPIO may like to decide to give information in larger public interest. Foreclosure of the judicial discretion of the SPIO is not a good prescription.

Recommendation

Form 'C' and related rules merits removal and replacement with rules which will carry out the provisions of the Act.

Salaries and Allowances of SCIC & SIC

It would be beneficial for the persons and officials concerned if, for other terms and conditions of service of SCIC, the provisions of the "Election Commission (Conditions of Service of Election Commissioners and Transaction of Business) Act, 1991" read with the relevant provisions of the "Supreme Court Judges (Salaries and Conditions of Service) Act, 1958" and the rules made there under are inserted in the rules.

5. Rules for carrying out other provisions of the Act: The rule making power of the State Government is for carrying out the provisions of the Act. Apart from the existing rules, some of the possibilities of making rules are:

(1) Identification and listing of public authorities, including NGO public authorities, as defined in clause (h) of section 2 of the Act.

(2) How and in what manner relevant facts should be

published by public authority while formulating or announcing important policies [See Section 4(1(c)]

(3) How and when public authorities should provide information suo motu under sub-section (2)

(4) How and in what manner dissemination of information is to be made. [See Section 4(3)]

(5) How and in what manner the SPIO should tackle sensitive issues like sovereignty of India, security etc. under Section 8(1)(a).

(6) What should be the procedure to be adopted by the SPIO as to what is, and what is not, larger public interest, under Section 8.

Rules Framed by Competent Authorities SECTION 28.

Section 28 of the Act empowers Competent Authorities to frames rules to carry out the provisions of the Act. Of the three Competent Authorities, namely, His Excellency, the Governor of Mizoram, the Hon'ble Speaker of Legislative Assembly and the Hon'ble Chief Justice of Gauhati High Court, only the Hon'ble Speaker framed rules in exercise of powers under Section 28 of the Act.

Section 15 of The R.T.I Act, 2005? Constitution of Mizoram State information Commission

The provisions of section 15 for Constitution of State Information Commission came into force with effect from 15th June, 2005. However, the Constitution of the Mizoram State Information Commission was notified by Notification No.13011/11/2005-IPR dated 29.6.2006. The Constitution of the Mizoram State Information Commission was complete when, by Notification No.F.13011/11/ 2005-IPR, dated the 3rd July, 2006 Pu Robert Hrangdawla, I.A.S. Rtd. was appointed the Mizoram State Chief Information Commissioner, and, Pu K. Tlanthanga IB(P)S Rtd. as Mizoram State Information Commissioner and, when, on the 5th of July, 2006 they were sworn in by His Excellency, the Governor of Mizoram. Thus, the provisions of sub-sections (1) and (2) section 15 of the Act was implemented during the year under report.

Autonomy of the Commission— Sub-section (4) of section 15 of the Act provides for autonomy of the Commission in the following words:

"(4) The general superintendence, direction and management of the affairs of the State Information Commission shall vest in the State Chief Information Commissioner who shall be assisted by the State Information Commissioners and may exercise all such powers and do all such acts and things which may be exercised or done by the State Information Commission autonomously without being subjected to directions by any authority under this Act."

Full Financial Powers: Accordingly, full financial powers has been delegated to the State Chief Information Commissioner in respect of the establishment of Mizoram State Information Commission in pursuance of Rule 3 (1)(a) of Delegation of Financial Power Rules, 1978 read with para 5 of the State of Mizoram Adaptation of Laws and Order.

(No.2) of 1978 vide Notification No. G17012/1/2000-F.Est., dated 11.10.2006 issued by Finance Department of the Government. of Mizoram.

Section 16 : Terms and Conditions of Service

Section 16 of the Act prescribes the terms and conditions of service of the State Chief Information Commissioner and the State Information Commissioners.

1. Period of office: is to be 5 years in all or till the age of 65 years, whichever is earlier.
2. Salaries and other terms and conditions of service: Sub-section (5) of section 16 of the Act provides that the salaries and allowances payable to and other terms and conditions of service of —
   (a) the State Chief Information Commissioner shall be the same as that of an Election Commissioner; and
   (b) the State Information Commissioner shall be the same as that of the Chief Secretary to the State Government.

Accordingly, the State Government, in rule 8 of the Mizoram Right to Information Rules, 2006 fixed the scale of pay of—

(a) the State Chief Information Commissioner at Rs.30,000 fixed; and
(b) the State Information Commissioners at Rs.26,000 fixed.

No other terms and conditions of service were laid down in the said rules except stating in the rules 'subject to the conditions of sub-section (5) of section 16. More detailed rules in accordance with section 16(5) would be helpful.

3. No Regular Pay Slip : During the year under report, the State Chief Information Commissioner and the State Information Commissioner were not issued Regular Pay Slip, they had to draw their salaries on the basis of Provisional Pay Slip.

4. Other terms and conditions of service of SCIC &

SIC:Other terms and conditions of service of the State Chief Information Commissioner shall be the same as that of an Election Commissioner. The terms and conditions of service of an Election Commissioner is provided in the "Election Commission (Conditions of Service of Election Commissioners and Transaction of Business) Act, 1991" as amended in 1994 (vide No.4 of 1994) which provides under sections "3.

5. There shall be paid to the Chief Election Commissioner and other Election Commissioners a salary which is equal to the salary of a Judge of the Supreme Court."

"6(2) Where the Chief Election Commissioner or an Election Commissioner demits office (whether in any manner specified in sub-section (3) or by resignation, he shall, on such demission be entitled to—

"(a) a pension which is equal to the pension payable to a Judge of the Supreme Court in accordance with the provisions of Part III of the Schedule to the Supreme Court Judges (Conditions of Service) Act, 1958, as amended from time to time" and

"(b) such pension (including commutation of pension), family pension and gratuity as are admissible to a Judge of the Supreme Court under the said Act and the rules made there under, as amended from time to time."

"7. Every person holding office as the Chief Election Commissioner or an Election Commissioner shall be entitled to subscribed to the General Provident Fund (Central Services)."

"8. Save as otherwise provided in this Act, the conditions of service relating to traveling allowance, provision of rent-free residence and exemption from payment of income-tax on the value of such rent-free residence, conveyance facilities, sumptuary allowance, medical facilities and such other conditions of service as are for the time being applicable to a Judge of the Supreme Court under Chapter IV of the Supreme Court Judges (Conditions of Service) Act, 1958 and the rules made there under, shall, so far as may be, apply to the Chief Election Commissioner and other Election Commissioners."

Thus, in terms of the conditions of service applicable to an Election Commissioner, which is also applicable to the SCIC under sub-section (5) of section 16 of the Act, the salaries and other terms and conditions of service of a Judge of the Supreme Court as specified in Supreme Court Judges (Conditions of Service) Act, 1958 and the rules made there under are applicable to the SCIC.

The State Government, in I & P.R., with the concurrence of Finance Department, vide No. F. 13011/14/2005 – IPR, dated 12.2.2007 fixed provisional entitlement and other terms and conditions of the services of the State Chief Information Commissioner and State Information Commissioner as at annexure – 8, most of which are totally at variance with the provisions of the said terms and conditions as are applicable to an Election Commissioner or to the Chief Secretary to the State Government. State Government had been requested for rectification. The State Government did not respond during the yea under report.

5. Official Residence of SCIC: In terms of the provisions of sub-section (5) of section 16 of the Act, read with the provisions of the "Election Commission

(Conditions of Service of Election Commissioners and Transaction of Business) Act, 1991" as amended in 1994 (vide No.4 of 1994) read with the provision of CHAPTER IV of the "Supreme Court Judges (Salaries and Conditions of Service) Act, 1958" and the rules made there under as applicable to an Election Commissioner and the SCIC, the SCIC is entitled without payment of rent to the use of furnished official residence which includes the staff quarters and other buildings appurtenant thereto and the garden thereof. It was not possible for the State Government to provide the SCIC an official residence as entitled by the post.

6. Official Residence of SIC: In terms of the provisions of sub-section (5) of section 16 of the Act, the terms and conditions of service SIC is the same as that of the Chief Secretary to the State Government. Official Residence is a part of the terms and conditions of service of the Chief Secretary. However, the SIC was not provided with an Official Residence similar to that of the Chief Secretary to the State Government.

Recommendation

The terms and conditions of service may be finalized with retros pective effect in accordance with the terms and conditions of service—

(a) as are applicable to an Election Commissioner in the case of SCIC;
(b) as are applicable to the Chief Secretary to the State in the case of SIC

Section18 : Complaints

Section 18 of the R.T.I. Act, 2005 empowers and obliges the State Information Commission to receive and inquire into complaint received from any person. Such a complaint can be made by a person.—

(a) who has been unable to submit a request to the State Public Information Officer (SPIO) either by reasons that no such officer had been appointed under this Act, or because the State Assistant Public Information Officer (SAPIO) has refused to accept his/her application for information or appeal under this Act for forwarding the same to the State Public Information Officer or Senior Officer designated as Departmental Appellate Authority (DAA) or the State Information Commission (SIC), as the case may be.

(b) who has been refused access to any information requested under the Act.

(c) who has not been given a response to a request for information or access to information within the time limits specified under this Act.

(d) who has been required to pay an amount of fee which he or she considers unreasonable.

(e) who believes that he or she has been given incomplete, misleading or false information under this Act.

(f) in respect of any other matter relating to requesting or obtaining access to records under this Act.

During the year under report, the Commission received six (6) complaints and disposed of 6. Four decisions were complied with and two remained pending for compliance.

Section19 : Appeals

Section 19 of the Act provides for First or Departmental Appeal to a designated senior officer and, second and final appeal to the Information Commission.

First Appeal : During the first year of implementation of

the R.T.I. Act, 2005, covering a period of roughly 9 months, 4 (four) appeals were preferred before the First/Departmental Appellate Authorities, who disposed of all the four appeals during the same year. Out of four appeals decided by them, three (3) were allowed and one was rejected. It is an excellent job performed by the First Appellate Authorities.

Second Appeal: No application for second appeal was received during the first year of implementation in Mizoram.

V. Section 20 (1): Penal Ties

Sub-section (1) of Section 20 of the R.T.I. Act, 2005 has obliged the Information Commission to impose penalty on the SPIO if, at the time of deciding any complaint or appeal, the Commission is of the opinion that the SPIO has , without any reasonable cause—

- (i) refused to receive an application for information;
- (ii) has not furnished information within the time specified under sub-section (1) of section 7;
- (iii) mal-afidely denied the request for information;
- (iv) knowingly given incorrect, incomplete or misleading information;
- (v) destroyed information which was the subject of the request, and
- (vi) obstructed in any manner in furnishing the information.

During the period under report, the Commission had no occasion for proceeding and for imposing any penalty on any SPIO. Annexure– 6.

VII. Section 20 (2) : Disciplinary Action Against SPIO

Sub-section (2) of Section 20 of the R.T.I. Act, 2005 obliges the Information Commission to recommend for disciplinary action against the SPIO if, at the time of deciding any complaint or appeal, the Commission is of the opinion that the SPIO has, without any reasonable cause and persistently—

(i) failed to receive an application for information;
(ii) has not furnished information within the time specified under sub-section (1) of section 7;
(iii) malafidely denied the request for information;
(iv) knowingly given incorrect, incomplete or misleading information;
(v) destroyed information which was the subject of the request; and
(vi) obstructed in any manner in furnishing the information.

During the period under report, the Commission had no occasion for proceeding and for recommendation of disciplinary action against any SPIO.

Section 24(4) Proviso : Approval of Commission

Certain intelligence and security organizations notified by the State Government under sub-section (4) of section 24 of the Act, though are exempt from the operation of the Act in normal course, are also liable to furnish information, with the approval of the State Information Commission, pertaining to the allegations of corruption and human rights violation.

During the year under report, no approval under this sub-section was give by the Commission.

Section 25 : Monitoring and Reporting

It is the duty of the Information Commission to prepare a report on the implementation of the provisions of the Act, each year and forward a copy thereof to the appropriate Government under Section 25 of the Act. This Report is the

First Report of the Mizoram State Information Commission on the implementation of the provisions of the Right to Information Act, 2005 in Mizoram.

Section 26 : The appropriate (State) Government is required by sub-section (1) of section 26 to perform the following:—

1. To develop and organize educational programmes to advance the understanding of the public as to how to exercise the rights contemplated under the Act;
2. To encourage public authorities to participate in the development and organization of educational programmes and to undertake such programmes themselves;
3. To promote timely and effective dissemination of accurate information by public authorities about their activities; and
4. To train SPIOs of public authorities and produce relevant training materials for use by the public authorities themselves.

Implementation

The Commission has no information about the implementation of the provisions of sub-section (1) of section 26 for the public by the State Government during the year under report. However, seven training programmes were organized for the PIOs, for 14 days for seven districts of the State with total number of 183 participants.

Second Schedule

[See Rules 4 and 10]

(A) Fees/Amount to be Charged for Providing Information

PART-I(A) Application fee Rupees ten per application Mode of Fee Payment — Treasury Challan/ Cash / Court fee stamp

Fee for 1st Appeal forty
2nd appeal — Rupees fifty
Mode: Court fee stamp

PART –II(B) Amount to be charged for providing information.

(B) (i) Inspection of documents no fee for the first hour by cash and a fee of Rupees five per each subsequent hour or fraction thereof;

(ii) A4 size paper/A3 size paper for each folio:

1. Type copy/photocopy Rupees two by cash per page.
2. Print out from computer Rupees five by cash per page.

(iii) CD with cover Rupees fifty per CD by cash;

(iv) Floppy Diskette (1.44MB) Rupees fifty per Floppy by cash;

(v) Maps & Plans Reasonable cost to be fixed by P.I.O. depending upon the cost of labour and material and equipment and other ancillary expenses;

(vi) Video Cassettedo-by cash Microfilm/Microfiche; and

(vii) Certified sample of material -do- by cash

N.B: Proper and authenticated money receipt to be issued for all cash payment. The office is to state the cash receipt No. on the application Form. Revenue Head : 0070 : Other Admistrative Services 60 : Others 118 : Receipt under RTI Act,2005

Nagaland RTI Rules, 2005

Dated, the 30th November, 2005.

NO. AR-3/Gen-1471200S (A)

In exercise of the powers conferred by clauses (b) and (c) of sub-section (2) of section 27 of the Right to Information Act, 2005 (Government. of India Act No. 22 of 2005), the Government of Nagaland hereby makes the following rules, namely:—

1. Short Title and commencement—

   (i) These Rules may be called the Nagaland State Right to Information (Regulation of Fcc and Cost) Rules, 2005.
   (ii) They shall come into force on the date of their publication in the Official Gazette.

2. Definitions— In the rules, unless the context otherwise requires—

   (a) 'Act' means the Right to Information Act, 2005 (Govt. of India Act No. 22 of 20(5)
   (b) 'Section' means section of the Act;
   (c) all other words and expressions used herein and not defined but defined in the Act shall have the meanings assigned to them in the Act.

3. A request for obtaining information under sub-section (I) of section 6 shall be accompanied by an application fee of rupees ten by way of cash against proper receipt or by demand draft or bankers cheque payable to the Accounts Officer/Head of Department/Head of Office of the public authority or the Government Department/ Office.
4. For inspection or records, no fee for the first hour and a fee of rupees five for each fifteen minutes (or fraction thereof) thereafter for providing the information under sub-section (I) of section 7, the fee shall be charged by way of cash against proper receipt or by demand draft or bankers cheque payable to the Accounts Officer /

Head of Department/Head of Office of the public authority or Government Department/Office at the following rates:—

(a) rupees two for each page (in A-4 or A-3 size paper) created or copied;
(b) actual charge or cost price of a copy if given in larger size paper;
(c) actual cost or price for samples or models; and
(d) for inspection of records, no fee for the first hour; and a fee of rupees five for each subsequent hour (or fraction thereof).

5. For providing the information under sub-section (5) of section 7 the fee shall be charged of cash by way of cash against proper receipt or by demand draft or bankers cheque payable to the Accounts Officer/Head of Department/Head of Office of the public authority or Government Department/Office at the following rates:—

(a) for information provided in diskette or floppy rupees fifty per diskette or floppy; and
(b) for information provided in printed form at the price fixed for such publication or rupees two per page of photocopy for extracts from the publication.

6. In respect of all Government Departments/Offices and other Public Authority, whose establishment costs are met from the State's exchequers, the fees collected under these rules shall be deposited at the end of every month, in the Government Treasury through a Treasury Challan and credited to the head of Account '0070':'Other Administrative Services'.

The Nagaland SIC RTI Rules, 2005

Notification

Dated: 30th November, 2005

No: AR-3/Gen-147/2005/B

In exercise of the powers conferred by Section 27 of the Right to Information Act, 2005 (Central Act 22 of 2005), the Government of Nagaland hereby makes the following rules, namely:—

1. Short title and commencement —

    (1) These rules may be called the Goa State Information Commission (Appeal Procedure) Rules, 2005.

    (2) They shall come into force from the date of their publication in the Official Gazette.

2. Definitions – In these rules, unless the context other wise requires—

    (a) "Act" means the Right to Information Act, 2005 (Central Act No. 22 of 2005);

    (b) "Section" means a section of the Act;

    (c) "Commission" means the State Information Commission; and

    (d) words and expressions used herein and not defined but defined in the Act, shall have the same meaning respectively assigned to them in the Act.

3. Contents of appeal – An appeal to the Commission shall contain the following information, namely :—

    (i) name and address of the appellant;

    (ii) name and address of the State Public Information

Officer against whose decision the appeal is preferred;

(iii) particulars of the order including number, if any, against which the appeal is preferred;

(iv) brief facts leading to the appeal;

(v) If the appeal is preferred against deemed refusal, the particulars of the application, including number and date as also the name and address of the State Public Information Officer to whom the application was made;

(vi) prayer or relief sought;

(vii) grounds for the prayer or relief;

(viii) verification by the appellant; and

(ix) any other information which the Commission may deem necessary for deciding the appeal.

4. Documents to accompany appeal – Every appeal made to the Commission shall be accompanied by the following documents, namely:—

(i) self-attested copies of the Orders or documents against which the appeal is being preferred, unless the appeal is preferred against deemed refusal;

(ii) copies of documents relied upon by the appellant and referred to in the appeal; and

(iii) an index of the documents referred to in the appeal.

5. Procedure in deciding appeal – In deciding an appeal, the Commission may—

(i) take oral or written evidence on oath or on affidavit from the concerned or interested person;

(ii) peruse or inspect documents, public records or copies thereof;

(iii) inquire, through authorised officer, about further details or facts;

(iv) hear State Public Information Officer, State Assistant Public Information Officer or such Senior Officer who had decided the first appeal, or such person against whom the complaint is made, as the case may be ;

(v) hear a third party ; and

(vi) receive evidence on affidavits from State Public Information Officer, State Assistant Public Information Officer, such Senior Officer who decided the first appeal, such person against whom the complaint lies or the third party.

6. Service of notice by Commission – Notice to be issued by the Commission may be served in any of the following modes, namely :—

(i) service by the party itself;

(ii) by hand delivery (dasti) through Process Server;

(iii) by registered post with acknowledgement due; or\

(iv) through the Head of Office or Department.

8. Order of the Commission – Order of the Commission shall be pronounced in proceeding and shall be in writing duly authenticated by the Registrar or any other officer authorised by the Commission for this purpose.

The Orissa Right to Information Rules, 2005.

Notification
Dated: 1st October, 2005
S.R.O.No.477/2005

In exercise of the power conferred by Section 27 of the Right to Information Act (No.22 of 2005), the State Government do hereby make the following rules, namely: —

1. Short title and commencement :

   (1) These rules may be called the Orissa Right to Information Rules, 2005.
   (2) They shall come into force on the date of their publication in the Orissa Gazette.

2. Definitions :

   (1) In these rules, unless there is anything repugnant in the subject or context —

      (a) *'Act'* means the Right to Information Act, 2005 (No. 22 of 2005);
      (b) *'BPL Card'* means a card issued to any citizen who is below the poverty line;
      (c) *'fee'* means amount payable by the applicant for obtaining any information under the provisions of sub-section (1) of section 6 and sub-sections (1) and (5) of section 7 excluding the cost of providing information;
      (d) *'form'* means a form appended to these rules;
      (e) *'identity'* means an evidence to show the citizenship like an electoral photo identity

card, a passport or any other document which can satisfy the authority about the citizenship of the person;

(f) *'Nodal Officer'* means the Commissioner-cum-Secretary to Government, Information and Public Relations Department;

(g) *'Public Information Officer'* means the State Public Information Officer designated under sub-section (1) of section 5 of the Act and includes an Assistant Public Information Officer designated as such under sub-section (2) thereof;

(h) *'Schedule'* means a Schedule appended to these rules; *and*

(i) *'State Government'* means the Government of Orissa

(2) Words and expressions used but not defined in these rules shall have the meaning as assigned to them in the Act.

3. Appointment and Obligations of Public Information Officers.—

(1) A public authority, if it is a department of State Government, shall designate as many officers as it deem proper, not below the rank of Under Secretary as Public Information Officers.

(2) In each sub-ordinate office of the Department of Government including the Heads of Department and offices in the district and Sub-divisional level the head of such offices shall designate as many officers as they deem proper as Public Information Officers and Assistant Public Information Officers.

(3) Every public authority other than those mentioned in sub-rules (1) and (2) of the said rule 3 shall designate one or more Public

Information Officers in all administrative units and offices under such authority: Provided that every such public authority shall, while designating such officers as Public Information Officers so designated, ensure that an officer higher in rank to public Information Officer, is available to be specified as Appellate Authority.

(4) If, for any reason beyond the control of Public Information Officer furnishing of information is delayed, he shall record reasons with justification thereof and shall communicate the Head of the office about such delay.

4. Procedure to obtain information. –

(1) A citizen desirous of any information may apply for information in Form 'A' to the Public Information Officer, with the required fee in shape of Treasury Challan or cash as specified in the Schedule under the appropriate head of Account: Provided that application fee shall not be payable in case of a person whose name appears in the latest list of persons below poverty line for which he has to produce BPL Card.
Provided that a citizen seeking information through electronic means has to submit evidence regarding deposit of prescribed application fee.

(2) The Public Information Officer or any other officer authorized by him shall furnish the acknowledgement and after being satisfied with the identity of the applicant shall also intimate in Form 'B' as soon as possible the amount of cost for providing information required to be paid by the applicant in cash, as mentioned in the Schedule.

(3) The applicant may deposit the said amount within a period of fifteen days from the date of receipt of such information, failing which the application shall stand rejected.

5. Information regarding rejection.—

(1) Where a request has been rejected under sub-section (1) of section 7, the Public Information Officer shall intimate the applicant, the reasons for such rejection in Form 'C'.

(2) Wherever, information applied for is available in electronic means, the Public Information Officer may advise in Form 'C' to the applicant to obtain the information from the appropriate website to be specified by the Public Information Officer.

6. *Meeting of the recommending Committee.*—For the purpose of appointment of the State Chief Information Commissioner and the State Information Commissioner under sub-section (3) of section 15, the Nodal Officer shall, in consultation with the State Government, convene the meeting of the Committee for their recommendation.

7. Memorandum of appeal.—

(1) An appeal under sub-section (1) of section 19 shall be filed in Form 'D' to the officer as designated by the Public Authority to hear such appeal.

(2) The Memorandum of appeal shall be accompanied with such fee as specified in the Schedule which shall be paid in the shape of court fee stamp.

(3) Any person aggrieved by the decision under sub-section (1) of section 19, may prefer a second appeal before the State Information Commission under sub-section (3) thereof in form E which shall be accompanied with such fee in the shape of court fee stamp as specified in the Schedule.

(4) The appeal preferred under sub-rules (1) and (3), if not accompanied with the required fee, shall be rejected by the concerned Appellate Authority, but no fee is payable by the applicant holding a BPL Card.

(5) Every order of the Appellate Authority shall be communicated to the appellant concerned and to the Public Information Officer where such appeal is from the order of the Public Information Officer and to the first Appellate Authority in case it is a second appeal.

8. Guidelines by the State Government.— The State Government shall have the power to issue guidelines not inconsistent with the provisions of the Act and these rules for smooth implementation of the provisions of the Act and the rules.

9. Penalties – In the event of imposition of penalty under section 20 on the Public Information Officer concerned, such penalty may be deposited by the said officer by Treasury Challan under the appropriate receip. Head of the State Budget within a period of thirty days, failing which the amount shall be recovered from the salary of the officer concerned.

10. Calculation of cost of damage. — If any damage is caused to the public property in the course of giving any information in the form of samples of materials, the damage caused to such property shall be included while calculating further fees representing the cost of providing the information.

11. Maintenance of Register –

(1) The Public Information Officer shall maintain a register in Form 'F' for recording the details of the applications received and the information supplied by him and keep the Head of Office informed after furnishing any information and it shall be the duty of the Head of Office to ensure required assistance if any, as would be sought for by the Public Information Officer to facilitate providing information.

(2) The Public Information Officer shall maintain a cash register in Form 'G' for recording the details

of money received by him relating to providing information and deposit the money in such head of account or in any Scheduled Bank in the name of such officer as the concerned Head of Office decides.

12. Deposit of expenditure—The expenditure to be incurred for production of witness or documents before the State Information Commission shall be deposited before the Commission by the party at whose instance the witnesses or the documents are to be produced.

13. Realisation of penalties or damages—Any penalty or damage or any other sum payable under the Act, if not paid within thirty days of the date of receipt of the order for realization of the same or cannot be recovered, it can be realized from such person as arrears of land revenue.

[No.- 27163 – I & P.R.]

The Orissa Gazette

Notification

The 29th May 2006

S. R. O. No.251/2006

In exercise of the powers conferred by Section 27 of the Right to Information Act, 2005 (Act No.22 of 2005), the State Government do hereby make the following rules, to amend the Orissa Right to Information Rules, 2005, namely:—

1. Short title and commencement —

    (1) These rules may be called the Orissa Right to Information (Amendment) Rules, 2006.
    (2) They shall come into force on the date of their publication in the Orissa Gazette.

2. In the Orissa Right to Information Rules, 2005 for rule 11, the following rule shall be substituted, namely:—

"11. *Maintenance of Register*"—

(1) The Public Information Officer shall maintain a register in Form 'F' for recording the details of the applications received and the information supplied by him and keep the Head of Office informed after furnishing any information and it shall be the duty of the Head of Office to ensure required assistance if any, as would be sought for by the Public Information Officer to facilitate providing information and the said Register shall remain always open to inspection by the members of public as required in respect of the proactive disclosures under Section 4 (1b) of the Act.

(2) Each public authority shall maintain a Register for day-to-day record of the members of public who visit its office in connection with accessing or inspecting suo motto information proactively disclosed by the said authority under Section 4 of the Act.

(3) The Public Information Officer shall maintain a cash register in Form 'G' for recording the details of money received by him relating to providing information and deposit the money in such Head of Account or in any Scheduled Bank in the name of such officer as the concerned Head of Office decides."

3. In the said rules, in Form 'A' :

(i) for the entries appearing against item 5, the following shall be substituted namely:— "(d) Whether information is required by post/in person/E-Mail
(The actual postal charges shall be included in providing information)"; and

(ii) for item 6, alongwith the entries made, thereof the following shall be substituted, namely:— "6 Address/E-mail ID to which information will be sent & in which form".

4. In the said rules, the existing Schedule shall be substituted by the following, namely:—

Schedule

(See Rules 4 and 7)

Fees/Amount to be charged for providing information

	PART – I		
(A)	Application fee	*Rate to be charged*	*Mode of deposit*
(i)	Application fee seeking information	Rupees ten per Application	Treasury Challan / cash
(ii)	Application fee for Ist Appeal	Rupees twenty	Court fee stamp
(iii)	Application fee for 2nd Appeal	Rupees twenty-five	Court fee stamp

	PART – II		
(B)	*Amount to be charged for Providing information*		
(i)	A4 or A3 size paper created or copied	Rupees two per each folio	By cash
(ii)	Paper size larger than A4 or A3	Actual charge or cost price of a copy	By cash
(iii)	Inspection of records	No fee for the first hour and Rs.5.00 for each 15 minutes (or fraction thereof) thereafter.	By cash
(iv)	CD with cover	Rupees 50 per CD	By cash
(v)	Floppy Diskette (1.44MB)	Rupees 50 per Floppy	By cash
(vi)	Maps and Plans	Reasonable cost to be fixed by P.I.O.	By cash

(Contd...)

(Contd...)

		depending upon the cost of labour and material and equipment and other ancillary expenses	
(vii)	Video Cassette/ Microfilm/Microfiche	Reasonable cost to be fixed by P.I.O. depending upon the cost of labour and material and equipment and other ancillary expenses	By cash
(viii)	Certified sample or or models of material	Actual cost of price for sample or models	By cash
(ix)	Information in printed form	Price fixed for such publication	By cash

N.B.–Proper and authenticated money receipt to be issued for all cash payment. The office is to state the cash receipt No. on the application Form 'A'. "

Note–The Principal rules were published in the Gazette of Orissa vide I & P.R. Department Notification No.27163, dated the 1st October 2005 [S.R.O. No.477/2005, dated the 1st October 2005].

The Punjab RTI Rules, 2007

NOTIFICATION

No.G.S.R.16/C.A.22/2005/S.27/2007

In exercise of the powers conferred by sub-section (1) of section 27 of the Right to Information Act, 2005 (Central Act No.22 of 2005), and all other powers enabling him in this behalf, the Governor of Punjab is pleased to make the following rules to provide for the matters specified in subsection (2) of the said section, namely:—

Rules

1. Short title and commencement:—
   (1) These rules may be called the Punjab Right to Information Rules, 2007.
   (2) They shall come into force on and with effect from the date of their publication in the Official Gazette

2. Definitions :

   (1) In these rules, unless the context otherwise requires—

   1. "Act" means the Right to Information Act, 2005(Central Act No.22 of 2005);
   2. "Commission" means the Punjab Information Commission, constituted under section 15 of the Act;
   3. "Form" means a Form, appended to these rules; and
   4. "Section" means a section of the Act.

(2) The words and expressions used in these rules, but not defined, shall have the same meanings as assigned to them in the Act.

3. Application obtaining information:— (Sections 2(m), 6 and 27)

1. A person, who desires to obtain any information admissible under the Act, shall make an application in Form 'A' to the State Public Information Officer alongwith a fee, as specified in sub-rule (1) of rule 5 of these rules.
2. On the receipt of an application, made under sub-rule (1), the State Public Information Officer shall give a receipt in token thereof to the applicant in Form 'B'.
3. Each public authority shall maintain the information register in Form 'C' in respect of the records of requests received from the applicants for seeking information under the Act.
4. The application, received without requisite fee, shall not be entertained and shall be liable to be rejected straightway without giving any notice to the applicant.

4. Deposit of fee:- (Section 6)

1. The fee may be paid in the following modes, namely:—

(a) by Crossed Bank Draft/Banker's Chequie/IPO or in cash in favour of concerned Drawing and Disbursing Officer from where the information is to be obtained;
(b) in cash with the concerned Drawing and Disbursing Officer ; and
(c) through Treasury Challan in the following Heads of Account:—

Major Head	..	0070-Other Administrative Services
Sub-Major Head	..	60 - Other Services
Minor Head	..	800 -Other Receipts
Sub-Head	..	86-Fee under the Right to Information Act, 2005
Detailed Head	..	0070 Other Administrative Services 60 Other Services-800-Other Receipts 86-Fees under the Right to Information Act, 2005.

2. The amount of fee shall be credited to the account as referred to in clause (c) of sub-rule (1) : Provided that the Board, Corporations and other Autonomous bodies of the State, may get the amount of requisite fee deposited in their own accounts maintained by them
3. On receipt of an application, submitted under sub-rule (1) of rule 3, the State Public Information Officer shall scrutinize the application and shall assess how much fee is required to be paid by the applicant for obtaining the information.
4. The fee, assessed under sub-rule (3), shall be informed to the applicant by the State Public Information Officer in Form 'D' within a period of ten days from the receipt of application.
5. The intimation of rejection of an application of the applicant seeking information under the Act, shall be intimated by the State Public Information Officer concerned, in Form 'E'.
6. The amount of fee collected under this rule, shall be maintained in the Cash register as specified in Form 'F'.

5. *Quantum of fee:—* (Section 6 and 7)

1. An application for obtaining any information under sub-section (1) of section 6 shall be accompanied with a fee of rupees ten only.

2. The following fee shall be charged for providing information under sub-section (1) of section 7, namely:—
   (a) Rupees two for each page in A-4 or A-3 size paper, created or copied;
   (b) Actual charge or cost price of a copy in larger size paper;
   (c) Actual cost or price for samples or models;
   (d) for inspection of records, no fee for the first hour; and a fee of rupees five for each fifteen minutes (or fraction thereof) thereafter;
   (e) for information provided in diskette or floppy rupees fifty per diskette or floppy; and
   (f) for information provided in printed from at the price fixed for such publication or rupees two per page of photocopy for extracts from the publication.

3. The applicant shall, while depositing fee under sub-rule(2) of rule 4, shall also submit a self addressed envelope duly stamped for supplying the information. Stamps on the envelope shall be affixed according the mode of supplying the information, as desired by the applicant i.e. through ordinary registered or speed post.

6. Procedure to be followed in deciding appeal:—(Section 19 (10))

Before deciding an appeal, the Commission shall,—

(a) serve notice to the concerned persons;
(b) entertain any evidence in support of appeal, which may be oral or in writing from the concerned persons;
(c) examine on oath or by having affidavits from the persons concerned;
(d) peruse or inspect the documents or any records or copies thereof ;

(e) inquire through the authorized officer the facts of an appeal or may require facts in detail, if it so deems appropriate, hear the State Public Information Officer or any other senior officer, who had decided the first appeal, as the case may be; and

(f) receive evidence on affidavits from the officer senior in rank to State Information Officer who had decided the first appeal or from any other officer or person authorized in this behalf from whom the evidence may be deemed necessary.

7. *Mode of serving notice:-* (Section 19 (10))

The Commission may serve notice to the persons concerned in any of the following modes, namely:—

(a) by hand delivery(dasti) through process server; or
(b) by registered post with acknowledgment due; or
(c) by publication in the news paper;.

8. *Order by the Commission:-*Section 19 (10))

1. The Commission shall make order in writing and pronounce the same in the presence of the concerned parties.
2. After the decision is pronounced by the Commission, it shall intimate the same to the complainant and the State Information Officer of the Department or the public authority concerned

9. *Repeal and Saveing.*— The Punjab Right to Information Rules 2006 are hereby repealed:

Provided that any order made or action taken under the rules so repealed shall be deemed to have been made or taken under the corresponding provisions of these rules.

The Rajasthan RTI Rules, 2005

Notification

Dated: 12.10.2005

No. F.9.(23) Gr-5/2005

In exercise of the powers conferred by section 27 of Right to Information Act 2005 (Central Act No. 22 of 2005), the State Government hereby makes the following rules, namely:—

1. Short title and commencement: —

   (1) These rules may be called by the Rajasthan Right to Information Rules, 2005.

   (2) They shall come into force on the date of their publication in the official Gazette.

2. Definitions

   (1) In these rules, unless the context otherwise requires:—

      (a) 'Act' means the Right to Information Act, 2005.

      (b) 'Commission' means the Rajasthan Information Commission

      (c) 'Section' means section of the Act

   (2) The words and expressions used herein, but not defined, shall have the meaning assigned to them in that Act

3. Application Fee: -

   A request for obtaining information under sub section (1) of section 6 shall be accompanied by an application fee of Rs. 10 by way of cash against proper receipt or by demand draft or bankers' cheque payable to public authority.

4. Fee for providing information: —

(1) For providing the information under sub-section (1) of section 7, the fee shall be charged by way of cash against proper receipt or by demand draft or bankers cheque payable to the public, authority at the following rates:

(a) rupees two for each page (in A4 and A3 size paper) created or copied;
(b) actual charge or cost price of a copy in large size paper;
(c) actual cost or price for samples or models; and
(d) for inspection of records, no fee for the first hour and a fee of rupees five for each 15 minutes or fraction thereof thereafter.

(2) For Providing information under sub-section (5) of section 7, the fee shall be charged by way of cash against proper receipt or by demand draft or bankers cheque payable to the public authority at the following rates: —

(a) for information provided in diskette or floppy rupees fifty per diskette or floppy; and
(b) for information provided in printed form at the price for such publication or rupees two per page of photocopy for extracts from the publication.

5. Contents of appeal:—
An appeal to the Commission shall contain the following information, namely:—

(i) name and address of the appellant;

(ii) name and address of the State Public Information Officer ;

(iii) particulars of the orders against which the appeal is made including number and date;

(iv) brief facts leading to the appeal;

(v) grounds for the prayer or relief;

(vi) provisions of the Act or the rules;

(vii) prayer or relief sought;

(viii) verification by the appellant; and

(ix) any other information which the commission may deem necessary for deciding the appeal.

6. Documents to accompany appeal: — Every appeal made to the Commission shall be accompanied by the following documents namely:—

(i) attested true copy of the order against which the appeal is being preferred;

(ii) copies of documents relied upon by the appellant and referred in the appeal; and

(iii) an index of the documents referred to in the appeal

7. Procedure in deciding appeal:— In deciding the appeal the Commission shall—

(i) consider oral and written evidence on oath or on affidavit from concerned or interested person;

(ii) peruse or inspect documents, public record or copies thereof;

(iii) inquire through authorized officer further details or facts;

(iv) hear State Public Information Officer, Assistant State Public Information Officer or Senior officer, who decided the first appeal, as the case may be;

(v) hear third party; and

(vi) receive evidence on affidavit from State Public Information Officer, Assistant State Public

Information Officer or Senior officer, who decided the first appeal, as the case may be ; (iv) (v) (vi) (vii) (viii) (ix)

8. Service of notice by Commission:— Notice to be issued by the Commission may be served in any of the following modes, namely:—

   (i) service by the party itself;
   (ii) by hand delivery (dasti) through processes;
   (iii) by registered post with one acknowledgement.

9. Signing of order:—Order of the Commission pronounced in open. Proceedings shall be in writing and authenticated by the Registrar or any other officer authorized by the Commission for the purpose.

The Sikkim Right to Information Rules, 2005

NOTIFICATION
Dated: 22.12.2005
No.230/GEN/DOP

In exercise of the power conferred by section 27 of the Right to Information Act, 2005 (22 of 2005), the State Government hereby makes the following rules namely:—

1. Short title and commencement—

   (1) These rules may be called the Sikkim State to Information (Regulation of Fee Cost and Miscellaneous) Rules, 2005.

   (2) They shall come into force on the date of their publication in the Official Gazette.

2. Definition :

   (1) In this Rules, unless the context otherwise requires:—

      (a) "Act" means the Right to Information Act, 2005.

      (b) "Section" means section of the Act.

      (c) Appellate Authority refers to the officers appointed to hear first appeals under Section 1(1) of the Act; and

      (d) All other words and expressions used in these rules but not defined and defined in the Act shall have the same meanings assigned to them, in the Act.

3. There shall be a State Public Information Officer (PIO for short) in each Department of the Government to perform the functions and discharge the responsibilities s provided under the Act. Such Public Information Officers shall not be below the rank of a Joint Secretary of the State Government.

4. (1) There shall be a State Assistant Public Information Officers (Asstt. P.I.O. for short) in every Sub-Division and the Districts of the State to be appointed by the State Government. Such Assistant Public Information Officers shall be from among the Gazetted Class - I or Class - II State Government Officers posted in the Sub-Division or the District levels. The Assistant Public Information Officers should be such who is accessible and who the people would fee comfortable to approach.

   (2) The official receipt for the fees shall be issued by the receiving State Assistant Public Information Officers.

Procedure for Seeking Information

5. Applications:

   (1). A request for obtaining information under sub-section (1) of section 6 shall be made to the concerned State Public Information Officer in an application preferably in the form as given in Annexure "A" accompanied by an application fee of Rs. 100 (One Hundred) by way of bank receipt to be deposited under Major head 0070. OAS (E) RTI Fee payable to the public authority with a copy of such order appealed against.

(2) Whatever form an application is received in, it shall include the following:

(i) Name, father's name, permanent address of the applicant;
(ii) Documentary proof of being a citizen of India. (*Explanation*: Certified copy of Sikkim Subject Certificate, certified copy of Certificate of Identification, Attested copy of Passport, certified copy of Electoral Roll will suffice for this purpose)
(iii) An address to which notices and information can be sent;
(iv) The date of the application is submitted;
(v) Subject mater of the information requested, including if relevant the period and/or geographic area to which the information relates; and
(vi) Form of access preferred (optional).

(3) Where an electronic application is made, the application shall send a money order/cheque/ demand draft to the PIO for the application fee or send a copy of a payment receipt either by post, fax, PDF or in person.
(4) The period of 30 days referred to in Sec. 7(1) shall be counted from the day the application fee is received by the public authority.
(5) If the information sought for does not fall within the jurisdiction of the State Public Information Officer he shall refer the application to such authority having jurisdiction over the matter within five days with intimation to the application advising him to contact such authority.
(6) If the requested Information falls within the jurisdiction of the State Public Information Officer and/or in any one or more of the category of

restrictions listed in Section 6 of the Act and Rule 6 of these rules, the State Public Information Officer, on being satisfied, will issue a rejection order in form of Annexure "C" within 30 days from the date of receipt of the application.

(7) If the requested information falls with in the competent authority's jurisdiction but not in one or more of the category listed in Section 6 of the Act or Rule 6 of these Rules, the State Public Information Officer, on being so satisfied shall supply the information to the application in the form Annexure "D" in these Rules, falling within his jurisdiction. In case the information sought is party outside the jurisdiction of the State Public Information Officer or partly falls in the categories listed in Section 6 of the Act or Rule 6 of these Rules, the State Public Information Officer shall supply only such information as is permissible under the Act and the Rules and is within his jurisdiction and reject the remaining part giving reasons thereof.

6. Application relating to life and liberty:

(1) Where an application is made which purports to affect a person's life and liberty as referred to under Sec. 7(1), the applicant should note this clearly on the application and should include an explanation as to why the application should be expedited under this provision.

(2) Where Sec. 7(1) is invoked in respect of information relating to life and liberty, the PIO should examine the applicants application liberally, and should, when processing the request, apply the interpretation of the Act which is most beneficial to the applicant.

(3) For the purpose of applying Sec. 7(1), the PIO should at a minimum expedite an application where the information requested relates to a person's confinement, internment, arbitrary detention, imminent death at the hands of the State or another individual, torture or violation of due process rights.

7. Application for Samples or Inspection:

(1) Where an application is made for taking a sample of inspecting a record or public works, the PIO shall intimate the date, time and venue when the application and/or his/her authorized representative (s) can obtain a sample or material or inspect information or works.
(2) In accordance with Sec. 7(1), the date for providing a sample and/or permitting inspection shall not exceed 30 days from the date of receipt of application unless the applicant requests a later date for inspection.
(3) The sample shall be provided to the applicant in the same manner and following the same procedure as followed when the sample is taken by a vigilance or an investigation agency. As far as possible, the sample shall be provided from the spot of applicant's choice indicated by the applicant on the spot.
(4) The PIO shall ensure that all the records sought by the applicant are available for inspection, during the inspection.
(5) At the time of inspection, at least one official should be present to follow inspection
(6) If the applicant desires to take copies of any parts of the records inspected by him or a sample of the work inspected by him, he/she may request such copies/samples without having to make an

additional application (or pay and additional application fee) and the PIO shall provide such copies/samples within 5 days, subject to payment of any fees.

8. Receiving and Acknowledging Applications:

(1) In accordance with Section 5(4) and 5(5), any officer in any public authority shall be under an obligation to receive an application for information under the Act.

(2) It will be the responsibility of any officer who receives an application for information under the Act to pass the application on to the relevant PIO or Assistant PIO as soon as possible and no later than 3 days from receiving the application, although the date of receipt for the purpose of the time limits in Sec. 7 shall be the date the application was initially received by the officer.

(3) The person who receives the application shall acknowledge the receipt of every application in writing. The receipt must include, at a minimum, the application reference No. the receiver's name, position, department/public body, the date of the application was received and the date by which a response must be provided.

(4) Where an application is received by post, the date of receipt is taken to be the date, the application is logged into the mail register of the Department or public body, whether or not that date is the same date the application is received by the PIO.

(5) Where an application is received electronically, the date of receipt is taken to be the date the application is sent to the Department or public body, whether or not that date is the same date the application is received by the PIO.

9. (1) *Fee for Information*: For providing the information under sub-section (1) of section 7 and Rule 5 under these Rules, the fee shall be charged by way of bank receipt under Major Head 0070. OAS(E) RTI Fee payable to the public authority, at the following rates, namely: —

(A) (a) When the concerned department has already fixed the price of charges some documents, samples, model, maps etc. The price so fixed plus postal.

(b) When the information is readily available, either by way of photocopying or by other way or by other (copy). (i) Rupees 10 (ten) for each page (in A-4 or A-3 size paper) created or copied plus post charges, or (ii) actual charge or cost price a copy in large size paper plus postal charges.

(B) For inspection of records, no fee for the first hour, and a fee of Rupees five for each fifteen minutes (or fraction thereof) thereafter:

Provided that no postal charges shall be charged if the application collects the information personally.

Provided further that if on a particular day it is not administratively feasible the matter of inspection may be postponed.

10. For providing the information under sub-section (5) of section 7, the fee shall be charged by way of bank receipt payable to the public authority at the following rates—

(a) For information provided in printed form at the price fixed for such publication or rupees five per page of photocopy for extracts from the publication plus Postal charges. The above charges are to be accompanied by a bank receipt deposited under Major Head 0070.OAS (E) RTI Fee.

Provided that no postal charges shall be charges if the applicant collects the information personally.

11. On receipt of an application seeking information under Rule 3, the concerned State Public Information Officer shall consider as to whether :—

(a) The Information sought for relates to any occurrence, event or matter which has taken place, occurred or happened 20 years before the date on which any request is made under these rules and if such information is found to be more than 20 years from such date, the request shall no be entertained, and in any case the information sought for falling under clauses (b), (d) and (j) below shall not be furnished subject to the extent of permissibility provided therein;

(b) Disclosure of which would prejudicially affect the sovereignty and integrity of India, the security, strategic, or economic interest of the State, relation with foreign State or lead to incitement of an offence;

(c) The information sought for has been expressly forbidden to be published by any court of law or tribunal or the disclosure of which may constitute contempt of court;

(d) The disclosure of the information would cause a prejudice of privilege of Parliament or the State Legislature;

(e) The disclosure of the information including commercial, confidence, trade, secrets or intellectual property would harm the competition position of a third party, unless he is satisfied that larger public interest warrants the disclosure of such information;

(f) Information available to a person in his fiduciary relationship, unless the competent authority is satisfied that the larger public interest warrants the disclosure of such information;

(g) Information received in confidence from foreign Government;

(h) Information, the disclosure of which would endanger the life or physical safety of any person or identify the source of information or assistance given in confidence for law enforcement or security purposes;

(i) Information which would impele the process of investigation or apprehension or prosecution of offenders;

(j) As to whether the information sought for is a decision/decisions of the Council of Ministers and in such case and if asked for, the reasons of such decision and the materials on the basis of which the decisions were taken only after the decision have been taken by the Council of Ministers and the decision-making process is complete or over. However, if the decision of the Council of Ministers come under the exemption specified under sub-section (1) of Section 8 of the Act, 2005, and under this rule, such information shall not be disclosed.

(k) In any case, information which relates to personal information the disclosure of which has no relationship to any public activity or interest, or which would cause unwarranted invasion of the privacy of the individual, and shall not be disclosed if in larger public interest justifies the disclosure of such information.

While deciding the question as to what is larger public interest, the State Public Information Officer shall decide in his discretion by first deciding as to whether such information relates to personal information the disclosure of which has no relation to any public activity or interest and would amount to unwarranted invasion of privacy. But information which cannot be denied to the Parliament or the State Legislature shall not be denied to any person.

12. *Appeal:* Any person who, does not receive a decision within the time specified in sub-section (1) or clause (a) of sub-section (3) of section 7, or is aggrieved by an order of the State Public Information Officer may, within thirty days from the date of receipt of the order of the State Public Information Officer, prefer an appeal to the Law Secretary who shall be the Appellate Authority Under Section 19(1) of the Right to Information Act, 2005, which shall be accompanied by an appeal fee of Rs.100 (Rupees One Hundred) by way of bank receipt to be deposited under Major Head 0070.OAS(E)RTI. Fee payable to the public authority with a copy of such order appealed against.

13. Monitoring Applications and Appeals:

(1) A register of applications received shall be maintained by each PIO and Assistant PIO. The register may be electronic or in hard copy. At a minimum, the register will note the following information:—

(i) Application reference number;
(ii) Name of applicant;
(iii) Date of application;
(iv) Summary of applicant's request;
(v) Date response provided to applicant;
(vi) Where information was provided, summary of information provided;

(vii) Where application was rejected, specific clause relied upon and brief explanation of reasons;
(viii) Whether appeal filed and outcome;
(ix) Any additional remarks.

(2) At the end of every month, every PIO and Assistant PIO will provide a monthly report containing the information collected under sub-section (1) above to the Head of the public authority or his/her delegate.

(3) A register of appeals received shall be maintained by each Appellate Authority and Information Commission. At a minimum, the register will note the following information:—

(i) Application reference number;
(ii) Name of applicant:
(iii) Date of appeal;
(iv) Date response provided to applicant;
(v) Outcome of the appeal, including the provision(s) of the law being disputed, the interpretation of the provision(s) relied upon and a summary of the order passed;
(vi) Any additional remarks.

(4) At the end of every month, each Appellate Authority will provide a monthly report containing the information collected under sub-section (3) above to the Head of the Department or public body or his/her delegate.

(5) Within 14 days from the end of each month, the Head of the Department or public body or his/her delegate will collate all of the information received in accordance with sub-section (2) and (4) above and publish this information on the internet.

(6) Within 14 days from the end of the every month,

each Information Commission will publish the information collected under sub-section (3) on the internet.

14. Any person aggrieved by an order of the appellate authority under sub-section (1) of section 19 may, within ninety days from the date of receipt of the order of the appellate authority, prefer a second appeal to the State Information Commission on plain paper in the format given in Annexure "F", which shall be accompanied by an appeal fee of Rs.100 (Rupe One Hundred) by way of bank receipt to be deposited under Major Head 0070.OAS (E) RTI Fee payable to the State Information Commission.

15. Records Management:

(1) In accordance with Sec. 4(1) of the Act, every public authority shall ensure that their records are computerized within a period of 3 years from the enactment of this Act.

(2) Every authority shall, immediately upon the enactment of this Act, make a time bound plan for achieving implanting Rule 14(1) above and said plan shall be made public. Every six months, the public authority shall publish a progress statement in respect of the plan.

The Tamil Nadu Right to Information Rules, 2005

NOTIFICATION

Dated:07.10.2005

No. G.O.Ms.NO.989

In exercise of the powers conferred by section 27 of the Right to Information Act, 2005 (Central Act 22 of 2005), the Governor of Tamil Nadu hereby makes the following Rules:—

Rules—

1. Short title— These rules may be called the Tamil Nadu Right to Information (Fees) Rules, 2005.
2. Definitions—In these rules unless the context otherwise requires—

   (a) "Act" means the Right to Information Act, 2005 (Central Act 22 of 2005);
   (b) Words and expressions used in these Rules and not defined shall have the same meaning assigned to them in the Act.

3. Fee—

   (a) Every application for obtaining information under sub-section (1) of section 6 of the Act shall be accompanied by an application fee of rupees fifty by cash or by demand draft or bankers cheque payable in the head of account, as may be specified by the Public Authority.
   (b) For providing the information under sub-section (1) of section 7 of the Act, a fee shall be charged

by way of cash against proper receipt or by demand draft or banker's cheque payable in the head of account, as specified by Public Authority at the following rates:—

(i) rupees two for each page (in A-4 or A-3 size paper) created or copied;

(ii) Actual charges or cost price of a copy in the larger size paper;

(iii) Actual cost of price for samples or models; and

(iv) For inspection of records, no fee for the first hour and a fee of rupees five for each fifteen minutes (or fraction thereof)

(c) For providing the information under sub-section (5) of section 7 the fee shall be charged by way of cash against proper receipt or by demand draft or banker's cheque payable in the head of account, as specified by the Public Authority at the following rates:

(i) for information provided in diskette or floppy rupees fifty per diskette and floppy; and

(ii) for information provided in printed form at the price fixed for publication

The Tripura Right to Information Rules, 2005

NOTIFICATION

Dated: 7th March,2006

No.F.3(5)-GA (AR)/2005

In exercise of the powers conferred by Section 27 of the Right to Information Act, 2005, the State Government hereby makes the following rules, namely; —

CHAPTER -1
Preliminary

1. Short title and commencement :

   (a) These rules may be called the Tripura Right to Information Rules, 2008 .

   (b) They shall come into force from the date of their publication in the Official Gazettee.

2. Definitions: —

   In these rules, unless there is anything repugnant to the subject or context—

   (a) "Act"" means the Right to Information Act, 2005.

   (b) "Administrative Department* means the General Administration (Administrative Reforms) Department of the Government of Tripura.

   (c) "Appellate Authority" means an officer senior in rank to the State Public Information Officer as designated by the public authority under section 19(1) of the Act.

   (d) "Commission" means the Tripura Information Commission.

(e) " Form" means form appended to these rules in Appendix.

(f) Government* means the Government of Tripura.

(g) "Sample" means specimen for small part or quantity of any material to be supplied for any scientific testing or analysis for the purpose of ascertaining what the whole like;

(h) "Secretary" means the Secretary of the Tripura Information Commission;

(i) "Section" means section of the Act:

(J) " Year" means the financial year from Ist April to 31st March; and

(k) The words and expressions used in these rules but not defined shall have the same meaning as assigned them in the Act.

CHAPTER - II
Public Authorities

3. *Publication of Nat of Public Authorities* : The Administrative Department shall publish a list of public authorities as defined in section **2**(h) of the Act in Form No.1.

4. *Pro-Active disclosure of information:* Each public authority shall connect through a network all over the country on different systems so that access to such records is facilitated to the information showing the particulars of the functions and duties of the public authorities in Form No. 2.

5. *Publication of directory:* The Administrative Department shall publish a directory showing the particulars of the public authorities, Appellate Authorities in each public authority, State Public Information Officers and State Assistant Public Information Officers designated by

the different public authorities of the state within 6(six) months from 12th October, 2005 and the directory shall be updated immediately after any change is made.

CHAPTER –III

Disposal of request for Information by State Public Information Officer/ State Assistant Public Information Officer.

6. *Assistance to SPIO:* The public authority may allow the State Public Information Officer to entrust someone of his office for assisting him for maintaining registers and other official works in connection with the implementation of the provisions of the Act.
7. *Rates of Fees* :(1) Rates of fees for providing information shall be as follows:
   (a) Application fee at the time of making the request for obtaining information - Rupees ten
   (b) Fee for any information or record in paper.

      (i) Rupees two per page (per impression) for A-4 or A-3 size paper or part thereof.
      (ii) Actual charge or cost price of a copy in larger size paper.

   (c) Fee for samples or models — actual cost or price for samples or models.
   (d) Fee for Inspection of records—No fee for the first hour and a fee of Rs. 5 for each subsequent hour or fraction thereof.
   (e) For Information to be provided in computer diskette or floppy Rupees fifty per diskette or floppy provided the computerized information is available.
   (f) For information in printed publication. At the price

fixed for such publication or Rupees two per page of photocopy for extracts for the publication.

(2) *Mode off payment of fee:* Application fee which shall accompany the request for obtaining information under sub section (1) of Section 6 of the Act and further fees required to be paid under sub-sections (1) and (5) of Section 7 of the Act shall be paid by way of either in cash or treasury challan or Indian postal order.

8. *Form of request for Information:* A request for information shall ordinarily be made in writing in Form No. 3. If the request is made orally, the State Public Information Officer or the State Assistant Public Information Officer to whom the request is presented shall reduce it into writing in the prescribed form and obtain the signature/thumb impression of the person-making request for information on it. The State Assistant Public Information Officer shall issue a receipt as appended to the bottom of the application form—making request for information. However, application in plain paper should also be accepted.

9. *Receipt for payment of fees:* The person-making request for information shall pay the application fee or furthers fee, if any, in any of the manner prescribed in sub-rule (2) of Rule 7 against the money receipt to be issued by the State Assistant Public Information Officer or the State Public Information Officer as the case may be in Form No. 4.

10. *Register of request for Information:* On receipt of the request for Information. It shall be entered into the register maintained for this purpose. In every application a year wise chronological number shall be put distinguishing its nature in the office of the State Public Information Officer or the State Assistant Public Information Officer as the case may be to whom the

request is presented. The following registers shall be maintained for the purposes as shown against their names and on the body of the request for Information, the chronological number shall be noted in the manner as mentioned against the name of the registers as shown below:

(a) General register of request for information in the nature of copy/extracts etc,— Gl/Sr-No/Year.
(b) Register of request for information in the nature of inspection of records and taking notes etc,— INS/Sr No/Year.
(c) Register of request for information in the nature of sample/model etc,— SM/Sr No/ year.
(d) Register of request for information in the nature of diskette/floppy/printed material — El/Sr. No./year.
The registers as mentioned here-in-before at (a),(b),(c) and (d) shall be maintained in Form No— 5,6,7, and 8 respectively.

11. Maintenance of Cash Book and deposit of fees to Treasury: Every State Public Information Officer or State Assistant Public Information Officer, as the case may be, shall maintain in his office a cash book in Form No. 9 for receipt and deposit of fees paid by the person requesting for information. Fees received in a week shall be deposited to the treasury by challan by the State Public Information Officer or the State Assistant Public Information Officer as the case may be in the receipt head of accounts as may be specified by the Finance Department, Government of Tripura, on the first working day of the following week.
The cash book shall be signed duly by the State Public Information Officer or the State Assistant Public Information Officer as the case may be on every day of transaction.

12. *SAPIO to produce the requests for Information before SPIO*: After registration of the request for information, the State Assistant Public Information Officer shall present before the State Public Information Officer within 5 days of receipt of the request for Information for disposal.

13. *Disposal of request for Information by SPIO:*

    (1) If the request for information is found to be in order, the equisition for information may be sent to the custodian of the information directly if it is not available within the custody of the State Public Information Officer after making necessary entry in a register to be maintained in Form No. 10 known as the Register of Requisition for Information in the office of the State Public Information Officer and on receipt of such requisition, the custodian shall at once forward such information in original to the State Public Information Officer.

    (2) After receipt of the information from the custodian of such information, the State Public Information Officer shall determine further fees to be paid by the person for making request for information and show the details of such determination on the reverse side of the written request for information.

    (3) When the State Public Information Officer accepts the application for providing Information as sought for he has to send an intimation to the person for making request for information in Form No. 11 about the exact amount of further fees to be deposited by the person for making request for information along with the calculation as to how the amount has been determined specifying a reasonable time by which such further fee is to be deposited.

(4) If in any request for information, interest of any third party relates, such third party shall be noticed in Form No. 12 and be provided the opportunity of making submission before disclosure of the information as sought for as required under Section 11 of the Act.

(5) When a request for obtaining information is accepted for part supply of information or rejected by the State Public Information Officer, the applicant shall be given intimation to that effect in Form No. 13.

(6) If the State Public Information Officer or the State Assistant Public Information Officer on any working day remains out of office on any ground, he may authorize in writing a subordinate officer to receive any request for information together with application fee as well as further fee from any person.

(7) If any person presents any request for information to a State Public Information Officer or the State Assistant Public Information Officer held by another public authority, the former shall transfer the request for information to the concerned public authority by a forwarding letter in Form No. 14 under intimation to the person-making request for information.

14. *Supply of Information in electronic mode:* Supply of Information or copy of record in computer diskette or floppy shall depend on the availability of information in electronic form and the facility for providing such information in diskette or floppy with the public authority.

15. *Mode of providing sample:*

(1) In supplying sample of any material used by a public authority for any work, the State Public

Information Officer shall intimate the applicant the date, time and venue when the applicant can obtain a sample of the material or inspect the information or work. The State Public Information Officer shall also give notice in writing to the authority who has got the work done or from whose custody the sample is to be taken.

(2) While supplying a sample all precautionary measures should be taken to prevent tempering with the sample and the sample should be properly packed and sealed in presence of witnesses and may be handed over to the applicant.

(3) At the time of Inspection of any Information or work, at least one official should remain present to supervise the inspection.

(4) For the purpose of obtaining a sample or making an inspection, the applicant may bring with him a helper of his choice.

16. *Copy of Information to be certified:* Copy of Information in the form of document or record may be certified to be copy of the original by the State Public Information Officer under his seal, signature and date.

CHAPTER -IV

Constitution of the State Information Commission

17. *Recommendation for appointment of State Chief Information Commissioner and State Information Cornmissioner* : If there is any difference of opinion among the members of the three members' Committee constituted under sub-section (3) of Section 15 of the Act to recommend names of suitable persons to be appointed as the State Chief Information Commi-ssioner or State information Cornmissioner (s), the decision of the majority shall prevail.

18. *Subscription to oath or affirmation*: The person appointed as State Chief Information Commissioner or State Information Commissioner shall, before he enters upon his office by making or subscribing to an oath or affirmation under sub- section (3) of Section 16 of the Act in the form set out for the purpose in the First Schedule to the Act. and shall also make a declaration in Form No. 15 appended to these rules.

CHAPTER -V
Disposal of Complaint by the State Information Commission

19. *Lodging of complaint and Its disposal :*

(1) A complaint under Section 18(1) of the Act shall be made in plain paper directly to the State Information Commission addressing to the State Chief Information Commissioner containing the following particulars: —

(i) name and address of the complainant;
(ii) name and particulars of the Public Authority/ First Appellate Authority/State Public Information Officer against whom the complaint is lodged;
(iii) brief facts leading to the complaint;
(iv) relief sought for;
(v) any other information and copies of the documents relied on by the complainant; and
(vi) referred to In the complaint shall accompany the complaint.

(2) No fee is required to be paid for making a complaint.
(3) On receipt of the complaint, the Secretary shall cause it to be entered In the complaint register in Form No. 16 and a year wise chronological number

shall be put on the body of the complaint It shall also be entered in the daily list of complaint/ appeals in Form No. 17 and be presented before the State Chief Information Commissioner.

(4) In any case, if interest of any third party relates, such third party shall be noticed in Form No. 18 giving him an opportunity of making submission within a specific time to be fixed by the Commission and such submission shall be considered at the time of disposal of the complaint.

(5) Summons to the opposite party shall be issued in Form No. 19.

(6) The Complainant shall be noticed of the date of hearing of complaint In Form No. 20.

(7) The complainant or the opposite party may appear in hearing of the complaint either in person or through their duly authorized representatives unless their appearance is specially required by the Commission.

(8) A daily cause list for hearing of complaint/appeal in the Commission shall be maintained in Form No. 21.

(9) Summons to a witness may be issued in Form No. 22.

(10) The deposition of a witness to a complaint or appeal for either of the parties or the Commission may be recorded in Form No. 23.

Appeal from order passed by the State Public Information Officer

20. *Lodging of first appeal and its disposal:*

(1) Every appeal against the order passed by the State Public Information Officer under sub-sections (1) and (2) of Section 19 of the Act shall be preferred in the form of memorandum in Form No. 24 signed by the appellant and presented to the State

Assistant Public Information Officer or State Public Information Officer or to the Appellate Authority. A copy of the written request seeking information and order appealed from shall accompany the memorandum of Appeal.

(2) On receipt of an appeal either directly or through the State Assistant Public Information Officer, the Appellate Authority shall enter it in a register of appeal Form No. 25.

(3) If in an appeal preferred to the Appellate Authority, interest of a third party relates, such third party shall be noticed in Form No. 26 giving him an opportunity to make submission, if any, within a specific time to be fixed by the Appellate Authority and such submission shall be considered at the time of disposal of the appeal.

(4) No fee is required to be paid for preferring an appeal to the Appellate Authority under Sections 19(1) and 19(2) of the Act.

CHAPTER-VI
Appeal to the Commission

21. *Lodging of second appeal and Its disposal:* The second appeal under sub-section (3) of Section 19 of the Act shall normally be submitted directly to the Commission in Form No. 27. However, if such appeal is presented to the State Assistant Public Information Officer he shall forward it to the Commission at once with intimation to the appellant—

(2) Every second appeal made to the Commission shall be accompanied by the following documents, namely—

(i) self attested copies of the judgment and orders against which the appealis preferred;

(ii) copies of documents relied upon by the appellant and referred to in the appeal;

(iii) an Index of the document referred to in the appeal; and

(iv) any other information/documents, the Commission may ask for to decide the appeal.

(3) The Secretary shall maintain a register of second appeal in Form No. 28. A year-wise chronological number shall be put on the body of the appeal. The Secretary shall cause the appeal to be entered in the appeal register as well as in the daily list of complaint/appeal.

(4) The memorandum of appeal shall set forth concisely and under distinct heads, the grounds of objection of the order appealed from without any argument or narrative and such grounds shall be numbered consecutively.

(5) The appellant or the respondent may appear in hearing of the appeal either in person or through their duly authorized representatives unless their appearance is specially required by the Commission.

(6) The respondent may be summoned in Form No. 29. The appellant may be noticed of the date of hearing in Form No. 29.

(7) For preferring an appeal to the Commission under Section 19(3) of the Act, no fee is required to be paid.

(8) Where memorandum of an appeal has not been drawn up specifying the grounds, it may be rejected or be returned to the appellant for the purpose of being amended within the time to be fixed by the Commission.

(9) Where the Commission rejects any memorandum of appeal, it shall record reasons for such rejection.

(10) When an appeal is presented after the expiry of the period of limitation specified in the Act, it should be accompanied by an application supported by a declaration stating the facts on

which the appellant relies to satisfy the Commission that he had sufficient cause for not preferring the appeal within such period.

(11) The Commission, if sees no reason to reject the application, may admit and decide the appeal accordingly.

(12) If in an appeal, interest of any third party relates, he shall be noticed in Form No. 26 and be given an opportunity of making submission, if any, within a specific time to be fixed by the Commission and such submission shall be considered at the time of disposal of the appeal.

(13) The Commission shall fix a date for hearing of appeal and notice shall be served on the appellant and the respondent in the manner as provided for service of summons to appear and answer and all the provisions applicable to such summons and to proceedings with reference to service thereof shall apply to the service of such notice, as in the Code of Civil Procedure 1908.

22. *Dismissal of second appeal for default—*

(1) Where on the date fixed, or on any other date to which the hearing to be adjourned, in spite of receipt of notice of the Commission to appear, the appellant does not appear when the appeal called on for hearing, the Commission may make an order that the appeal be dismissed. Such disposal on default shall not be construed as dismissal on merit.

(2) Where the appellant appears and the respondent does not appear, the appeal shall be heard in absence of the latter.

23. *Re-admission of appeal:* Where an appeal is dismissed

for default the appellant may apply to the Commission for re-admission of the appeal within a period of thirty days of such dismissal, and, where it Is proved that he was prevented by sufficient cause from appearing when the appeal was called on for hearing, the Commission may admit the appeal.

24. *Batting aside of ex-parte order:* Re-hearing of application of the respondent against whom ex-parte order made: Where an appeal is heard ex-parte, judgment Is pronounced against the respondent, he may apply to the Commission within a period of thirty days of pronouncing the judgment to re-hear the appeal and if he satisfies the Commission that the notice was not duly served or he was prevented by sufficient cause from appearing when an appeal was called on for hearing, the Commission may re-hear the appeal.

25. *Judgment in complaint and appeal:* The judgment on the complaint or appeal under the Act shall be in writing and at the time of pronouncing the judgment, it shall be signed and dated by the Commission.

26. *Pronouncement of judgment:* —

(i) The Judgment shall be pronounced in open office either at once or on a future day of which notice shall be given to the parties or their representative, if any; and

(ii) It shall not be necessary for the Commission to read out the whole judgment, but a copy of the whole judgment shall be made available for the parties immediately after the judgment is pronounced free of cost.

27. The Rules from 21 to 26 shall also apply, so far as may be, to appeals to the Appellate Authority.

CHAPTER-VIII
Secretariat of the Commission

28 *Secretariat:—*

(1) There shall be a secretariat in the Commission. The Secretary shall be the Chief Executive Officer of the Commission. All correspondences with the Commission other than filing complaints and appeal to the Commission shall be addressed to the Secretary and the Secretary shall make all correspondences on behalf of the Commission subject to approval of the Commission on policy matters.

(2) The Secretary shall authenticate copies of all judgment and orders passed by the Commission in deciding complaint, appeal and applications under the Act.

(3) The Secretary shall have the power to administer oath or affirmation to any person for making any affidavit in connection with any complaint or appeal or application preferred in the Commission under the Act

(4) The Secretary shall also do the following functions on behalf of the Commission:

(a) to receive complaint, appeal and applications.

(b) to call for records from any public authority, appellate authority and state public information officer as and when directed by the Commission.

(c) to receive and dispose of any application for return of records and documents.

(d) to maintain and sign the daily cause list.

(e) to deal with all matters relating to service of notice, no service and defect of service.

(f) to dispose of all application for copies of

information relating to complaints and appeals.

(g) to sign other registers and papers to be maintained in the office of the Commission.

(h) any other duties as and when entrusted by the Commission.

(5) The Commission may authorize any other official of the Secretariat of the Commission to discharge the functions and duties of the Secretary in his absence from duties.

CHAPTER -IX
Miscellaneous

29. Report on implementation of the provisions of the Act:

(1) Every State Public Information Officer and the Appellate Authority at the end of each year shall submit an annual report in Forms Nos. 30 and 31 respectively to the concerned public authority by 30th April of the year.

(2) Every public authority shall submit an annual report for every year in Form Nos-32 to the concerned head of the department of the Government of Tripura, the Head of the General Administration (Administrative Reforms) Department, Government of Tripura and the Secretary to the information Commission by 31st May of the following year.

(3) Every head of the department at the end of the each year shall submit a consolidated report in Form No. 33 on the implementation of the Act to the Commission by 30th June of the following year.

30. *Disposal of complaint and appeal by the Commission:* A complaint under Section 18 and an appeal under

Section 19(3) of the Act may be disposed of either jointly by the State Chief Information Commissioner and the State Information Commissioners together or Independently by themselves as the State Chief Information Commissioner decides and allocates. When the State Chief Information Commissioner and the State Information Commissioner act in collegiate, the decision shall be unanimous.

31. If any request for information or appeal is not made in the forms prescribed by these rules, but contains the requisite materials, such request for information or appeal shall be admitted.

32 *Repeal and Savings:* —

(1) The Tripura Right to Information Rules. 2005 are hereby repealed.

(2) Notwithstanding such repeal orders issued, action taken or anything whatsoever done under the rules so repealed shall be deemed to have been issued, taken or done under the corresponding provisions of these rules.

Uttranchal Right to Information (Regulation of Fee and Cost) Rules, 2005

In exercise of the powers conferred by clauses (b) and (c) of sub-section (2) of section 27 of the Right to Information Act, 2005 (22 of 2005), the Governor bereby makes the following rules, namely:—

1. Short title and commencement:—

   (1) These rules may be called the Right to Information (Regulation of Fee and Cost) Rules, 2005.
   (2) They shall come into force on the date of their publication in the Official Gazette.

2. Definitions:—
   In the rules, unless the context otherwise requires—

   (a) "Act" means the Right to Information Act, 2005.
   (b) "Section" means section of the Act.
   (c) All other words and expressions used herein but not defined in the Right to Information Act shall have the meanings assigned to them in that Act.

3. A request for obtaining information under sub-section (1) of section 6 shall be accompanied by an application fee of rupees ten by way of cash against proper receipt or by demand draft or bankers cheque payable to the Finance/Accounts Officer of the public authority .
4. For providing the information under sub-section (1) of section 7, the fee shall be charged by way of cash against proper receipt or by demand draft or bankers

cheque payable to the Finance/Account Officer of the public authority at the following rates:—

(a) rupees two for each page (in A4 and A3 size paper) created or copied and actual charge or cost price of a copy in large size paper;
(b) for inspection of records, no fee for the first hour and a fee of rupees five for each subsequent hour (or fraction thereof); and
(c) actual cost or price for samples or models.

5. For Providing the information under sub-section (5) of section 7, the fee shall be charged by way of cash against proper receipt or by demand draft or bankers cheque payable to the Finance/Accounts Officer of the public authority at the following rates:—

(a) for information provided in diskette floppy rupees fifty per diskette or floppy; and
(b) for information provided in the printed form at the price fixed for publication or rupees two per page of photocopy for extracts from the publication.

The Uttar Pradesh Right to Information (Regulation of Fee and Cost) Rules, 2006

NOTIFICATION

No. 528/43-2-2006

Dated 13 April, 2006

In exercise of the power conferred by section 27 of the Right to Information Act, 2005 (Act No. 22 of 2005) the Governor is please to make the following Rules:—

1. These rules may be called the Uttar Pradesh Right to Information (Regulation of Fee and Cost) Rules, 2006
2. They shall come into force at once. In these rules:—

   (a) 'Act' means the Right to Information Act (Act No. 22 of 2005)
   (b) 'Section' means section of the Act
   (c) All other words and expression used herein but not defined and defined in the Act shall have the meanings assigned to them in the Act.

3. Any person who wants to have access to any information prescribed under the Act shall make an application to the concerned state Public Information Officer or State Assistant Public Information Officer mentioning therein name and address of the applicant along with his contact phone number if any, proof of payment of prescribed fee for inspection or proof of his being a member or below poverty line family and the details of information he want to access.
4. A request for obtaining information under sub-section (I0 of section 6 of the act shall be accompanied by an

application fee or rupees 10 by way of cash against proper receipt or by demand draft or bankers cheque payable to the concerned public authority.

5. For providing the information under sub-section (1) of section 7 of the act, the fee shall be charged by way of cash against proper receipt or by demand draft or bakers cheque payable to the public authority at the following rates:—

(a) Rupees two for each pager (in A-4 or A-3 size paper) created or copied;
(b) Actual charge or cost price of a copy in larger size paper;
(c) Actual cost or price for samples or models and where the information is available in the form of priced publication, price so fixed; and
(d) For inspection of records, a fee of rupees ten for the first hour; and a fee of rupees five for each fifteen minutes (or traction thereof) thereafter.

6. For providing the information under sub-section (5) of the section 7 the fee shall be charged by way of cash against proper receipt or by demand drat or bankers cheque payable to the public authority at the following rates:—

(a) for information provided in diskette or floppy or compact disk rupees fifty per diskette or floppy or compact disk; and
(b) for information provided in the printed form at the price fixed for such publication or rupees two per page of photocopy for extracts from the publication

7. In the case of maps and plans etc, the fee shall be fixed by the concerned public information officer in each case depending upon the cost of labour and material required to be employed.

8. The amount of fee shall be deposited in following head of account. "0070" – Other administrative service , 800 other receipts, 11 fees received on account of implementation of Right to Information Act, 2005.

The West Bengal Right to Information Rules, 2005

NOTIFICATION

Dated:10 March, 2006

No. 1 57 – PAR(AR)

In exercise of the power conferred by Sub-Section (I) read with sub-section (2) of Section 27 of the Right to Information Act, 2005 (22 of 2005), the Governor is pleased hereby to make the following rules namely:

Rules—

1. Short title and commencement:

   (i) These rules may be called the West Bengal Right to Information Rules, 2006.

   (ii) They shall come into force on the date of their publication in the Official Gazette.

2. Definitions:

   1. In these rules, unless the context otherwise requires—

      (a) "Act" means the Right to Information Act, 2005 (22 of 2005)

      (b) "Commission" means the West Bengal Information Commission;

      (c) "Registrar" means the Registrar of the Commission;

      (d) "Section " means section of the Act;

      (e) "State Government" means the Government of West.

2. Words and Expression used and not defined in these rules but defined in the Act, shall have the same meanings as respectively assigned to them in the act.

3. *Application Fee:* An application containing a request in writing to the State Public Information Officer the State Assistant Public Information Officer, as the case may be, made under sub-section (1) of Section 6 for obtaining information, shall be accompanied with a fee of rupees ten.

4. *Fee for providing information:* Save as otherwise provided in the provision to sub-section (5) of Section (7) the State Public Information Officer or the State Assistant Public Information Officer, as the case may be, shall provide information under sub-section (1) and sub-section (5) of Section 7 upon receipt of a request under section 6, on payment of a fee of:—

(a) rupees two, for each page (in A – 4 or A-3 size paper) created or copied;
(b) Actual charge or cost price for a copy in large size paper;
(c) Actual cost price for sample or model;
(d) Rupees five for each fifteen minutes or fraction there off for inspection of records;
(e)R upees fifty per diskette or floppy, for information provided in the diskette or floppy; and
(f) Actual charge fixed for publication or rupees two per page of photocopy for extracts there from for information provided in printed form.

5. Content of appeal to Commission under Sub-Section(3) of Section 19-An appeal to the Commission under sub-section (3) of Section 19, shall contain the following information, namely :—

(a) Name and Address of the applicant.

(b) Name and Address of the State Public Information Officer or the State Assistant Public Information officer, as the case may be, who passed the order;
(c) Particular of the order against which the appeal is made including its number and date;
(d) Brief facts of the case
(e) Prayer or relief sought for by the appellant;
(f) Ground for such prayer relief ; and
(g) Verification by the appellant

6. Documents to accompany appeal to Commission under sub-section (3) of Section 19. Every appeal made to the Commission shall be accompanied by the following documents, namely—

(a) the attested true copy of the order against which the appeal is being preferred;
(b) the copies of the documents relied upon the appellant and referred to in the appeal; and
(c) an index of the document referred to in the appeal

7. Procedure in deciding appeal to Commission under sub-section (3) of section 20 —

1. In deciding the appeal to the Commission, the commission shall:—

(a) Hear oral or written evidence on oath or on affidavit from the concerned interested person
(b) Pursue or inspect documents, public records or copies thereof
(c) Enquire through the authorized, officer for further details or facts
(d) Here the State Public Information Officer or the State Assistant Public Information Officer or such Officer who decided the first appeal

mentioned sub-section (1) of section 19, as the case may be.

(e)H ere the third party if required; and

(f) Receive evidence on "affidavits from State Public Information Officer, State Assistant Public Information Officer or such officer who decided it appeal mentioned in sub-section 19 or from the third party;

2. In deciding the appeal the commission may ask the appellant to add any information other than the information included in the contents of the second appeal under rule 5.

8. *Service of notice by Commission* : The notice required to be issued under sub-section (9) of Section 19 by Commission may be served in any of the following modes, namely:—

(a) Service by itself;

(b) Service by hand delivery through the process server;

(c) Service the registered post with acknowledgement due; and

(d) Service through the head of office or the department.

9. *Signing of order*: The order of the Commission pronounced in open proceedings shall be in writing authenticated by the Registrar of any other officer authorized by the Commission in the behalf.

10. *Terms and conditions of officer and other employees of Commission*—The officers and other employees of the Commission shall be placed on deputation from the State Government on the usual terms and conditions.

Annexure V

RTI Fee Structure : Centre and States

Name of the State	*Form*	*Application Fee*	*Modes of Fee Payment*	*Additional Fee*	*Appeal Fee*
Centre and Delhi	No	Rs. 10	Cash/Demand Draft/ Bankers Cheque	• A3/A4-Rs. 2 • Larger Size Paper - Actual Cost • Floppy/CD-Rs.50 • Sample/Model – Actual Cost • Published Documents-Printed Price • Inspection of Record-No charge for Ist hour and there-after Rs. 5 per hour or fraction thereof.	No
Andhra Pradesh	No	• No fee at the village level. • Rs. 5 at the Mandal level • Rs. 10 for other public authorities	Cash/Demand Draft/ Bankers Cheque	• A3/A4-Rs. 2 • Larger Size Paper - Actual Cost • 1.44 Floppy/ CD-Rs. 50, 700 MBCD Rs. 100, DVD Rs. 200 • Maps / Plans Actual cost • Sample/Model– Actual Cost • Published Documents-Printed Price • Inspection of Record-No charge for Ist hour and thereafter Rs. 5 per fifteen minutes or fraction thereof. • Postal charges extra-	No

(Contd...)

(Contd...)

Arunachal Pradesh	Yes	Rs. 50 for general information. Rs. 500 for information relating to tender document/ bids/ quotation/ business contract	Treasury Challan	• Rs. 5 per page • Published document-printed Price	First appeal-Rs. 50 Second Appeal Appeal Zero
Assam	No	Rs. 10	Cash/Demand Draft/ Bankers Cheque	• A3/A4-Rs. 2 • Larger Size . Paper - Actual Cost • Floppy/CD-Rs. 50 • Sample/Model–Actual Cost • Published Documents-Printed Price • Inspection of Record-No charge for Ist hour and thereafter Rs. 5 per fifteen minutes or fraction thereof.	No
Bihar	Yes	Rs. 10	Cash , Demand Draft, judicial Stamp, Pay order	• A3/A4-Rs. 2 • Bigger size paper actual cost • Floppy /CD Rs. 50 • Sample/Model Actual cost • Published document printed price • Inspection of record for first hour free and after that Rs. 5 per hour.	First Appeal Rs. 50
Chattisgarh		Rs. 10	Cash/Treasury Challan/Non-Judicial Stamp Paper	• A3/A4-Rs. 2 • Larger Size Paper - Actual Cost • Floppy/CD-	First appeal-Rs. 50 (by post Rs. 75)

(Contd...)

(Contd...)

			Rs. 50 • Sample/Model–Actual Cost • Published Documents-Printed Price • Inspection of Record- Rs. 5 per hour or fraction thereof. • For in'ormation sought in q/a form (non-BPL people) cost per page is Rs. 100 or the cost of producing such information. Choice will be of the applicant. • BPL-(i) if the information relates to applicants life it would be provided in the form in which it is sought. • (ii) If the information does not relate to applicant's life and is in 50 pages or the cost is Rs. 100 would be provided in the form in which it is sought.	Second Appeal Rs. 100 (by post Rs.125)
Goa	Rs. 10	Cash/Demand Draft/ Bankers Cheque	• A3/A4-Rs. 2 • Larger Size Paper - Actual Cost • Floppy/CD-Rs. 50 • Sample/Model–Actual Cost • Published Documents-Printed Price • Inspection of Record-No charge for Ist hour and thereafter Rs. 5 per hour or fraction thereof.	No

(Contd...)

(Contd...)

Gujarat	Yes	Rs. 20	Cash/Demand Draft/ Pay Order	• A3/A4-Rs. 2 • Larger Size Paper - Actual Cost • Floppy/CD- Rs. 50 • Sample/Model– Actual Cost • Published Documents- Printed Price • Inspection of Record-No charge for Ist hour and thereafter Rs. 20 for half an hour or fraction thereof.	No
Haryana	Yes	Rs. 50	Cash/Demand Draft/ IPO/ Treasury Challan	• A3/A4-Rs. 10 • Larger Size Paper - Actual Cost • Floppy/CD- Rs. 50 • Sample/Model– Actual Cost • Published Documents- Printed Price • Inspection of Record-No charge for Ist hour and thereafter Rs. 10 per fifteen minute or fraction thereof.	No
Himachal Pradesh	Yes	Rs. 10	Treasury Challan/ Demand Draft	• A3/A4-Rs. 2 • Larger Size Paper— Actual Cost • Floppy-Rs.50 • CD-Rs. 100 • Sample/Model– Actual Cost • Published Documents- Printed Price • Postal charges extra • Inspection of Record Rs.10 per fifteen minutes or fraction thereof.	No
J&K				•	

(Contd...)

(Contd...)

Jharkhand	No	Rs. 10	Cash/Demand Draft/ Bankers Cheque	• A3/A4-Rs. 2 • Larger Size Paper - Actual Cost • Floppy/CD- Rs. 50 • Sample/Model– Actual Cost • Published Documents- Printed Price • Inspection of Record-No charge for Ist hour and thereafter Rs. 5 per fifteen minutes or fraction thereof.	No
Karnataka	Yes	Rs. 10	Cash/Demand Draft/Bankers Cheque IPO/ Treasury Challan/ Court Stamp	• A3/A4-Rs. 2 • Larger Size Paper - Actual Cost • Map/ Plans/ Reports / Technical Data/ Sample/Model – price decided by PIO on the basis of labour and material cost • Floppy/CD- Rs. 50 • Published Documents- Printed Price • Inspection of Record-No charge for Ist hour and thereafter Rs. 20 per half an hour or fraction thereof.	
Kerala	Yes	Rs. 10	Cash/Demand Draft/ Bankers Cheque/Treasury Challan/Court Stamp	• A3/A4-Rs. 2 • Larger Size Paper - Actual Cost • Floppy/CD- Rs. 50 • Sample/Model– Actual Cost • Published Documents- Printed Price • Inspection of Record-No charge	No

(Contd...)

(Contd...)

				for Ist hour and thereafter Rs. 10 per half an hour or fraction thereof.	
Madhya Pradesh	No	Rs. 10	Cash/None Judicial Stamp	• A3/A4-Rs. 2 • Bigger size paper actual cost • Floppy /CD - price decided by PIO/APIO • Sample price decided by PIO/APIO • Published document printed price • Inspection of record first hour. Rs. 50 and after that Rs. 25 per 15 minutes.	First Appeal Rs. 50 Second appeal Rs. 100
Maharashtra	Yes	Rs.10	Cash/Demand Draft/Bankers Cheque/Court Stamp	• A3/A4-Rs. 2 • Bigger size paper actual cost • Floppy /CD Rs. 50 • Sample/Model Actual cost • Published document printed price • Inspection of record: No fee for first hour and after that Rs.5 per 15 minutes or fraction thereof. • Postal Charges-Extra	First and Second Appeals-Rs. 20/.
Manipur	No	Rs.10	Cash/Demand Draft/Bankers Cheque	• A3/A4-Rs. 2 • Bigger size paper actual cost • Floppy /CD Rs. 50 • Sample/Model Actual cost • Published document printed price • Inspection of	No

(Contd...)

(Contd...)

				record for first hour. No fee for first hour and after that Rs. 5 per 15 minutes or fraction thereof.	
Meghalya	No	Rs.10	Cash/Demand Draft/Bankers Cheque	• A3/A4-Rs. 2 • Bigger size paper actual cost • Floppy /CD Rs. 50 • Sample/Model Actual cost • Published document printed price • Inspection of record: No fee for first hour and after that Rs. 5 per 15 minutes or fraction thereof. • Postal Charges-Extra	No
Mizoram	Yes	Rs. 10	Cash/Demand Draft/Bankers/ Cheque/ Court Stamp/Treasury challan	• A3/A4-Rs. 2 • Bigger size paper actual cost • Floppy /CD Rs. 50 • Sample/Model/ Video/Microfilm actual cost • Published document printed price • Inspection of record for first hour. No fee for first hour and after that Rs. 5 per hour or fraction theof.	No
Nagaland	No	Rs. 10	Cash/Demand Draft/Bankers Cheque	• A3/A4-Rs. 2 • Bigger size paper actual cost • Floppy /CD Rs. 50 • Sample/Model Actual cost • Published document printed price • Inspection of	No

(Contd...)

(Contd...)

				record for first hour. No fee and thereafter for every subsequent hour or fraction thereto- Rs. 5	
Orissa	Yes	Rs. 10	Cash/ Treasury Challan	• A3/A4-Rs. 2 • Larger Size Paper - Actual Cost • 1.44 Floppy/ CD-Rs. 50 • Video Cassettes/ Map/Plans-Price decided by PIO on the basis of effort and investment made • Sample/Model– Actual Cost • Published Documents- Printed Price • Inspection of Record-No charge for Ist hour and thereafter Rs. 5 per fifteen minutes or fraction thereof.	First and second appeal Rs. 20
Punjab	Yes	Rs. 10	Cash/Demand Draft/Bankers Cheque/IPO Treasury Challan	• A3/A4-Rs. 2 • Bigger size paper actual cost • Floppy /CD Rs. 50 • Sample/Model Actual cost • Published document printed price • Inspection of record for first hour. No fee for first hour and after that Rs. 5 per 15 minutes.	
Rajasthan	Yes	Rs.50	Cash/Demand Draft/Bankers Cheque/ IPO	• A3/A4-Rs. 2 • Bigger size paper actual cost • Floppy /CD Rs. 50 • Sample/Model	No

(Contd...)

(Contd...)

				Actual cost • Published document printed price • Inspection of record: No fee for first hour and after that Rs. 5 per 15 minutes or fraction thereof. • Postal Charges-Extra	
Sikkim	Yes	Rs.100	Court Fee/Money Order/Cheque/ Demand Draft/ Bank Receipt	• A3/A4-Rs. 2 • Bigger size paper actual cost • Floppy /CD Rs. 50 • Sample/Model Actual cost • Published document printed price or Rs. 5 per page of photocopy or extracts from publication. • Inspection of record : No fee for first hour and after that Rs. 5 per 15 minutes or fraction thereof.	First and Second Appeal Rs. 100
Tamil Nadu	No	Rs. 50	Cash/Demand Draft/ Bankers Cheque	• A3/A4-Rs. 2 • Larger Size Paper - Actual Cost • Floppy/CD-Rs. 50 • Sample/Model – Actual Cost • Published Documents-Printed Price • Inspection of Record-No charge for Ist hour and thereafter Rs. 5 per fifteen minutes or fraction thereof.	No

(Contd...)

(Contd...)

Tripura	Yes	Rs. 10	Cash/IPO/ Treasury Challan	• A3/A4-Rs. 2 • Larger Size Paper - Actual Cost • Floppy/CD- Rs. 50 • Sample/Model– Actual Cost • Published Documents- Printed Price • Inspection of Record-No charge for Ist hour and thereafter Rs. 5 each subsequent hour or fraction thereof.	No
Uttranchal	No	Rs. 10	Cash/Demand Draft/ Bankers Cheque	• A3/A4-Rs. 2 • Larger Size Paper - Actual Cost • Floppy/CD- Rs. 50 • Sample/Model– Actual Cost • Published Documents- Printed Price • Inspection of Record-No charge for Ist hour and thereafter Rs. 5 per an hour or fraction thereof.	
Uttar Pradesh	No	Rs. 10	Cash/Demand Draft/ Bankers Cheque	• A3/A4-Rs. 2 • Larger Size Paper - Actual Cost • Floppy/CD- Rs. 50 • Sample/Model– Actual Cost • Published Documents- Printed Price • Inspection of Record- Rs. 10 for first hour and thereafter Rs. 5 per fifteen minutes or fraction thereof.	

(Contd...)

(Contd...)

West Bengal	No	Rs. 10	Court Fee	• A3/A4-Rs. 2 • Larger Size Paper - Actual Cost • Floppy/CD- Rs. 50 • Sample/Model– Actual Cost • Published Documents- Printed Price • Inspection of Record-Rs. 5 per fifteen minutes or fraction thereof.	No

Source :

1.RTI Rules - Centre, States and Union Territories.
2.Arun Kumar Ojha and Rupa Manglani, Suchna Ka Adhikar—Sidh and awam vavhar, Centre for Good Governance, RIPA, Jaipur, 2008.
3.Kabir, NGO, New Delhi.

Annexure - VI

Information Commissions in India

State	Name of the Chief Information Commissioner	Address	Phone	E-mail
Central Government and Delhi	Shri Wajahat Habibullah	Club Building, Old JNU Campus, New Delhi-110067	Off. 011-2161137 Fax. 011-26185336	htp://cic.gov.in
Arunachal Pradesh	Shri Nyodek Yonggam	Block 2(A), 3&4, Secretariat Annexe Adjacent to MLA Cottage P.O: Itanagar District Pa um Pare PIN-791 111	Off: 0360-2290853 Resi :0360-2291664 Mob: 09436256881 Fax: 0360-2291051	
Andhra Pradesh	Shri. C D Arha	Ground Floor, HACA Bhawan, Opposite Public Gardens, Hvderabad - 500004	Off 040-23452620 040-23230607 Fax.040-23230591	http:/www.apic.gov.in info.apic@gmail.com
Assam	Shri. R.S. Mooshahary	Janata Bhawan, Dispur Guwahati -781006	Off : 0361- 2261676 Fax: 0361- 2261900 2261676	cic@sicassam.ir scic-as@nic.in hftp://www.sicassam.in
Bihar	Justice Shri Shashank Kumar Singh	Fourth Floor, Soochna Bhawan Bailey Road, Patna - 800021		http://wwwbsic.co.in query@bsic.co.in
Chattisgarh	Shri. A K Vijayavargiya	Nirmal Chhaya Bhavan Meera Datar Road, Shankar Nagar, Raiour - 492 001	Off: 0771-4024406 Fax: 0771024140 Resi: 0771-2331012	akvijayargiya@nic.in http://www.cq.nic.in/sic avr@nic.in

(Contd...)

Goa	Shri. A Venkatratnam	Shrama Shakthi Bhavan, Ground Floor, Patto Panaji, GOA. Pin 403 401	Off : 0832-2413774 Mobile: 09860287282	http://egov.goa.nic.in/rb publish/sic.aspx
Gujarat	Shri. R N Das	1st Floor, Bureau of Economics & Statistics, Building, Sector-18, Gandhina ar-382 018	Off :079-23252701,706 Secy: 079-23252966 Resi : 079-23230993	gscic@gujrat.nic.in http://gic.guj.nic.in
Haryana	Shri. G Madhavan	SCO No. 70-71, Sector 8C, Madhya Marg, Chandiqarh	Office: 0172-2726568 (Tele-Fax) Resi: 0172-2793628	madhavang@hry.nic.in http://cicharyana.gov.in
Himachal Pradesh	Shri P.S. Rana	Room No.222,Armsdale Building HP Secretariat Shimla-171 002	Office: 0177-2621904, 2880726 Resi: 0177-2812236 2652538	scic-hp@nic.in hftp://admis.hp.nic.in/sic
Jharkhand		Engineers Hostel: 2, Near Golchakkar, Dhurwa, Ranchi, 834004		http://210.212.20.92tjsic
Karnataka	Shri. K K Misra	3rd floor, 3rd Stage, Multistoried Buildings, Dr.Ambedkar Road, Bangalore- 560 001.	Ph.No.080-22371191 Off :+91-80 - 22371191 Fax: +91-80 - 22371192	scic@kamataka.gov.in h2p://www.kic.gov.in
Kerala	Shri. Palat Mohandas	T.C. 26/298, Punnen Road Thiruvananthaouram, Pin 695039	Phone: 0471- 2335199, 2320920 Fax : 0471- 330 920 Off: +91 -471- 2333147	sic@kerala.nic.in hftp://kerala.nic.in http://keralasic.gov.in

(Contd...)

Madhya Pradesh	Shri. T N Shrivastava	Nirwachan Bhawan, Second Floor, 58, Arera Hills, Bhopal - 462011	Of f: +91-755 - 2761367 Mobile: 9425365434	hftp://www.mpsic.nic.in
Maharashtra	Shri. Suresh Vinayakrao Joshi	15th Floor, New Administrative Building, Madame Cama Road, Opposite Mantralaya, Mumbai- 400 0032	Res: +91- 22 - 22022859 Off: +91-22-22856078 Mobile: 9821525427	htp://sic.maharastra.gov.in
Meghalaya	Shri. G P Wahlang,IAS	New Administrative Building Lower Lachumiere Shillona -3	Off: +91-0364 -2500160	rti-meg@nic.in
Mizoram	Shri. Robert Hrangdawla	New Capital Complex, Khatla, Aizawl- 796 001	Off :2334825 Res: 2316001 Mobile: 943140247	mizoram.sic@gmail.com http://msic.mizoram.gov.in
Nagaland	Shri. P. Talitemjen Ao	Post Box -148 Kohima-797 001 Nagaland	Off :0370-2292595 Fax: 0370-2291798 Res: 0370-2242983	cic nagaland@.yahoo:co.in hftp://nlsic.gov.in
Orissa	Shri. Ohirendra Nath Padhi	State Guest House Annexe, Room No. 44, Unit 5, Bhubaneshwar 751001	Off: 91-674 - 2534300	hon scic@ori.nic.in httpa/orissasoochanacommission.nic.in
Punjab	Shri. Rajan Kashyap	SCO No.84-85, Sector 17-C, Chandigarh	Off: +91-172-2740543 Fax: +91-172-2740353	http://www.infocommpunjab.com
Rajasthan	Shri M.D. Kaurani			hftp://dc.rajasthan.gov.in

(Contd...)

Sikkim	Shri O.K. Gajmer	Lower Secretariat Opp Super Market Gangtok-737101	off : 03592-205710 Tele Fax : 03592-228526 Res: 03592-203048 Mobile: 9434023532	gajmerdk@yahoo.co.in http://www cicsikkim.gov.in
Tamil Nadu	Shri. S Ramakrishnan	Kamadhenu Co- operative Supermarket Building, 1st Floor, Teynampet, (Near Vanavil) Old No. 273, New No. 378, Anna Salai, Teynampet, Chennai - 600 018 (Post Box No. 6405,	Phone: 044-24357580 Fax: 044 - 24357580	sic@tn.nic.in htm://www.tnsic.gov.in
Tripura	Shri. B K Ctiakraborty	Civil Secretariat, Agartala West Tripura - 799001	Off: +91-381-2218021 Mobile: 9436120039	sic-tic-tr@nic.in http:/ lrtitripura.nic.in
Uttaranchal	Shri. R.S. Tolia	4 Subhash Road, 4th Floor Dehradun - 248001	Off: +91-135-2712100 2712200, 2712079	htm://gov.ua.nic.in
Uttar Pradesh	Justice Shri. Mohd Asgar Khan	6th Floor, Indira Bhawan, Lucknow - 226001	Off : 0522-2288598 0522- 2235798 Telefax: 0522-2288600	
West Bengal	Shri. Arun Bhattacharya	2nd Floor, Bhabani Bhaban, Ali re, Kolkata - 700 027	Telefax: 033 - 24791966	scic@wb.nic.in http://wbic.gov.in/

Source: www.cic.gov.in

Annexure VII

Quiz on the Subject

1. Only a citizen can have access to the information under RTI Act.

   Yes/No

2. A Public Authority is supposed to maintain their records in duly cataloged and indexed form .

   Y es/No

3. A Public authority is required to publish various details about itself.

   Yes/No

4. A Public authority shall provide reasons for its administrative and quasi-judicial decisions to the affected persons.

   Yes/No

5. A Public authority designates only one Public Information Officer and one Assistant Public Information Officer.

   Yes/No

6. An applicant can make a verbal request to the Public Information Officer.

   Yes/No

7. A RTI application can be submitted on the prescribed format only.

   Yes/No

8. A uniform format for RTI application has been prescribed under the Act .

   Yes/No

9. Public Information Officer can verify the intention the information seeker.

   Yes/No

10. An applicant is required to give reasons for seeking information.

    Yes/No

11. If the same information has been sought by a large number of people, then to save Public Information Officer's time and resources, such information should be put on the website of the public authority.

    Yes/No

12. There is limit on the number and types of information sought in a single application.

    Yes/No

13. Information is to be provided in the form in which it is asked unless it does not disproportionately divert the resources of public authority.

    Yes/No

14. No penalty is imposed upon Public Information Officer if proved that she/he took necessary action in good faith.

    Yes/No

15. Only the designated Public Information Officer is penalized by the Information Commission.

    Yes/No

16. If the RTI application is wrongly addressed, then Public Information Officer has to transfer the application to concerned public authority.

    Yes/No

17. Public Information Officer has to transfer the application to the concerned public authority within a week.

    Yes/No

18. Time limit for providing information has been prescribed under the Act.

Yes/No

19. BPL applicant is not required to pay application fee instead he/she has to pay additional fee.

Yes/No

20. Information is provided free to the applicant, if it is provided after the time limit.

Yes/No

21 An applicant can have accessed to the information even from the investigation related file.

Yes/No

22 Request for information can be made in writing or on email.

Yes/No

23 Information provided in confidence by the third party or treated as confidential by third party, can be given to the applicant without giving a notice to third party in this regard.

Yes/No

24. Like Public Information Officer, Assistant Public Information Officer is also supposed to give information to the applicant.

Yes/No

25. Penalty can be imposed on the Assistant Public Information Officer also, if she/he refuses to receive or forward an application or appeal to the Public Information Officer and First Appellate Authority/ Information Commission respectively as the case may be.

Yes/No

26. Assistant Public Information Officer is assistant to the Public Information Officer

Yes/No

27. Public Information Officer has to refund the RTI fee i.e. both application fee and additional fee received from the applicant, if information is not provided within the time limit.

Yes/No

28. BPL applicant is provided information free of cost even, if it is in floppy or CD

Yes/No

29. Information has to be provided even if the applicant does not pay additional pay within the prescribed 15 days time limit in Haryana.

Yes/No

30. Application can be filed if additional has not been received within the prescribed time limit.

Yes/No

31. If the information requested relates the work of several departments, the Public Information Officer has to transfer it to the concerned departments.

Yes/No

32. The Act has overriding effect over the Official Secret Act, 1923

Yes/No

33. Public Information Officer can reject the request if taking of sample/model causes damage to the concerned public work.

Yes/No

34. Instead of daily, Public Information Officer can fix certain days in the month for inspection of records.

Yes/No

35. A Public Information Officer is bound to certify the information given to the applicant.

Yes/No

36. A citizen can seek information which is 40 years old, if record retention schedule permits the preservation such information.

Yes/No

37. Section 8 covers the exemptions from providing certain types of information.

Yes/No

38. In case, information is available with the Public Authority from the third party in confidence, Public Information Officer has to give ten days notice of the intention to disclose the information to the third party.

Yes/No

39 If third party says no to such notice, information can't be disclosed to the applicant.

Yes/No

40. File and notings can be given to the applicant .

Yes/No

41. A Public Information Officer has to assist the illiterate applicant in writing the application.

Yes/No

42. The decision of Information Commission is final and its decision can not be challenged in High Court/ Supreme Court.

Yes/No

43. The applicant can approach the First Appellate Authority within the 30 days of the Public Information Officer's decision.

Yes/No

44. The aggrieved applicant instead of approaching the First Appellate Authority, can directly make a complaint to the Information Commission.

Yes/No

45. Only Information Commission can impose penalty.

Yes/No

46. There is time limit to decide the the appeal by the First Appellate Authority.

Yes/No

47. IC can summon the First Appellate Authority to appear before it.

Yes/No

48. The Committee meant for recommending the name of Chief Information Commissioner/Information Commissioner at the Central level for appointment by President consists of PM, leader of Opposition in Lok Sabha and Speaker of Lok Sabha.

Yes/No

49. The Committee meant for recommending the name of Chief Information Commissioner/Information Commissioner at the state level for appointment by Governor consists of CM, leader of Opposition in assembly and a cabinet minister nominated by CM.

Yes/No

50. Maximum age of the Chief Information Commissioner and Information Commissioner is 62 years

Yes/No

51. The term of the office of Information Commissioner and that of Chief Information Commissioner both as Information Commissioner and Chief Information Commissioner shall not be more than five years in aggregate.

Yes/No

52. The salary of the Chief Information Commissioner in

the State Information Commission and that of Information Commissioner in the Central Information Commission is equivalent to that of a Central election Commissioner.

Yes/No

53. The applicant in case of damages and harassment by Public Information Officer can request Information Commission for compensation.

Yes/No

54. Compensation is paid by the concerned public authority to the applicant.

Yes/No

55. Information Commission can't recommend disciplinary action against the Public Information Officer.

Yes/No

56. The Central or State Government as the case may be, can exempt certain agencies & organisations from the ambit of the Act.

Yes/No

57. The appropriate government can make rules for effective implementation of the Act.

Yes/No

58 Information which can not be denied to MP or MLA also can't be denied to the citizen of the country.

Yes/No

59 The Information Commission can summon the First Appellate Authority to appear before it .

Yes/No

60 The appellant can make an appeal to the Information Commission within the 75 days of the decision of the First Appellate Authority

Yes/No

Guidelines for applying

1. Decide the exact information you desire to have with period etc. Do not ask questions. Seek information and copies of record relating to your matter.
2. Locate the exact SPIO/Asstt SPIO and his address of concerned Government office by visiting website of relevant ministry/dept/undertaking etc (called Public Authority i.e. PA) or by visiting/contacting on phone local office of PA.
3. If you cannot get it as above, address application to SPIO of concerned office or Head Office or Ministry to whom the information may pertain. He will mail to correct. SPIO within five days of receipt of your application.
4. Please pay application fee as prescribed.
5. Attach self-attested photocopies of papers, wihch you think would help locate the information by SPIO.
6. Retain photocopy of entire set.
7. Mail by speed/registered post. Avoid courier/hand delivery. Usually RTI applicants are not welcome at Government offices.
8. Carefully retain postal proof of mailing.
9. Remit other charges promptly as mentioned above, if requested by SPIO.
10. If you do not receive reply within 35 days, including postal delay, from the date of mailing by you; perpare to file complaint Information Commission instead of appeal to First Appellate Authority.
11. If you receive reply and are not satisfied with it, then within 30 days of receipt of reply by you, you should file appeal. After the SPIO's reply, you have 30 days time to file the first appeal to the First Appellate Authority.
12. It is advisable to consult local RTI NGO/activists/ useful website like *www.Saji.net.in/www. human-rightsinitiative.org/www.cic.gov.in/cichar-yana.gov.in/ www.rtiindia.org* for first and second appeals or complaint for better results.

Index